SUCH IS

A Handbook For Living

Who am I? What is my purpose? How should I live my life? How do I acquire happiness and recognize it when it is within my grasp?

Man has grappled with these fundamental questions since the beginnings of recorded history. **SUCH IS LIFE** opens a dialogue between generations of our greatest philosophers in search of the answers.

Confucius, Aristotle, Samuel Johnson, Sigmund Freud, Mark Twain and a thousand other such personages join in the debate. Their topic of discussion is life itself: the ages of man; the passions that influence his fate; the effect of society upon the individual; the private, internal search for identity and one's sense of self. In the flow of their conversation they attempt to isolate and define the Human Condition. Their insight bridges the whole of our earthly tenure from birth to death and offers a conclusion as to how to make your life work for you.

Here you will find the accumulated wisdom of the ages presented in an enjoyable and accessible manner. **SUCH IS LIFE** will broaden your understanding while guiding you towards a happier and more fulfilling life experience.

SUCH IS LIFE is a resource and handmaiden for your journey through life.

SUCH IS LIFE

A Handbook For Living

L. J. Field

FOR MY DEAR FRIEND
DEAN

WITH WARM WISHES

BLEAK HOUSE BOOKS

Such Is Life, A Handbook For Living
Copyright © L. J. Field, 2014

Published by Bleak House Books
Contact: bleakhousebookZ@gmail.com

Front cover painting
Child at Bath, 1886
Adolphe-William Bouguereau

Back cover painting
Study of an Elderly Lady, c. 1900
Frederick James McNamara Evans

Cover design and colophon by Colin Martin
Contact: pwherman@gmail.com

ISBN-978-1505207668

First Edition
1 3 5 7 9 8 6 4 2

This book is dedicated to the ladies in my life:
my wife, Zusia,
our daughters, Leilah and Ashlei,
and our granddaughters, Ava, Riley, and Elsa

J'aime et j'espere

Contents

Such Is Life

Despair of nothing.

—Horace

Such Is Life

INTRODUCTION

What a piece of work man is!
How noble in reason!
how infinite in faculty!
in form, in moving how express and admirable!
in action how like an angel!
in apprehension how like a god!
the beauty of the world!
the paragon of animals!
And yet, to me, what is this quintessence of dust?
—William Shakespeare

The gods alone live forever under the divine sun;
but as for mankind, their days are numbered,
all their activities will be nothing but wind.

The words above were written in cuneiform on a clay tablet sometime before 2150 BC. This relic was unearthed by archaeologists in the ruins of the lost city of Ebla in ancient Mesopotamia, the birthplace of civilization.

The scribe who wrote this epigram could not have guessed that his private thought, carefully etched in clay, would be shared with his ancestors 4000 years after his death. Nor could he have dreamt that these words would be one of our earliest captured examples of man's attempt to understand and describe the human condition.

It was probably not long after man gained the capacity to reason that he began to ponder on the mystery of his own life. There are several concepts that are essential as a foundation for successful contemplation. An understanding of death is primary: that there is a limit imposed on the capacity for experience. A conception of the past and the future are also important: that past actions influence the present and present activities design the future. The process of aging must be comprehended: that one is born dependent, grows to adulthood and is ultimately destroyed by nature. Finally, the realization that one's interactions within the society in which one lives can result in good or bad consequences dependent on the individual's behavior and adherence to the norms of his community.

The acquisition of these fundamental perceptions allowed man the ability to rationalize his life experience and impose order on the chaos of everyday living.

While the world we live in bears little resemblance to our dark beginnings, the interior landscape of our life is essentially the same. We hope for a better future, fret over past mistakes and redefine our expectations as we age. Our families and friends, our passions and loves continue to shape our lives. The society we are immersed in dictates our desires and behavior. Our thoughts and feelings—our sense of identity itself, are for most of us the riddles of our existence.

The subjects of human life and the conditions of typical living have interested the greatest intellects in history. To the benefit of mankind, many of these people have left a written testament of the vital truths they realized in moments of profound clarity. The buried and sometimes obscure books of centuries past teem with these acute observations. Others appear unexpectedly in works published in our lifetimes by our contemporaries.

In this era of conventions and symposiums, it is not unusual to find the experts of any particular subject brought together to discuss or debate their views. However, these discussions are limited to the people inhabiting the present. Our ancestors cannot join in and contribute their own knowledge and enlightenment. Their ability to communicate is confined to the written word.

This book is an attempt to open a discussion between generations of thinkers. Their topic of investigation is life itself: the ages of man, the passions that influence his fate, the effect of society upon the individual, the private, internal search for identity and one's sense of self. In the flow of their conversation they attempt to isolate and define the human condition. They are unconcerned with politics, religion or history. Their thoughts concentrate on the interior life of men and women and the intrinsic qualities that make our species what it is.

Over one thousand people have been gathered here. They come from diverse centuries, continents and cultures and yet find sympathy and understanding with one another. We all live the same lives inside—and we always have. The subjects encompassed in this book are timeless. They were as significant and consequential to our ancestors as they are to us today. We have all known the prickle of pride, the cherished hopes and dreams, the sadness and grief of loss. We have all experienced the first flutter of love, the illusions of its foundations and the reality that time imposes upon it. Happiness, pleasure; adversity, anxiety, regret; all of these await us on our journey through life. These topics and the many others that are inherent to the human condition are examined here.

The book has an outward appearance of being a volume of quotations. After a few pages of reading, however, the actual architecture of the book becomes apparent. The work is constructed as a dialogue and resembles the interplay of actual conversation. Each sentence leads to and suggests the next. It is a symposium of thought and an interchange of ideas, checkered by disputes.

The book is structured to resemble one's actual journey through life. It begins with birth, followed by youth and education. As maturity approaches, the individual enters adult society, garners friendships and falls under the thrall of one's escalating passions. The grand passion—love—has an individual part devoted to it followed by reflections on the family and one's experience in the great arena of life's occupations.

With middle age the individual becomes more introspective and judgmental as to his own place in the world and his ultimate value. Hence, the mind and one's self are explored.

As old age looms, opinions have been formed of humanity in general and the human condition and life specifically. With age also comes the certainty of approaching death.

Part 19 records the final spoken thoughts of thirty-seven people as they joined eternity. In their few words they encapsulate some of the mysteries and wonders of life.

In Part 20, the "Moral", the speakers attempt to identify the fundamentals necessary to having a happy and fulfilling life.

In the rush of everyday living we often fail to take the necessary time to reflect on our life and present it to ourselves in terms that can bring some clarity to our experience. It is the great tragedy of life that so many people leave this world in as great a state of ignorance of their place in it as when they arrived.

—L. J. Field
December, 2014

I have only made a nosegay of culled flowers,
and have brought nothing of my own but the
thread that ties them together.
—Michel de Montaigne

Such Is Life

PART 1

BIRTH

Thou know'st the first time that we smell the air,
We wawl and cry. . . .
When we are born we cry that we are come
To this great stage of fools.
—William Shakespeare

Such Is Life

Thy home is not here!
—Aztec (First words to newborn baby)

Our birth is but a sleep and a forgetting.
—William Wordsworth

It is not true, it is not true that we come on this earth to live. We come only to sleep, only to dream. Our body is a flower. As grass becomes green in the springtime, so our hearts will open and give forth buds, and then they whither.
—Aztec

Life is but a day;
A fragile dewdrop on its perilous way
From a tree's summit.
—John Keats

The cradle rocks above an abyss, and common sense tells us that our existence is but a brief crack of light between two eternities of darkness.
—Vladimir Nabokov

The first Breath is the Beginning of Death.
—Thomas Fuller (II)

Our birth is nothing but our death begun, as tapers waste the moment they take fire.
—Edward Young

It is as natural to die as to be born; and to a little infant, perhaps, the one is as painful as the other.
—Francis Bacon

One must not mourn the death of men, but their birth.
—Charles de Secondat Montesquieu

Why is it that we rejoice at a birth and grieve at a funeral? It is because we are not the person involved.
—Mark Twain

Such Is Life

All men come into this world alone and leave it alone.
—Thomas De Quincey

We are all in positions of passengers from a ship which has reached an island. We have gone on shore, we will walk about and gather shells, but we must always remember that, when the whistle sounds, all the little shells will have to be thrown away and we must run to the boat.
—Leo Tolstoy

The end of birth is death. The end of death is birth.
—Bhagavadgita

From small beginnings come great things.
—Proverb

All that lies between the cradle and the grave is uncertain.
—Seneca

PART 2

YOUTH

In early youth, as we contemplate our coming life,
we are like children in a theatre before the curtain
is raised, sitting there in high spirits
and eagerly waiting for the play to begin.
—Arthur Schopenhauer

Such Is Life

Childhood is the sleep of reason.
—Jean Jacques Rosseau

Childhood has no forebodings; but then it is soothed by no memories of outlived sorrow.
—George Eliot

Childhood is only the beautiful and happy time in contemplation and retrospect.
—George Eliot

I can remember, at the age of five, being told that childhood was the happiest period of life (a blank lie, in those days). I wept inconsolably, wished I were dead, and wondered how I should endure the boredom of the years to come.
—Bertrand Russell

The myth of childhood happiness flourishes so wildly not because it satisfies the needs of children but because it satisfies the needs of adults. In a culture of alienated people, the belief that everyone has at least one good period in life free of care and drudgery dies hard. And obviously you can't expect it in your old age. So it must be you've already had it.
—Shulamith Firestone

Childhood is not only the childhood we really had but also the impressions we formed of it in our adolescence and maturity. That is why childhood seems so long. Probably every period of life is multiplied by our reflections upon it in the next. The shortest is old age because we shall never be able to think back on it.
—Cesare Pavese

Childhood is less clear to me than to many people: when it ended I turned my face away from it for no reason that I know about, certainly without the usual reason of unhappy memories. For many years that worried me, but then I discovered that the tales of former children are seldom to be trusted. Some people supply

23

too many past victories or pleasures with which to comfort themselves, and other people cling to pains, real and imagined, to excuse what they have become.
—Lillian Hellman

In our play we reveal what kind of people we are.
—Ovid

The most powerful ties are the ones to the people who gave us birth . . . it hardly seems to matter how many years have passed, how many betrayals there may have been, how much misery in the family: We remain connected, even against our wills.
—Anthony Brandt

A brother is a friend given by nature.
—Gabriel Marie Legouvé

A sister is both your mirror—and your opposite.
—Elizabeth Fishel

You don't choose your family. They are God's gift to you, as you are to them.
—Desmond Tutu

You never get over being a child, long as you have a mother to go to.
—Sarah Orne Jewett

People who lose their parents when young are permanently in love with them.
—Aharon Appelfeld

Love your parent, if he is just: if not, bear with him.
—Publilius Syrus

Conduct thyself towards thy parents as thou wouldst wish thy children to conduct themselves toward thee.
—Isocrates

People are always rather bored with their parents. That's human nature.
—W. Somerset Maugham

The first half of our lives is ruined by our parents and the second half by our children.
—Clarence Darrow

We never know the love of the parent till we become parents ourselves.
—Henry Ward Beecher

The joys of parents are secret, and so are their griefs and fears.
—Francis Bacon

Parents can only give good advice or put them on the right paths, but the final forming of a person's character lies in their own hands.
—Anne Frank

I have not much interest in anyone's personal history after the tenth year, not even my own. Whatever one was going to be was all prepared before that.
—Katherine Anne Porter

The ten year old gives a fair indication of the man or woman he or she is to be.
—Arnold Gesell

We become adolescents when the words that adults exchange with one another become intelligible to us.
—Natalia Ginzburg

If youth is the season of hope, it is often so only in the sense that our elders are hopeful about us; for no age is so apt as youth to think its emotions, partings, and resolves are the last of their kind. Each crisis seems final, simply because it is new.
—George Eliot

For youth, the future is long, the past short. . . . It is easily deceived, because it is quick to hope.
—Aristotle

When you understand what you see, you will no longer be children. You will know that life is pain, that each of us hangs always on the cross of himself. And when you know that this is true of every man, woman and child on earth you will be wiser.
—Whittaker Chambers

It is an illusion that youth is happy, an illusion of those who have lost it.
—W. Somerset Maugham

In no order of things is adolescence the time of the simple life.
—Janet Erskine Stuart

The old know what they want; the young are sad and bewildered.
—Logan Pearsall Smith

The eyes of young men are curious and penetrating, their imaginations are of a roving nature, and their passion under no discipline or restraint.
—Joseph Addison

As I grew to adolescence, I imagined, from closely observing the boredom and vexations of matrimony, that the act my parents committed and the one I longed to commit must be two different things.
—Shirley Abbott

Adolescence: a stage between infancy and adultery.
—Author Unknown

Youth is quick in feeling but weak in judgment.
—Homer

No young man believes he shall ever die.
—William Hazlitt

Young men are as apt to think themselves wise enough, as drunken men are to think themselves sober enough.
—Lord Chesterfield

There is a strong disposition in youth, from which some individuals never escape, to suppose that everyone else is having a more enjoyable time than we are ourselves.
—Anthony Powell

A man's worse difficulties begin when he is able to do as he likes.
—Thomas H. Huxley

The greatest part of mankind employ their first years to make their last miserable.
—Jean de La Bruyère

It is the height of absurdity to sow little but weeds in the first half of one's lifetime and expect to harvest a valuable crop in the second half.
—Percy Johnston

Youth is in danger until it learns to look upon debts as furies.
—Edward G. Bulwer-Lytton

The excesses of our youth are drafts upon our old age, payable with interest, about thirty years after the date.
—Charles Caleb Colton

Bestow thy youth so that thou mayst have comfort to remember it, when it hath forsaken thee, and not sigh and grieve at the account thereof. Whilst thou art young thou will think it will never have an end; but behold, the longest day hath his evening, and thou shalt enjoy it but once; it never turns again; use it therefore as the spring-time, which soon departeth, and wherein thou oughtest to plant and sow all provisions for a long and happy life.
—Sir Walter Raleigh

Youth, what man's age is to be, doth show;
We may our ends by our beginnings know.
—Sir John Denham

Youth lasts much longer than the young imagine.
—Comtesse Diane

'Tis a maxim with me to be young as long as one can: there is nothing can pay one for that invaluable ignorance which is the companion of youth; those sanguine groundless hopes, and lively vanity, which make all the happiness of life. To my extreme mortification I grow wiser every day.
—Lady Mary Wortley Montagu

If youth is a fault, one soon gets rid of it.
—Johann Wolfgang von Goethe

A boy becomes an adult three years before his parents think he does, and about two years after he thinks he does.
—Lewis B. Hershey

How do you know that the fruit is ripe? Simply because it leaves the branch.
—André Gide

The disappointment of manhood succeeds the delusion of youth.
—Benjamin Disraeli

PART 3

EDUCATION

To endure is the first thing that a child ought to learn,
and that which he will have the most need to know.
—Jean Jacques Rousseau

Such Is Life

Knowledge is the true organ of sight, not the eyes.
—Panchatantra

Nothing in this life, after health and virtue, is more estimable than knowledge—nor is there anything more easily attained, or so cheaply purchased—the labour, only sitting still, and the expense but time, which if we do not spend, we cannot save.
—Laurence Sterne

An extensive knowledge is needful to thinking people—it takes away the heat and fever; and helps, by widening speculation, to ease the burden of the mystery.
—John Keats

The reward of study is understanding.
—Babylonian Talmud

The more extensive a man's knowledge of what has been done, the greater will be his power of knowing what to do.
—Benjamin Disraeli

Education, then, beyond all other devices of human origin, is the great equalizer of the conditions of men,—the balance-wheel of the social machinery.
—Horace Mann

The desire of knowledge, like the thirst of riches, increases ever with the acquisition of it.
—Laurence Sterne

There is nothing so minute, or inconsiderable, that I would not rather know it than not.
—Samuel Johnson

As soon as a true thought has entered our mind, it gives a light which makes us see a crowd of other objects which we have never perceived before.
—François de Chateaubriand

Knowledge is a comfortable and necessary retreat and shelter for us in advanced age; and if we do not plant it while young it will give us no shade when we grow old.
—Lord Chesterfield

Learning makes a Man fit Company for himself.
—Thomas Fuller (II)

The highest purpose of intellectual cultivation is to give a man a perfect knowledge and mastery of his own inner self; to render our consciousness its own light and its own mirror.
—Novalis

As the soil, however rich it may be, cannot be productive without culture, so the mind without cultivation can never produce good fruit.
—Seneca

A man of learning is never bored.
—Jean Paul Richter

Curiosity is one of the permanent and certain characteristics of a vigorous mind.
—Samuel Johnson

Education is a companion which no misfortune can depress, no crime can destroy, no enemy can alienate, no despotism can enslave. At home a friend, abroad an introduction, in solitude a solace, and in society an ornament. It chastens vice, it guides virtue, it gives, at once, grace and government to genius. Without it, what is man? A splendid slave, a reasoning savage.
—Joseph Addison

The wise are instructed by reason; ordinary minds, by experience; the stupid, by necessity; and brutes by instinct.
—Cicero

All that a university or final highest-school can do for us is still but what the first school began doing—teach us to read. We learn to read in various languages, in various sciences; we learn the

letters of the alphabet and letters of all manners of books. But the place where we are to get knowledge, even theoretic knowledge, is the books themselves. It depends on what we read, after all manner of professors have done their best for us. The true university of these days is a collection of books.
—Thomas Carlyle

I am part of all that I have read.
—John Kieran

Reading is to the mind what exercise is to the body.
—Sir Richard Steele

Learning is acquired by reading books; but the much more necessary learning, the knowledge of the world, is only to be acquired by reading men, and studying all the various editions of them.
—Lord Chesterfield

If you wish to know yourself observe how others act.
If you wish to understand others look into your own heart.
—Johann Friedrich von Schiller

It is by imitation, far more than by precept, that we learn everything.
—Edmund Burke

Example is the school of mankind, and they will learn at no other.
—Edmund Burke

Intercourse with decent or bad people is the good or bad education which goes on throughout one's life.
—Eugène Delacroix

A vacant mind invites dangerous inmates, as a deserted mansion tempts wandering outcasts to enter and take up their abode in its desolate apartments.
—George Stillman Hilliard

Scratch the green rind of a sapling, or wantonly twist it in the soil, and a scarred or crooked oak will tell of the act for centuries to come. So it is with the teachings of youth, which makes impressions on the mind and heart that are to last forever.
—Author Unknown

Man learns more readily and remembers more willingly what excites his ridicule than what deserves his esteem and respect.
—Horace

The surest way to corrupt a young man is to teach him to esteem more highly those who think alike than those who think differently.
—Friedrich Wilhelm Nietzsche

We learn not in school, but in life.
—Seneca

No man's knowledge here can go beyond his experience.
—John Locke

Every man has two educations—that which is given to him, and the other, that which he gives to himself. Of the two kinds, the latter is by far the most valuable. Indeed, all that is most worthy in a man, he must work out and conquer for himself. It is that that constitutes our real and best nourishment. What we are merely taught seldom nourishes the mind like that which we teach ourselves.
—Jean Paul Richter

Perhaps the most valuable result of all education is the ability to make yourself do the thing you have to do, when it ought to be done, whether you like it or not; it is the first lesson that ought to be learned, and however early a man's training begins, it is probably the last lesson that he learns thoroughly.
—Thomas Huxley

Say not "When I have leisure I will study"; it may be that thou wilt have no leisure.
—Rabbi Hillel

Education is an ornament in prosperity and a refuge in adversity.
—Aristotle

Education is what survives when what has been learned has been
forgotten.
—B. F. Skinner

An education isn't how much you have committed to memory, or
even how much you know. It's being able to differentiate between
what you do know and what you don't.
—Anatole France

Education is a progressive discovery of our ignorance.
—Will Durant

Knowledge is realizing one's own ignorance and not being afraid
to ask questions.
—Author Unknown

I attribute the little I know to my not having been ashamed to ask
for information, and to my rule of conversing with all descrip-
tions of men on those topics that form their own peculiar
professions and pursuits.
—John Locke

Some people will never learn anything because they understand
everything too soon.
—Sir Thomas Pope Blount

Much learning does not teach understanding.
—Heraclitus

Learning without thought is labor lost.
—Confucius

Contemplation is to knowledge, what digestion is to food—the
way to get life out of it.
—Tryon Edwards

When you know a thing, to hold that you know it, and when you do not know it, to admit that you do not—this is true knowledge.
—Confucius

There is hardly any place, or any company, where you may not gain knowledge, if you please; almost everybody knows some one thing, and is glad to talk upon that one thing.
—Lord Chesterfield

When the most insignificant person tells us we are in error, we should listen, and examine ourselves, and see if it is so. To believe it possible we may be in error is the first step toward getting out of it.
—Author Unknown

The wisest mind has something yet to learn.
—George Santayana

Knowledge is proud that he has learn'd so much;
Wisdom is humble that he knows no more.
—William Cowper

The learning and knowledge that we have is, at the most, but little compared with that of which we are ignorant.
—Plato

I've known countless people who were reservoirs of learning, yet never had a thought.
—Wilson Mizner

The cultivated often treat practical matters as the ignorant do books, quite without understanding.
—Joseph Joubert

All wish to possess knowledge, but few, comparatively speaking, are willing to pay the price.
—Juvenal

The trouble with people is not that they don't know but that they know so much that ain't so.
—Josh Billings

Strange how much you've got to know before you know how little you know.
—Author Unknown

We only labor to stuff the memory, and leave the conscience and the understanding unfurnished and void.
—Michel de Montaigne

Mediocre men often have the most acquired knowledge.
—Tristan Bernard

Most men want knowledge not for itself, but the superiority which knowledge confers.
—Sydney Smith

There are various sorts of curiosity: one of interest, which leads us to desire to understand what may be useful to us; and another of pride, which comes from the desire to know what others are ignorant of.
—François de La Rochefoucauld

Wear your learning like your watch, in a private pocket, and do not pull it out and strike it merely to show that you have one. If asked what o'clock it is, tell it, but do not proclaim it hourly and unasked, like the watchman.
—Lord Chesterfield

Learning is a dangerous weapon, and apt to wound its master if it be wielded by a feeble hand, or by one not well acquainted with its use.
—Michel de Montaigne

Knowledge may not be as a courtesan, for pleasure and vanity only; or as a bondswoman, to acquire and gain for her master's use; but as a spouse, for generation, fruit, and comfort.
—Francis Bacon

Knowledge is always accompanied with accessories of emotion and purpose.
—Alfred North Whitehead

The three foundations of learning: Seeing much, suffering much, and studying much.
—Samuel Catherall

It is hard to find a man who has studied for three years without making some progress in virtue.
—Confucious

Learning is like a great house that requires a great charge to keep it in constant repair.
—Samuel Butler (I)

Studies grow into character.
—Ovid

Make wisdom your provision for the journey from youth to old age, for it is a more certain support than all other possessions.
—Bias

You know more than you think you do.
—Dr. Benjamin Spock

PART 4

SOCIETY

The humblest individual exerts some influence,
either for good or evil, upon others.
—Henry Ward Beecher

Such Is Life

The body is the shell of the soul, and dress the husk of that shell; but the husk often tells what the kernel is.
—Author Unknown

As you treat your body, so your house, your domestics, your enemies, your friends. Dress is the table of your contents.
—Johann Kaspar Lavater

The well-dressed man is he whose clothes you never notice.
—W. Somerset Maugham

A graceful and pleasing figure is a perpetual letter of recommend-dation.
—Francis Bacon

The face is the index of the mind.
—Latin Proverb

The voice is a second face.
—Gérard Bauër

A cheerful, easy, open countenance will make fools think you a good-natured man, and make designing men think you an undesigning one.
—Lord Chesterfield

Look in the face of the person to whom you are speaking, if you wish to know his real sentiments; for he can command his words more easily than his countenance.
—Lord Chesterfield

Eyes are more accurate witnesses than ears.
—Heraclitus

People unused to the world have babbling countenances; and are unskillful enough to show what they have sense enough not to tell.
—Lord Chesterfield

Mind not only what people say; and, if you have any sagacity, you may discover more truth by your eyes than by your ears. People

can say what they will but they cannot look what they will, and their looks frequently discover what their words are calculated to conceal.
—Lord Chesterfield

The eyes have one language everywhere.
—George Herbert

Looks are more expressive and reliable than words.
—Tryon Edwards

When the eyes say one thing, and the tongue another, a practiced man relies on the language of the first.
—Ralph Waldo Emerson

The eye speaks with an eloquence and truthfulness surpassing speech. It is the window out of which the winged thoughts often fly unwittingly. It is the tiny magic mirror on whose crystal surface the moods of feeling fitfully play, like the sunlight and shadow on a quiet stream.
—Henry Theodore Tuckerman

It is hard for the face to conceal the thoughts of the heart—the true character of the soul. The look without is an index of what is within.
— Author Unknown

Good nature is more agreeable in conversation than wit, and gives a certain air to the countenance which is more amiable than beauty.
—Joseph Addison

Good humor is one of the best articles of dress one can wear in society.
—William Makepeace Thackeray

Some men envelope themselves in such an impenetrable cloak of silence, that the tongue will afford us no symptoms of the mind. Such taciturnity, indeed, is wise if they are fools, but foolish if they are wise, and the only method to form a judgment of these mutes, is narrowly to observe when, where, and how they smile.
—Charles Caleb Colton

There are many kinds of smiles, each having a distinct character. Some announce goodness and sweetness, others betray sarcasm, bitterness and pride; some soften the countenance by their languishing tenderness, others brighten by their spiritual vivacity.
—Johann Kaspar Lavater

Laughter is the cipher-key, wherewith we decipher the whole man.
—Thomas Carlyle

I can usually judge a fellow by what he laughs at.
—Wilson Mizner

A cheerful temper, joined with innocence, will make beauty attractive, knowledge delightful and wit good-natured. It will lighten sickness, poverty and affliction, convert ignorance into an amiable simplicity, and render deformity itself agreeable.
—Joseph Addison

Everyone's manners make his fortune.
—Cornelius Nepos

Manners are especially the need of the plain. The pretty can get away with anything.
—Evelyn Waugh

A man's own good-breeding is the best security against other people's ill manners.
—Lord Chesterfield

We are more sociable and get on better with people by heart than the intellect.
—Jean de La Bruyère

The surest way to make ourselves agreeable to others is by seeming to think them so.
—William Hazlitt

Good manners is the art of making those people easy with whom we converse. Whoever makes the fewest persons uneasy is the best bred in the company.
—Jonathan Swift

Politeness is merely the art of choosing among your thoughts.
—Madame Germaine de Staël

Tact is after all a kind of mind reading.
—Sarah Orne Jewett

Not only to say the right thing in the right place, but far more difficult, to leave unsaid the wrong thing at the tempting moment.
—George Augustus Sala

Do not be smart at the expense of another.
—Baltasar Grácian

Nothing is more insulting, more mortifying, and less forgiven, then avowedly to take pains to make a man feel a mortifying inferiority in knowledge, rank, fortune, etc. In the last two articles it is unjust, they not being in his power; and in the first it is both ill-bred and ill-natured. Good breeding and good nature do incline us rather to help and raise people up to ourselves, than to mortify and depress them, and, in truth, our own private interest concurs in it, as it is making ourselves so many friends, instead of so many enemies.
—Lord Chesterfield

The most amiable people are those who least wound the self-love of others.
—Jean de La Bruyère

Politeness may be defined as a dexterous management of our words and actions whereby we make other people have better opinions of us and themselves.
—Author Unknown

There is one rule relative to behavior that ought to regulate every other; and it is simply to cherish such an habitual respect for mankind as may prevent us from disgusting a fellow-creature for the sake of a present indulgence.
—Mary Wollstonecraft

A gentleman is one who understands and shows every mark of deference to the claims of self-love in others, and exacts it in return from them.
—William Hazlitt

There is nothing that need be said in an unkind manner.
—Hosea Ballou

Most things must be left unnoticed among relatives and friends, and even among enemies.
—Baltasar Grácian

Abhor a knave and pity a fool in your heart, but let neither of them unnecessarily see that you do so.
—Lord Chesterfield

Tact: the ability to describe others as they see themselves.
—Abraham Lincoln

If we treat people too long with that pretended liking called politeness, we shall find it hard not to like them in the end.
—Logan Pearsall Smith

Hard to dislike a chap who likes you, isn't it? Well, there's your peace plan.
—Author Unknown

Politeness is the chief sign of culture.
—Baltasar Grácian

True politeness is perfect ease and freedom. It simply consists in treating others just as you love to be treated yourself.
—Lord Chesterfield

Whatever pleases you most, in others, will infallibly please others, in you.
—Lord Chesterfield

Politeness does not always evince goodness, equity, complaisance, or gratitude, but it gives at least the appearance of these qualities, and makes man appear outwardly as he should be within.
—Jean de La Bruyère

Politeness is a tacit agreement that people's miserable defects, whether moral or intellectual, shall on either side be ignored and not be made the subject of reproach.
—Arthur Schopenhauer

Great talent and success render a man famous; great merit procures respect; great learning, veneration; but politeness alone ensures love and affection.
—Author Unknown

No manners are finer than even the most awkward manifesttations of good will to others.
—Author Unknown

Politeness has been well defined as benevolence in small things.
—Thomas B. Macaulay

Courtesies of a small and trivial character are the ones which strike deepest in the grateful and appreciating heart.
—Henry Clay

The small courtesies sweeten life; the greater ennoble it.
—Christian Nestell Bovee

The secret of success in society is a certain heartiness and sympathy.
—Ralph Waldo Emerson

For the average man a sufficient rule of life is to follow his instincts controlled by the moral standard of the society in which he lives.
—W. Somerset Maugham

Life is livable because we know that wherever we go most of the people we meet will be restrained in their actions toward us by an almost instinctive network of taboos.
—Havelock Ellis

Politeness is the curb that holds our worse selves in check.
—Madame de Badanville

Civilization is an exercise in self-restraint.
—William Butler Yeats

Never underestimate the power of simple courtesy. Your courtesy may not be returned or remembered, but discourtesy will.
—Princess Jackson Smith

The test of good manners is to be patient with bad ones.
—Salomon Ibn Gabirol

Grace is the absence of everything that indicates pain or difficulty, hesitation or incongruity.
—William Hazlitt

Never seem wiser or more learned than the people you are with.
—Lord Chesterfield

There is an unseemly exposure of the mind, as well as of the body.
—William Hazlitt

A great man is always willing to be little.
—Ralph Waldo Emerson

If we would please in society, we must be prepared to be taught many things we know already by people who do not know them.
—Sébastien R. Nicholas Chamfort

A polite man is one who listens with interest to things he knows all about, when they are told him by a person who knows nothing about them.
—Phillipe de Mornay

Every man of sound brain whom you meet knows something worth knowing better than yourself.
—Edward G. Bulwer-Lytton

Everybody, my friend, everybody lives for something better to come. That's why we want to be considerate of every man—Who knows what's in him, why he was born and what he can do.
—Maxim Gorky

Real unselfishness consists in sharing the interests of others.
—George Santayana

Everyone alters and is altered by everyone else. We are all the time taking in portions of one another or else reacting against them, and by taking these involuntary acquisitions and repulsions modifying our behavior.
—Gerald Brenan

Treat your inferiors as you would be treated by your betters.
—Seneca

This is the final test of a gentleman: his respect for those who can be of no possible service to him.
—William Lyon Phelps

A bad manner spoils everything, even reason and justice.
—Baltasar Grácian

He that can please nobody is not so much to be pitied as he that nobody can please.
—Charles Caleb Colton

The first thing to learn in intercourse with others is non-interference with their own peculiar ways of being happy,

provided those ways do not assume to interfere by violence with ours.
—William James

Be not angry that you cannot make others as you wish them to be, since you cannot make yourself as you wish to be.
—Thomas á Kempis

What you dislike in another, take care to correct in yourself.
—Thomas Sprat

Be charitable and indulgent to every one but thyself.
—Joseph Joubert

Never be haughty to the humble; never be humble to the haughty.
—Jefferson Davis

If you would stand well with a great mind, leave him with a favorable impression of yourself; if with a little mind, leave him with a favorable opinion of himself.
—Samuel Taylor Coleridge

Good breeding consists in concealing how much we think of ourselves and how little we think of other persons.
—Mark Twain

Act in such a manner that I can esteem you, so that I should be sorry to lose your favor, or sorry I was never able to obtain it.
—Jean de La Bruyère

One can always be kind to people about whom one cares nothing.
—Oscar Wilde

A deserved and discriminating compliment is often one of the strongest encouragements and incentives to the diffident and self-distrustful.
—Tryon Edwards

A compliment is something like a kiss through a veil.
—Victor Hugo

You must not pay a person a compliment, and then straightaway
follow it with criticism.
—Mark Twain

Do not offer a compliment and ask a favor at the same time. A
compliment that is charged for is not valuable.
—Mark Twain

It is grace in flattery to let fall your compliments as that you shall
seem to consider them to be a matter of complete indifference to
him to whom they are addressed; for thus one flattery will
include another—and the other perhaps the most agreeable—
being that of attributing to the party a particular absence of self-
love.
—Sir Henry Taylor

To compliment often implies an assumption of superiority in the
complimenter. It is, in fact, a subtle detraction.
—Henry David Thoreau

Avoid flatterers, for they are thieves in disguise.
—William Penn

He who can lick can bite.
—French Proverb

Nothing is so great an instance of ill manners as flattery. If you
flatter all the company, you please none; if you flatter only one or
two, you affront the rest.
—Jonathan Swift

Flattery is like cologne water, to be smelt of, not swallowed.
—Josh Billings

Flattery is a kind of bad money, to which our vanity gives us
currency.
—François de La Rochefoucauld

Sometimes we think we dislike flattery, but it's only the way it is done that we dislike.
—François de La Rochefoucauld

We love flattery, even when we see through it, and are not deceived by it, for it shows that we are of importance enough to be courted.
—Ralph Waldo Emerson

I love flattery so well, I would fain have some circumstances of probability added to it, that I might swallow it with more comfort.
—Lady Mary Wortley Montagu

I hate careless flattery, the kind that exhausts you in your effort to believe it.
—Wilson Mizner

A flatterer: one who extremely exaggerates his opinion of your qualities so that it may come nearer to your opinion of them.
—Author Unknown

The love of flattery in most men proceeds from the mean opinion they have of themselves; in women, from the contrary.
—Jonathan Swift

Women who are either indisputably beautiful, or indisputably ugly, are best flattered upon the score of their understandings; but those who are in a state of mediocrity are best flattered upon their beauty, or at least their graces; for every woman who is not absolutely ugly thinks herself handsome.
—Lord Chesterfield

The aim of flattery is to soothe and encourage us by assuring us of some truth of an opinion we have already formed about ourselves.
—Edith Sitwell

Among all the diseases of the mind, there is not one more epidemical, or more pernicious, than the love of flattery. First we flatter ourselves, and then the flattery of others is sure of success.

It awakens our self-love within—a party who is ever ready to revolt from our better judgment, and join the enemy without.
—Sir Richard Steele

None are more taken in by flattery than the proud, who wish to be the first and are not.
—Benedict Baruch Spinoza

He who says he hates all kinds of flattery, and says so in earnest, simply says that he has not yet become acquainted with all kinds of it.
—George C. Lichtenberg

There is scarcely any man, how much soever he may despise the character of a flatterer, but will condescend in the meanest manner to flatter himself.
—Henry Fielding

A good listener is a silent flatterer.
—Author Unknown

No siren did ever so charm the ear of the listener as the listening ear has charmed the soul of the siren.
—Sir Henry Taylor

Most people have a furious itch to talk about themselves and are restrained only by the disinclination of others to listen. Reserve is an artificial quality that is developed in most of us as a result of innumerable rebuffs.
—W. Somerset Maugham

You will easily discover every man's prevailing vanity by observing his favourite topic of conversation.
—Lord Chesterfield

Never speak of yourself to others; make them talk about themselves instead: therein lies the whole art of pleasing. Everyone knows it and everyone forgets it.
—Edmund and Jules de Goncourt

There is no arena in which vanity displays itself under such a variety of forms as in conversation.
—Blaise Pascal

Conversation: A fair for the display of the minor mental commodities, each exhibitor being too intent upon the arrangement of his own wares to observe those of his neighbors.
—Ambrose Bierce

There are people who instead of listening to what is being said to them are already listening to what they are going to say themselves.
—Albert Guinon

One of the reasons that we find so few persons rational and agreeable in conversation is there is hardly a person who does not think more of what he wants to say than of his answer to what is said. The most clever and polite are content with only seeming attentive while we perceive in their mind and eyes that at the very time they are wandering from what is said and desire to return to what they want to say. Instead of considering that the worst way to persuade or please others is to try thus strongly to please ourselves, and that to listen well and to answer well are some of the greatest charms we can have in conversation.
—François de La Rochefoucauld

Accustom yourself to give careful attention to what others are saying, and try your best to enter into the mood of the speaker.
—Marcus Aurelius Antoninus

Avoid interruptive thinking. Everyone—and I mean everyone—has something good to offer you if you are astute enough to find it. Sometimes it means picking a small kernel out of a lot of chaff, but the kernel is always there. One way to get the best from people is to learn to avoid what I call interruptive thinking. This is where someone is saying something to you and you interrupt—and probably change the subject in doing so.
—David Mahoney

Cultivate the habit of attention and try to gain opportunities to hear wise men and women talk. Indifference and inattention are

the two most dangerous monsters that you ever meet. Interest and attention will insure to you an education.
—Robert A. Millikan

There is no such thing as a worthless conversation, provided you know what to listen for. And questions are the breath of life for a conversation.
—James Nathan Miller

Conversation is but carving!
Give no more to every guest
Than he's able to digest.
Give him always of the prime,
And but little at a time.
Carve to all but just enough,
Let them neither starve nor stuff,
And that you may have your due,
Let your neighbor carve for you.
—Jonathan Swift

Never talk for more than half a minute without pausing and giving others an opportunity to strike in.
—Sydney Smith

No man would listen to you talk if he didn't know it was his turn next.
—Edgar Watson Howe

Conversation is an art in which man has all mankind for competitors, for it is that which all are practicing every day while they live.
—Ralph Waldo Emerson

Do not put everything into the showcase at once, or none will pause to admire on another day. Always keep something new in reserve with which to dazzle to-morrow, for he who thus uncovers something fresh each day, maintains the interest, and never allows the limits of his treasury to be discovered.
—Baltasar Grácian

Never hold anyone by the button or the hand in order to be heard out; for if people are unwilling to hear you, you had better hold your tongue than them.
—Lord Chesterfield

It is a secret known to but few, but of no small use in the conduct of life, that when you fall into a man's conversation, the first thing you should consider is, whether he has a greater inclination to hear you, or that you should hear him.
—Sir Richard Steele

Do not fail to catch the other's mood; lest you give him pain instead of pleasure. . . . For when you do not sense another's mood, it is hard to bring him satisfaction.
—Baltasar Grácian

Do not betray even to your friend too much of your real purposes and thoughts; in conversation ask questions oftener than you express opinions; and when you speak offer data and information rather than beliefs and judgments.
—Will Durant

There is but one way of conversing safely with all men; that is, not by concealing what we say or do, but by saying or doing nothing that deserves to be concealed.
—Alexander Pope

Birds are entangled by their feet and men by their tongues.
—Thomas Fuller (II)

A well-bred man keeps his beliefs out of his conversation.
—André Maurois

Keep some opinions to yourself. Say what you please of others, but never repeat what you hear said of them to themselves. If you have nothing to offer yourself, laugh with the witty, assent to the wise; they will not think the worse of you for it. Listen to information on subjects you are unacquainted with, instead of always striving to lead the conversation to some favourite one of

your own. By the last method you will shine, but will not improve.
—William Hazlitt

Stay at home in your mind. Don't repeat other people's opinions.
—Ralph Waldo Emerson

Men who borrow their opinions can never repay their debts.
—Lord Halifax

It is as natural, and as allowable, that another man should differ in opinion from me, as that I should differ from him; and that, if we are both sincere, we are both blameless: and should consequently have mutual indulgence for each other.
—Lord Chesterfield

Don't judge a man by his opinions, but by what his opinions have made him.
—George C. Lichtenberg

We are most likely to get angry and excited in our opposition to some idea when we ourselves are not quite certain of our own position, and are inwardly tempted to take the other side.
—Thomas Mann

Obstinacy and heat in sticking to one's opinions is the surest proof of stupidity. Is there anything so assured, resolved, disdainful, contemplative, solemn and serious as an ass?
—Michel de Montaigne

We hardly find any persons of good sense save those who agree with us.
—François de La Rochefoucauld

The fellow that agrees with everything you say is either a fool or he is getting ready to skin you.
—Kin Hubbard

One often contradicts an opinion when what is uncongenial is really the tone in which it was conveyed.
—Friedrich Wilhelm Nietzsche

Do you know that the ready concession of minor points is a part of the grace of life?
—Henry Harland

Before you are frank with another, ask yourself: WHY? Is it to diminish the other, to make yourself feel better at his expense? The ethical question is to ask: will this foster the relationship? There is always a way to be honest without being brutal.
—Arthur Dobrin

Don't tell all that you know, or judge all that you see, if you wish to live in peace.
—Charles Cahier

Silence and modesty are very valuable qualities in the art of conversation.
—Michel de Montaigne

Some people talk simply because they think sound is more manageable than silence.
—Margaret Halsey

Silence propagates itself, and the longer talk has been suspended, the more difficult it is to find anything to say.
—Samuel Johnson

It is never more difficult to speak well than when we are ashamed of being silent.
—François de La Rochefoucauld

Nothing prevents our being natural so much as our desire to seem so.
—François de La Rochefoucauld

That we seldom repent of talking too little and very often of talking too much is a . . . maxim that everybody knows and nobody practices.
—Jean de La Bruyère

God has given to man a cloak whereby he can conceal his ignorance, and in this cloak he can enwrap himself at any moment, for it always lies near his hand. This cloak is silence.
—Bhartrihari

Nature has given us two ears, two eyes, and but one tongue, to the end that we should hear and see more than we speak.
—Socrates

A judicious reticence is hard to learn, but it is one of the great lessons of life.
—Lord Chesterfield

From listening comes wisdom, and from speaking repentance.
—Italian Proverb

When in the company of sensible men, we ought to be doubly cautious of talking too much, lest we lose two good things—their good opinion and our own improvement; for what we have to say we know, but what they have to say we know not.
—Charles Caleb Colton

Silence is always better than truth spoken without charity.
—Saint Francis de Sales

If you your lips would keep from slips,
    Five things observe with care;
To whom you speak, of whom you speak,
    And how, and when, and where.
—W. E. Norris

Look out for the fellow that lets you do all the talking.
—Kin Hubbard

Discretion in conversation is more important than eloquence.
—Baltasar Grácian

It (is) usually better not to walk through conversational doors other people (have) left open.
—Christopher Hale

Shun the inquisitive, for you will be sure to find him leaky. Open ears do not keep conscientiously what has been entrusted to them, and a word once spoken flies, never to be recalled.
—Horace

Never utter a word in private which you would regret to have heard in public.
—Saadi

The things most people want to know about are usually none of their business.
—George Bernard Shaw

Conversation has a kind of charm about it, an insinuating and insidious something that elicits secrets from us just like love or liquor.
—Seneca

We speak little if not egged on by vanity.
—François de La Rochefoucauld

Seldom do we talk of ourselves with success. If I condemn myself more is believed than is expressed; if I praise myself, much less.
—Henry Home

The more you speak of yourself, the more you are likely to lie.
—Johann G. Zimmermann

Man always talks about the most important things to perfect strangers.
—G. K. Chesterton

It is very disagreeable to seem reserved, and very dangerous not to be.
—Lord Chesterfield

Give not thy tongue too great liberty, lest it take thee prisoner, like the sword in the scabbard, thine. If vented, thy sword is in

another's hand. If thou desire to be held wise, be so wise as to hold thy tongue.
—Francis Quarles

Consider what you ought to say, and not what you think.
—Publilius Syrus

No one would talk much in society, if he only knew how often he misunderstood others.
—Johann Wolfgang von Goethe

For one word a man is often deemed to be wise, and for one word he is often doomed to be foolish. We should be careful indeed of what we say.
—Confucius

A wise man reflects before he speaks. A fool speaks, and then reflects on what he has uttered.
—Jacques Delille

No glass renders a man's form or likeness so true as his speech.
—Ben Jonson

Speech is a mirror of the soul: as a man speaks, so he is.
—Publilius Syrus

Words are the dress of thoughts; which should no more be presented in rags, tatters, and dirt, than your person should.
—Lord Chesterfield

Words, like eyeglasses, blur everything that they do not make more clear.
—Joseph Joubert

The more you say, the less people remember. The fewer the words, the greater the profit.
—François de Fénelon

If you would be pungent, be brief; for it is with words as with sunbeams—the more they are condensed the deeper they burn.
—Robert Southey

One great use of words is to hide our thoughts.
—François Marie de Voltaire

That character in conversation which commonly passes for agreeable is made up of civility and falsehood.
—Alexander Pope

Falsehood plays a larger part in the world than truth.
—Sir Thomas Overbury

So near is falsehood to truth that a wise man would be well not to trust himself on the narrow edge.
—Cicero

Falsehoods not only disagree with truths, but usually quarrel among themselves.
—Daniel Webster

A willful falsehood told is a cripple, not able to stand by itself without another to support it. It is easy to tell a lie, but hard to tell only one lie.
—Thomas Fuller (II)

One lie engenders another. Once committed, the liar has to go on in his course of lying; it is the penalty of his transgression.
—Francis Jacox

One lie must be thatched with another or it will soon rain through.
—John Jason Owen

A liar has many points to his favour,—but he has this against him, that unless he devote more time to the management of his lies than life will generally allow, he cannot make them tally.
—Anthony Trollope

One ought to have a good memory when he has told a lie.
—Pierre Corneille

Let the liar forget, and then ask him.
—Moroccan Proverb

If we suspect that a man is lying, we should pretend to believe him; for then he becomes bold and assured, lies more vigorously, and is unmasked.
—Arthur Schopenhauer

Falsehood, like poison, will generally be rejected, when administered alone; but when blended with wholesome ingredients, may be swallowed unperceived.
—Richard Whately

A little truth makes the lie go down.
—Italian Proverb

Clever liars give details, but the cleverest don't.
—Author Unknown

A liar begins with making falsehood appear like truth, and ends with making truth itself appear like falsehood.
—William Shenstone

Accuracy: A certain uninteresting quality carefully excluded from human statements.
—Ambrose Bierce

The moment a man talks to his fellows he begins to lie.
—Hilaire Belloc

Never to lie is to have no lock on your door.
—Elizabeth Bowen

We are all liars to people we don't care for.
—George Bernard Shaw

Seldom any splendid story is wholly true.
—Samuel Johnson

It is a rule of manners to avoid exaggeration.
—Ralph Waldo Emerson

Exaggeration is akin to lying; and through it you jeopardize your reputation for good taste, which is much, and for good judgment, which is more.
—Baltasar Grácian

There are people so addicted to exaggeration they can't tell the truth without lying.
—Josh Billings

Even if people's interests are not affected by what they say, it must not be definitely concluded that they are not lying for there are some people who lie simply for the sake of lying.
—Blaise Pascal

I myself could not open my mouth without misrepresenting things or people, for otherwise I should have seen no use in talking at all. Talking seemed to me an event in itself which must not be hampered by any other events.
—Italo Svevo

I have seldom known any one who deserted truth in trifles, that could be trusted in matters of importance.
—William Paley

The telling of a falsehood is like the cut of a sabre; for though the wound may heal, the scar of it will remain.
—Saadi

A liar will not be believed, even when he speaks the truth.
—Æsop

The liar's punishment is not in the least that he is not believed, but that he cannot believe anyone else.
—George Bernard Shaw

Liars share with those they deceive the desire not to be deceived.
—Sissela Bok

However much we may distrust men's sincerity, we always believe they speak to us more sincerely than to others.
—François de La Rochefoucauld

We are never deceived; we deceive ourselves.
—Johann Wolfgang von Goethe

The truth that survives is simply the lie that is pleasantest to believe.
—H. L. Mencken

No one escapes talking nonsense; the misfortune is to do it seriously.
—Michel de Montaigne

We often say things because we can say them well, rather than because they are sound and reasonable.
—Walter Savage Landor

Originality does not consist in saying what no one has ever said before, but in saying exactly what you think yourself.
—James Fitz-James Stephen

Never be afraid of the deafeningly obvious. It is always news to somebody.
—P. G. Kavanagh

Be yourself and speak your mind today, though it contradict all you have said before.
—Elbert Hubbard

If people would dare to speak to one another unreservedly, there would be a good deal less sorrow in the world a hundred years hence.
—Samuel Butler (II)

The soul of conversation is sympathy.
—William Hazlitt

One of the best rules in conversation is, never to say a thing which any of the company can reasonably wish had been left unsaid.
—Jonathan Swift

Conceit causes more conversation than wit.
—François de La Rochefoucauld

Wit is the salt of conversation, not the food.
—William Hazlitt

The true spirit of conversation consists more in bringing out the cleverness of others than in showing a great deal of it yourself; he who goes away pleased with himself and his own wit is also greatly pleased with you. Most men would rather please than admire you; they seek less to be instructed, and even to be amused, than to be praised and applauded; the most delicate of pleasures is to please another person.
—Jean de La Bruyère

The desire to seem clever often keeps us from being so.
—François de La Rochefoucauld

Those wanting wit affect gravity, and go by the name of solid men.
—John Dryden

Gravity is a trick of the body devised to conceal deficiencies of the mind.
—François de La Rochefoucauld

Reply with wit to gravity, and with gravity to wit.
—Charles Caleb Colton

Melancholy men are of all others the most witty.
—Aristotle

If you want to be witty, work on your character and say what you think on every occasion.
—Stendhal

The hapless wit has his own labors always to begin, the call for novelty is never satisfied, and one jest only raises expectation of another.
—Samuel Johnson

Wit consists in knowing the resemblance of things which differ, and the difference of things which are alike.
—Madame Germaine de Staël

Wit is the sudden marriage of ideas which, before their union, were not perceived to have any relation.
—Mark Twain

Wit's an unruly engine, wildly striking
Sometimes a friend, sometimes the engineer.
—George Herbert

If you have wit, use it to please, and not to hurt.
—Lord Chesterfield

Mockery is only too often mere poverty of wit.
—Jean de La Bruyère

It is not enough to possess wit. One must have enough of it to avoid having too much.
—André Maurois

If God gives you wit . . . wear it like your sword in the scabbard, and do not brandish it to the terror of the whole company.
—Lord Chesterfield

The temptation of saying a smart or witty thing, . . . and the malicious applause with which it is commonly received, have made people who can say them, and, still oftener, people who think they can, but cannot and yet try, more enemies, and implacable ones too, than any one thing that I can think of. When such things, then, shall happen to be said at your expense (as sometimes they certainly will) reflect seriously upon the sentiments of uneasiness, anger, and resentment, which they excite in you; and consider whether it can be prudent, by the same means, to excite the same sentiments in others against you.
—Lord Chesterfield

Who cares for anybody that has more wit than himself?
—William Congreve

Fools are only laugh'd at; wits are hated.
—Alexander Pope

Wit is so shining a quality that everybody admires it; most people aim at it, all people fear it, and few love it unless in themselves.
—Lord Chesterfield

One isn't amused long by the wit of someone else.
—Luc de Clapiers de Vauvenargues

There's no possibility of being witty without a little ill-nature; the malice of a good thing is the barb that makes it stick.
—Richard Brinsley Sheridan

Impropriety is the soul of wit.
—W. Somerset Maugham

Wit makes its own welcome, and levels all distinctions. No dignity, no learning, no force of character, can make any stand against good wit.
—Ralph Waldo Emerson

Men will let you abuse them if only you will make them laugh.
—Henry Ward Beecher

The finest satire is the one in which ridicule is combined with so little malice and so much conviction that it forces a laugh even from those it hits.
—George C. Lichtenberg

You are not angry with people when you laugh at them. Humour teaches tolerance.
—W. Somerset Maugham

It is the ability to take a joke, not make one, which proves you have a sense of humor.
—Max Eastman

He is not laughed at that laughs at himself first.
—Thomas Fuller (II)

A taste for irony has kept more hearts from breaking than a sense of humor for it takes irony to appreciate the joke which is on oneself.
—Jessamyn West

If you don't learn to laugh at trouble, you won't have anything to laugh at when you're old.
—Edgar Watson Howe

The most thoroughly wasted of all days is that on which one has not laughed.
—Sébastien R. Nicholas Chamfort

Conversation never sits easier upon us than when we now and then discharge ourselves in a symphony of laughter, which may not improperly be called the chorus of conversation.
—Sir Richard Steele

Jesting is often only indigence of intellect.
—Jean de La Bruyère

The jest loses its point when he who makes it is the first to laugh.
—Johann Friedrich von Schiller

Many a true word is spoken in jest.
—English Proverb

To smile at the jest which plants a thorn in another's breast is to become a principal in the mischief.
—Richard Brinsley Sheridan

Jests that give pains are no jests.
—Miguel de Cervantes

Better lose a jest than a friend.
—Thomas Fuller (II)

Those who cannot miss an opportunity of saying a good thing . . . are not to be trusted with the management of any great question.
—William Hazlitt

Take heed of jesting; many have been ruined by it. It is hard to jest, and not sometimes to jeer too, which often sinks deeper than we intended or expected.
—Thomas Fuller (I)

Never yield to that temptation, which, to most young men, is very strong, of exposing other people's weaknesses and infirmities, for the sake of diverting the company, or of showing your own superiority. You may get the laugh on your side by it, for the present; but you will make enemies by it for ever; and even those who laugh with you then, will, upon reflection, fear, and consequently hate you: besides that, it is ill-natured; and a good heart desires to conceal, than expose, other people's weaknesses or misfortunes.
—Lord Chesterfield

As long as a word remains unspoken, you are its master; once you utter it, you are its slave.
—Salomon Ibn Gabirol

Our words have wings, but fly not where we would.
—George Eliot

It is with a word as with an arrow—once let it loose and it does not return.
—Abd-El-Kader

Mark your words, as a matter of caution when with rivals, and as a matter of decency, when with the rest. There is always time to add a word, but none in which to take one back.
—Baltasar Grácian

A word ill-taken blots out the merit of ten years.
—Michel de Montaigne

We live at the mercy of a malevolent word. A sound, a mere disturbance of the air, sinks into our very soul.
—Joseph Conrad

A blow with a word strikes deeper than a blow with a sword.
—Robert Burton

Sharp words make more wounds than surgeons can heale.
—Thomas Churchyard

There are words which sever hearts more than sharp swords; there are words the point of which sting the heart through the course of a whole life.
—Frederika Bremer

Words can destroy. What we call each other ultimately becomes what we think of each other, and it matters.
—Jeane J. Kirkpatrick

People can bear hardship easily so long as there is no injury, and even injury so long as they do not have to cope with insult.
—Statius

Insults are like bad coins; we cannot help their being offered to us, but we need not take them.
—Charles Haddon Spurgeon

It is often better not to see an insult than to avenge it.
—Seneca

Whatever may be the motive of an insult it is always best to overlook it; for folly scarcely can deserve resentment, and malice is punished by neglect.
—Samuel Johnson

When people injure you, ask yourself what good or harm they thought would come of it. If you understand that, you'll feel sympathy rather than outrage or anger. Your sense of good and evil may be the same as theirs, or near it, in which case you have to excuse them. Or your sense of good and evil may differ from theirs. In which case, they're misguided and deserve your compassion.
—Marcus Aurelius Antoninus

An insult is either sustained or destroyed, not by the disposition of those who insult, but by the disposition of those who bear it.
—St. John Chrysostom

A very small offence may be a just cause for great resentment; it is often much less the particular instance which is obnoxious to us, than the proof it carries with it of the general tenor and disposition of the mind from whence it sprung.
—Lord Fulke Gréville

The words of some men are thrown forcibly against you and adhere like burs.
—Henry David Thoreau

Who offends writes on sand, who is offended on marble.
—Italian Proverb

Injuries may be atoned for and forgiven; but insults admit of no compensation; they degrade the mind of its own esteem, and force it to recover its level by revenge.
—Junius

There are innumerable modes of insults and tokens of contempt for which it is not easy to find a name, which vanish to nothing in an attempt to describe them, and yet may, by continual repetition, make day pass after day in sorrow and terror.
—Samuel Johnson

There are moments when petty slights are harder to bear than even a serious injury. Men have died of the festering of a gnat-bite.
—William Danby

The best way to procure insults is to submit to them. A man meets with no more respect than he exacts.
—William Hazlitt

Men are more ready to offend one who desires to be loved than one who wishes to be feared.
—Niccolò Machiavelli

By other's faults wise men correct their own offences.
—Nicholas Ling

If you speak insults, you shall also hear them.
—Plautus

Abuse a man unjustly, and you will make friends for him.
—Edgar Watson Howe

Offences ought to be pardoned, for few offend willingly, but only as led by some excitement.
—Hegesippus

He who regrets his offence offends without foresight.
—Publilius Syrus

Every man is of importance to himself.
—Samuel Johnson

No one considers himself contemptible.
—Jakob Burckhardt

There is nothing that people bear more impatiently, or forgive less, than contempt; and an injury is much sooner forgotten than an insult.
—Lord Chesterfield

Wrongs are often forgiven, but contempt never is. Our pride remembers it forever.
—Lord Chesterfield

Be not indifferent to contempt, even from very ordinary people, but rather look well to the cause of it.
—Charles Simmons

Be convinced that there are no persons so insignificant and inconsiderable, but may some time or other, have it in their power to be of use to you; which certainly they will not, if you have once shown them contempt.
—Lord Chesterfield

The insolent contempt of a proud man is, if possible, more shocking than his rudeness could be; because he shows you, by his manner, that he thinks it mere condescension in him; and

that his goodness alone bestows upon you what you have no pretense to claim.
—Lord Chesterfield

Superiority is always detested.
—Baltasar Grácian

No man who says "I am as good as you" believes it. The St. Bernard never says it to the toy dog, nor the scholar to the dunce, nor the employable to the bum, nor the pretty woman to the plain. The claim to equality is made only by those who feel themselves to be in some way inferior.
—C. S. Lewis

No one can make you feel inferior without your consent.
—Anna Eleanor Roosevelt

Arrogance in persons of merit affronts us more than arrogance in those without merit: merit itself is an affront.
—Friedrich Wilhelm Nietzsche

Rudeness is the weak man's imitation of strength.
—Eric Hoffer

Those who are contemptuous of everyone are more than anyone terrified of contempt.
—Logan Pearsall Smith

Contempt: The feeling of a prudent man for an enemy who is too formidable safely to oppose.
—Ambrose Bierce

Rudeness is better than any argument; it totally eclipses intellect.
—Arthur Schopenhauer

Silence—the most perfect expression of scorn.
—George Bernard Shaw

Arguments are to be avoided: they are always vulgar and often convincing.
—Oscar Wilde

It is easier to refrain than to retreat from a quarrel.
—Seneca

The test of a man or woman's breeding is how they behave in a quarrel.
—George Bernard Shaw

There is no such test of a man's superiority of character as in the well-conducting of an unavoidable quarrel.
—Sir Henry Taylor

Keep strong, if possible. In any case, keep cool. Have unlimited patience. Never corner an opponent, and always assist him to save his face. Put yourself in his shoes—so as to see things through his eyes. Avoid self-righteousness like the devil—nothing so self-blinding.
—Sir Basil Henry Liddell-Hart

The greatest mistake is the trying to be more agreeable than you can be.
—Walter Bagehot

Courtesy on one side can never last long.
—Author Unknown

Whenever two good people argue over principles, they are both right.
—Marie von Ebner-Eschenbach

When we would show any one that he is mistaken, our best course is to observe on what side he considers the subject,—for his view of it is generally right on this side—and to admit to him that he is right so far. He will be satisfied with this acknowledgment, that he was not wrong in his judgment, but only inadvertent in not looking at the whole case.
—Blaise Pascal

Do not carry a spirit of contradiction, for it is to be freighted with stupidity, and with peevishness, and your intelligence should plot against it; though it may well be the mark of mental genius to see objection, a wrangler about everything cannot escape being

marked the fool, for he makes guerrilla warfare of quiet conversation, and so becomes more of an enemy to his intimates, than to those with whom he will have nothing to do.
—Baltasar Grácian

Never contend with one that is foolish, proud, positive, testy, or with a superior, or a clown, in matter of argument.
—Thomas Fuller (I)

Behind every argument is someone's ignorance.
—Louis D. Brandeis

Men are apt to mistake the strength of their feeling for the strength of their argument. The heated mind resents the chill touch and relentless scrutiny of logic.
—William E. Gladstone

Argument seldom convinces anyone contrary to his inclinations.
—Thomas Fuller (I)

It is in disputes as in armies: where the weaker side set up false lights, and make a great noise to make the enemy believe them more numerous and strong than they really are.
—Jonathan Swift

Noise proves nothing. Often a hen who has merely laid an egg cackles as if she had laid an asteroid.
—Mark Twain

In quarreling the truth is always lost.
—Publilius Syrus

Discussion is an exchange of knowledge; argument an exchange of ignorance.
—Quillen

Some strand of our own misdoing is involved in every quarrel.
—Robert Louis Stevenson

A quarrel is quickly settled when deserted by one party: there is no battle unless there be two.
—Seneca

When worthy men fall out, only one of them may be faulty at first; but if the strife continue long, both commonly become guilty.
—Thomas Fuller (I)

A long dispute means that both parties are wrong.
—François Marie de Voltaire

When two quarrel, he who keeps silence first is the more praiseworthy.
—Babylonian Talmud

In private life I never knew anyone interfere with other people's disputes but that he heartily repented of it.
—Thomas Carlyle

Do not interfere when your opinion is not sought.
—Thomas á Kempis

He that blows the coals in quarrels he has nothing to do with has no right to complain if the sparks fly in his face.
—Benjamin Franklin

Always behave as if nothing had happened no matter what has happened.
—Arnold Bennett

There is no living in the world without a complaisant indulgence for people's weaknesses and innocent, though ridiculous, vanities.
—Lord Chesterfield

To be social is to be forgiving.
—Robert Frost

Life is not so short but that there is always time for courtesy.
—Ralph Waldo Emerson

Conduct is three-fourths of our life and its largest concern.
—Matthew Arnold

In civilized society we all depend upon each other, and our happiness is very much owing to the good opinion of mankind.
—Samuel Johnson

This is the sum of all true righteousness: deal with others as thou wouldst thyself be dealt by. Do nought to others which, if done to thee, would cause thee pain.
—Mahabharata

Such Is Life

PART 5

FRIENDSHIP

Each friend represents a world in us,
a world possibly not born until they arrive,
and it is only by this meeting
that a new world is born.
—Anaïs Nin

Such Is Life

We keep passing unseen through little moments of other people's lives.
—Robert M. Pirsig

We wander in this life together in a semi-darkness in which none of us can distinguish exactly the features of his neighbor. Only from time to time, through some experience that we have of our companion, or through some remark that he passes, he stands for a moment close to us, as though illuminated by a flash of lightning. Then we see him as he really is.
—Albert Schweitzer

The wisest man I have ever known once said to me: "Nine out of every ten people improve on acquaintance," and I have found his words true.
—Frank Swinnerton

You never know till you try to reach them how accessible men are; but you must approach each man by the right door.
—Henry Ward Beecher

Every man is a volume if you know how to read him.
—William Ellery Channing

No matter whom you meet, always begin by asking yourself, What are his views on the goodness or badness of things? For then, if his beliefs about pleasure and pain and their causes, or about repute and disrepute, or life and death are of a certain type, I shall not be surprised or scandalized to find his actions in keeping with them; I shall tell myself that he has no choice.
—Marcus Aurelius Antoninus

When the character of a man is not clear to you, look at his friends.
—Japanese Proverb

He is a good man whose intimate friends are all good, and whose enemies are decidedly bad.
—Johann Kaspar Lavater

As your enemies and friends, so are you.
—Johann Kaspar Lavater

All of us are more or less echoes; and despite ourselves, we repeat the good and bad qualities, the actions and the character of those among whom we live.
—Joseph Joubert

When we live habitually with the wicked, we become necessarily either their victim or their disciple; when we associate, on the contrary, with virtuous men, we form ourselves in imitation of their virtues, or, at least, lose every day something of our faults.
—Agapet

No man in effect doth accompany with others but he learneth, ere he is aware, some gesture, voice, or fashion.
—Francis Bacon

If you live with a lame man you will learn to limp.
—Plutarch

In any relationship we feel an unconscious need to create, as it were, a new picture, a new edition of ourselves to present to the fresh person who claims our interest; for them, we in a strange way wish to, and do, start life anew.
—Ann N. Bridge

In the presence of some people we inevitably depart from ourselves: we are inaccurate, say things we do not feel, and talk nonsense. When we get home we are conscious that we have made fools of ourselves. Never go near these people.
—Samuel Rutherford

Almost every man wastes parts of his life in attempts to display qualities which he does not possess, and to gain applause which he cannot keep; so that scarcely can two persons meet but one is offended or diverted by the ostentation of the other.
—Samuel Johnson

No two men can be half an hour together but one shall acquire an evident superiority over the other.
—Samuel Johnson

What makes us like new acquaintances is not so much any weariness of our old ones, or the pleasure of change, as disgust at not being sufficiently admired by those who know us too well, and the hope of being more so by those who do not know so much of us.
—François de La Rochefoucauld

I never knew a man so mean that I was not willing he should admire me.
—Edgar Watson Howe

We always love those who admire us; we do not always love those whom we admire.
—François de La Rochefoucauld

No man regards himself as in all ways inferior to the man he most admires.
—François de La Rochefoucauld

Admiration: Our polite recognition of another's resemblance to ourselves.
—Ambrose Bierce

Admiration is the daughter of ignorance.
—Benjamin Franklin

Admiration is a very short-lived passion that immediately decays upon growing familiar with its object.
—Joseph Addison

Admiration and familiarity are strangers.
—George Sand

Nothing is wonderful when you get used to it.
—Edgar Watson Howe

Familiarity is the root of the closest friendships, as well as the intensest hatreds.
—Antoine Rivarol

We not only love ourselves in others, but hate ourselves in others too.
—George C. Lichtenberg

At the heart of our friendly or purely social relations, there lurks a hostility momentarily cured but recurring in fits and starts.
—Marcel Proust

To really know someone is to have loved and hated him in turn.
—Marcel Jouhandeau

Almost all of our relationships begin and most of them continue as forms of mutual exploitation, a mental or physical barter, to be terminated when one or both parties run out of goods.
—W. H. Auden

It is the steady and merciless increase of occupations, the augmented speed at which we are always trying to live, the crowding of each day with more work than it can profitably hold, which has cost us, among other good things, the undisturbed enjoyment of friends. Friendship takes time, and we have no time to give it.
—Agnes Repplier

The bonds that unite another person to ourself exist only in our mind.
—Marcel Proust

The opinions which we hold of one another, our relations with friends and kinsfolk are in no sense permanent, save in appearance, but are as eternally fluid as the sea itself.
—Marcel Proust

We seek pitifully to convey to others the treasures of our heart, but they have not the power to accept them, and so we go lonely side by side but not together, unable to know our fellow and unknown by them.
—W. Somerset Maugham

Almost all our sorrows spring out of our relations with other people.
—Arthur Schopenhauer

I was taught when I was young that if people would only love one another, all would be well with the world. This seemed simple and very nice; but I found when I tried to put it in practice not only that other people were seldom lovable, but that I was not very lovable myself.
—George Bernard Shaw

People have generally three epochs in their confidence in man. In the first they believe him to be everything that is good, and they are lavish with their friendship and confidence. In the next, they have had experience, which has smitten down their confidence, and they have to be careful not to mistrust everyone, and to put the worst construction upon everything. Later in life, they learn that the greater number of men have much more good in them than bad, and that even when there is cause to blame, there is more reason to pity than to condemn; and then a spirit of confidence again awakens within them.
—Fredrika Bremer

Of all the means which wisdom uses to ensure happiness throughout the whole of life, by far the most important is the acquisition of friends.
—Epicurus

Life is to be fortified by many friendships. To love, and to be loved, is the greatest happiness of existence.
—Sydney Smith

Friends—those relations one makes for oneself.
—Émile Deschamps

Friendship is always a sweet responsibility, never an opportunity.
—Kahlil Gibran

The friendships which last are those wherein each friend respects the other's dignity to the point of not really wanting anything from him.
—Cyril Connolly

Friendship without self-interest is one of the rare and beautiful things of life.
—James F. Byrnes

A true friend is the greatest of all goods and that of which we think least of acquiring.
—François de La Rochefoucauld

Friendship is a strong and habitual inclination in two persons to promote the good and happiness of one another.
—Eustace Budgell

A companion loves some agreeable qualities which a man may possess, but a friend loves the man himself.
—James Boswell

We cannot tell the precise moment when friendship is formed. As in filling a vessel drop by drop, there is at last a drop which makes it run over; so in a series of kindnesses there is at last one which makes the heart run over.
—James Boswell

Do not let your vanity and self-love make you suppose that people become your friends at first sight, or even upon a short acquaintance. Real friendship is a slow grower and never thrives unless engrafted upon a stock of known and reciprocal merit.
—Lord Chesterfield

Friendship is seldom lasting but between equals, or where the superiority on one side is reduced by some equivalent advantage on the other.
—Samuel Johnson

Friendships last when each friend thinks he has a slight superiority over the other.
—Honoré de Balzac

Most people enjoy the inferiority of their best friends.
—Lord Chesterfield

Nobody who is afraid of laughing, and heartily too, at his friend, can be said to have a true and thorough love for him.
—Augustus and Julius Hare

The more we love our friends, the less we flatter them; it is by excusing nothing that pure love shows itself.
—Molière

Most men's friendships are too inarticulate.
—William James

Friendship is almost always the union of a part of one mind with a part of another: people are friends in spots.
—George Santayana

We often choose a friend as we do a mistress—for no particular excellence in themselves, but merely from some circumstance that flatters our self-love.
—William Hazlitt

We cherish our friends not for their ability to amuse us, but for ours to amuse them.
—Evelyn Waugh

Sweet is the scene where genial friendship plays
The pleasing game of interchanging praise.
—Oliver Wendell Holmes, Sr.

Never speak ill of yourself, your friends will always say enough on that subject.
—Charles de Talleyrand-Périgord

The desire of talking about ourselves, and of putting our faults in the light we wish them to be seen, forms a great part of our sincerity.
—François de La Rochefoucauld

We confess our bad qualities to others out of fear of appearing naïve or ridiculous by not being aware of them.
—Gerald Brenan

It is not our wrong actions which it requires courage to confess, so much as those which are ridiculous and foolish.
—Jean Jacques Rousseau

That I, or any man, should tell everything of himself, I hold to be impossible. Who could endure to own the doing of a mean thing? Who is there that has done none?
—Anthony Trollope

If we knew each others secrets, what comforts we should find.
—John Churton Collins

A person who has no secrets is a liar. We always fold ourselves away from others just enough to preserve a secret or two, something that we cannot share without destroying our inner landscape.
—Anne Roiphe

Confession is good for the soul only in the sense that a tweed coat is good for dandruff—it is a palliative rather than a remedy.
—Peter De Vries

Spilling your guts is just as charming as it sounds.
—Fran Lebowitz

All confidence placed in another is dangerous if it is not perfect, for on almost all occasions we ought to tell everything or to conceal everything. We have already told too much of our secret, if one single circumstance is to be kept back.
—Jean de La Bruyère

If you communicate your secret to another, you make yourself that other's slave.
—Baltasar Grácian

If you have let the secret slip from yourself and yet seek to confine it to another, you have taken refuge in another's good faith when you have already abandoned your own.
—Plutarch

How shall we hope that another person will keep our secret if we do not keep it ourselves?
—François de La Rochefoucauld

Thy friend has a friend, and thy friend's friend has a friend; be discreet.
—Babylonian Talmud

Be slow to count upon the respect or confidence of a man who shows interest in all your concerns, if he does not speak to you of his own also.
—Luc de Clapiers de Vauvenargues

Let us have a care not to disclose our hearts to those who shut up theirs against us.
—Francis Beaumont

To reveal imprudently the spot where we are most sensitive and vulnerable is to invite a blow.
—Madame Anne Sophie Swetchine

None are so fond of secrets as those who do not mean to keep them.
—Charles Caleb Colton

Those who are silent, self-effacing and attentive become the recipients of confidences.
—Thornton Wilder

Shy and unready men are great betrayers of secrets; for there are few wants more urgent for the moment than the want of something to say.
—Sir Henry Taylor

Women, and young men, are very apt to tell what secrets they know, from the vanity of having been trusted.
—Lord Chesterfield

The vanity of being known to be trusted with a secret is generally one of the chief motives to disclose it.
—Samuel Johnson

When a secret gets out it is the fault of whoever confided it.
—Jean de La Bruyère

If you want to keep something concealed from your enemy, do not disclose it to your friend.
—Salomon Ibn Gabirol

Tell your friend a lie; if he keeps it a secret then tell him the truth.
—Portuguese Proverb

Nobody will keep the things he hears to himself, and nobody will repeat just what he hears and no more.
—Seneca

Time and chance reveal all secrets.
—Mary de la Rivière Manley

The closer and more confidential our relationship with someone, the less we are entitled to ask about what we are not voluntarily told.
—Louis Kronenberger

Don't flatter yourself that friendship authorizes you to say disagreeable things to your intimates. The nearer you come into relation with a person, the more necessary do tact and courtesy become.
—Oliver Wendell Holmes, Sr.

It's important to our friends to believe that we are unreservedly frank with them, and important to friendship that we are not.
—Mignon McLaughlin

Don't believe your friends when they ask you to be honest with them. All they really want is to be maintained in the good opinion they have of themselves.
—Albert Camus

We want all our friends to tell us our bad qualities; it is only the particular ass that does so whom we can't tolerate.
—William James

There is no man so friendless but what he can find a friend sincere enough to tell him disagreeable truths.
—Edward G. Bulwer-Lytton

All men have their frailties; and whoever looks for a friend without imperfections, will never find what he seeks. We love ourselves not withstanding our faults, and we ought to love our friends in like manner.
—Cyrus the Great

Every man should keep a fair-sized cemetery in which to bring the faults of his friends.
—Henry Ward Beecher

We know our friends by their defects rather than their merits.
—W. Somerset Maugham

To find a friend one must close one eye. To keep him—two.
—Norman Douglas

Love is blind; friendship always closes its eyes.
—French Proverb

No man is much pleased with a companion who does not increase, in some respect, his fondness of himself.
—Samuel Johnson

We are not greatly pleased by our friends respecting our good qualities if they also venture to perceive our faults.
—Luc de Clapiers de Vauvenargues

It is well, when one is judging a friend, to remember that he is judging you with the same godlike and superior impartiality.
—Arnold Bennet

Two persons cannot long be friends if they cannot forgive each other's little failings.
—Jean de La Bruyère

We easily forgive in our friends those faults which do not affect us.
—François de La Rochefoucauld

Don't tell your friends their social faults; they will cure the fault and never forgive you.
—Logan Pearsall Smith

Never apologize for your terrible friends. We are all somebody's terrible friends.
—J. Gallagher

A man may love those with all his heart in whom he perceives grave faults. It would be absurd to claim that only perfection has a claim to our liking. Our failings sometimes bind us to one another as closely as could virtue itself.
—Luc de Clapiers de Vauvenargues

I like a friend better for having faults that one can talk about.
—William Hazlitt

Reprove your friends in secret, praise them openly.
—Publilius Syrus

Only friends will tell you the truth you need to hear to make the last part of your life bearable.
—Francine Du Plessix Gray

The preservative to keep the mind in health is the faithful admonition of a friend.
—Francis Bacon

If ever a friend tell thee a fault, imagine always that he telleth thee not the whole truth.
—Thomas Fuller (II)

Every man, however wise, requires the advice of some sagacious friend in the affairs of life.
—Plautus

No man is so foolish but he may sometimes give another good counsel, and no man so wise that he may not easily err if he takes no other counsel than his own. He that is taught only by himself has a fool for a master.
—Ben Jonson

Even the best pilots are willing to take advice from their passengers in bad weather.
—Cicero

He who is always his own counsellor will often have a fool for his client.
—John Hunter

Consult your friend on all things, especially on those which respect yourself. His counsel may then be useful where your own self-love might impair your judgment.
—Seneca

There is as much difference between the counsel that a friend giveth, and that a man giveth himself, as there is between the counsel of a friend and a flatterer.
—Francis Bacon

Write down the advice of him who loves you, though you like it not at present.
—Proverb

It takes nearly as much ability to know how to profit by good advice as to know how to act for one's self.
—François de La Rochefoucauld

Human nature is so constituted, that all see and judge better in the affairs of other men than in their own.
—Terence

It is far easier to be wise for others than to be so for oneself.
—François de La Rochefoucauld

How we admire the wisdom of those who come to us for advice!
—Author Unknown

Nothing makes one feel so strong as a call for help.
—George MacDonald

When a man has been guilty of any vice or folly, the best atonement he can make for it is to warn others not to fall into the like.
—Joseph Addison

It is one thing to show a man he is in error, and another to put him in possession of truth.
—John Locke

Advice is like castor oil, easy enough to give but dreadful uneasy to take.
—Josh Billings

The truest secret of giving advice is, after you have honestly given it, to be perfectly indifferent whether it is taken or not and never persist in trying to set people right.
—Hannah Whitall Smith

Advice is like snow; the softer it falls the longer it dwells upon, and the deeper it sinks into the mind.
—Samuel Taylor Coleridge

There is no use whatever trying to help people who do not help themselves. You cannot push anyone up a ladder unless he be willing to climb himself.
—Andrew Carnegie

It is always safe to learn, even from our enemies—seldom safe to venture to instruct, even our friends.
—Charles Caleb Colton

When we feel a strong desire to thrust our advice on others, it is usually because we suspect their weakness; but we ought rather to suspect our own.
—Charles Caleb Colton

Advice is always a confession.
—André Maurois

Give me the ready hand rather than the ready tongue.
—Giuseppe Garibaldi

It is not so much our friends' help that helps us as the confident knowledge that they will help us.
—Epicurus

Our chief want in life is somebody who will make us do what we can.
—Ralph Waldo Emerson

We only make a dupe of the friend whose advice we ask, for we never tell him all; and it is usually what we have left unsaid that decides our conduct.
—Comtesse Diane

When we ask for advice we are usually looking for an accomplice.
—Marquis de La Grange

Someone will always tell you what you want to hear.
—Delia Ephron

No one wants advice—only corroboration.
—John Steinbeck

To ask advice is in nine cases out of ten to tout for flattery.
—John Churton Collins

What advice can one give to people who ask for it? If you see that they are determined to take a particular course, and ask for encouragement only, give it to them in abundance. If they are still undecided, try to help them find what they really want and what it would cost. Put the facts before them, as they themselves shy off from seeing them. Help them to see the situation as the consequences of taking one course of action rather than another. Then if they really want a decision, they can make it themselves.
—Bernard Berenson

Advice is seldom welcome, and those who need it the most always like it the least.
—Lord Chesterfield

The usual pretext of those who make others unhappy is that they do it for their own good.
—Luc de Clapiers de Vauvenargues

Advice is offensive, not because it lays us open to unexpected regret, or convicts us of any fault which has escaped our notice, but because it shows us that we are known to others as well as ourselves; and the officious monitor is persecuted with hatred, not because his accusation is false, but because he assumes the superiority which we are not willing to grant him, and has dared to detect what we desire to conceal.
—Samuel Johnson

There is nothing which we receive with so much reluctance as advice. We look upon the man who gives it us as offering an affront to our understanding, and treating us like children or idiots. We consider the instruction as an implicit censure, and the zeal which anyone shows for our good on such an occasion as a piece of presumption or impertinence. The truth of it is, the person who pretends to advise does, in that particular, exercise a superiority over us, and can have no other reason for it but that, in comparing us with himself, he thinks us defective either in our conduct or our understanding. For these reasons, there is nothing so difficult as the art of making advice agreeable.
—Joseph Addison

It is by no means necessary to imagine that he who is offended at advice was ignorant of the fault, and resents admonition as a false charge; for perhaps it is most natural to be enraged when there is the strongest conviction of our own guilt. . . . When a man feels the reprehension of a friend seconded by his own heart, he is easily heated into resentment and revenge, either because he hoped that the fault of which he was conscious had escaped the notice of others; or that his friend had looked upon it with tenderness and extenuation, and excused it for the sake of his other virtues; or had considered him as too wise to need advice.
—Samuel Johnson

Don't expect others to take as much interest in you as you do yourself. . . . No person should be expected to distort the main lines of his life for the sake of another individual. On occasion there may exist such a strong affection that even the greatest sacrifices become natural, but if they are not natural they should not be made, and no person should be held blameworthy for not making them.
—Bertrand Russell

We see more clearly what others fail to do for us than what they actually do.
—Author Unknown

Never claim as a right what you can accept as a favour.
—John Churton Collins

When we call on our friends to sacrifice themselves, we generally wish them also to declare that they like being sacrificed.
—Anthony Trollope

To make large sacrifices in big things is easy, but to make sacrifices in little things is what we are seldom capable of.
—Johann Wolfgang von Goethe

Learn how to refuse favors. This is a great and very useful art.
—Thomas Fuller (II)

"No" and "Yes" are words quickly said, but they need a great amount of thought before you utter them.
—Baltasar Grácian

We cannot always oblige, but we can always speak obligingly.
—François Marie de Voltaire

A courteous way of saying no, is to change the conversation.
—Baltasar Grácian

The prompter the refusal, the less disappointment.
—Publilius Syrus

It is more tolerable to be refused than deceived.
—Publilius Syrus

Better a friendly refusal than an unwilling promise.
—German Proverb

A soft refusal is not always taken, but a rude one is immediately believed.
—Alexander Chase

Men are never attached to you by favors.
—Napoleon Bonaparte

If something is to be granted, then the gift well considered is cherished more than that bestowed in the rush of the moment; for what has been longed for, is always prized more highly, and if something must be refused, time gives opportunity for discovering how best, and most softly, to say No.
—Baltasar Grácian

He who is most slow in making a promise is the most faithful in its performance.
—Jean Jacques Rousseau

We should keep our word even to the undeserving.
—Publilius Syrus

The pleasure we derive from doing favors is partly in the feeling it gives us that we are not altogether worthless.
—Eric Hoffer

If you confer a benefit, never remember it; if you receive one, never forget it.
—Chilon

Friendship consists in forgetting what one gives, and remembering what one receives.
—Alexander Dumas *fils*

To remind a man of the good turns you have done him is very much like a reproach.
—Demosthenes

We should give as we would receive, cheerfully, quickly, and without hesitation; for there is no grace in a benefit that sticks to the fingers.
—Seneca

Never look a gift horse in the mouth. A gift ought to rise in our esteem in proportion to the friendship and respect of the donor; not to the intrinsic excellency or worth. . . . To make a judgment of the donor's affection by the value of the present is often a false estimate; for if it be but a small matter, 'tis more than you could insist upon, and may be the effect of the giver's sincerest affection, as well as equal to his fortunes.
—Samuel Palmer

The charity that is a trifle to us can be precious to others.
—Homer

The manner of giving shows the character of the giver, more than the gift itself.
—Johann Kasper Lavater

Gratitude is one of the least articulate of the emotions, especially when it is deep.
—Felix Frankfurter

Gratitude is not only the greatest of virtues, but the parent of all the others.
—Cicero

Gratitude is one of those things that cannot be bought. It must be born with men, or else all the obligations in the world will not create it.
—Lord Halifax

Do not neglect gratitude. Say thank you. Better still, say it in writing. A simple note of thanks is money in the bank and you will be remembered.
—Princess Jackson Smith

Gratitude is a duty which ought to be paid, but which none have a right to expect.
—Jean Jacques Rousseau

The man who returns his thanks only when witnesses have been removed shows himself ungrateful.
—Seneca

Let him that hath done the good office conceal it, let him that hath received it disclose it.
—Seneca

Most men remember obligations, but not often to be grateful; the proud are made sour by the remembrance and the vain silent.
—William G. Simms

We more often set limits on our gratitude than on our hopes and desires.
—François de La Rochefoucauld

What soon grows old? Gratitude.
—Aristotle

Wretches are ungrateful; it is part of their wretchedness.
—Victor Hugo

If you pick up a starving dog and make him prosperous, he will not bite you. This is the principal difference between a dog and a man.
—Mark Twain

Gratitude: A sentiment lying midway between a benefit received and a benefit expected.
—Ambrose Bierce

Gratitude is merely a secret hope of further favours.
—François de La Rochefoucauld

We should hear little of ingratitude, unless we were so apt to exaggerate the worth of our better deeds, and to look for a return in proportion to our own exorbitant estimate.
—Augustus and Julius Hare

We often fancy we suffer from ingratitude, while in reality we suffer from self-love.
—Walter Savage Landor

O you who complain of ingratitude, have you not had the pleasure of doing good?
—Sébastien R. Nicolas Chamfort

True friendship is like sound health, the value of it is seldom known until it be lost.
—Charles Caleb Colton

Friendships, like marriages, are dependent on avoiding the unforgivable.
—John D. MacDonald

Sooner or later you've heard all your best friends have to say. Then comes the tolerance of real love.
—Ned Rorem

The most fatal disease of friendship is gradual decay, or dislike hourly increased by causes too slender for complaint, and too numerous for removal.
—Samuel Johnson

Probably no man ever had a friend he did not dislike a little; we are all so constituted by nature no one can possibly entirely approve of us.
—Edgar Watson Howe

When friends quarrel the truth comes to light.
—Spanish Proverb

To make our peace with a friend, with whom we had broken, is a weakness for which we shall have to atone when at the first opportunity he again does the very same thing that has brought about the breach; indeed he does it again with more audacity and assurance because he is secretly aware of his being indispensable.
—Arthur Schopenhauer

We do not always regret the loss of our friends because of their worth, but because of our own needs and the flattering opinion they had of us.
—François de La Rochefoucauld

We ought always to make choice of persons of such worth and honour for our friends, that if they should ever cease to be so, they will not abuse our confidence, nor give us cause to fear them as enemies.
—Joseph Addison

Never cut what you can untie.
—Joseph Joubert

He who has a thousand friends has not a friend to spare.
And he who has one enemy will meet him everywhere.
—Ali Ibn-Abi-Talib

He who is capable of being a bitter enemy can never possess the necessary virtues that constitute a true friend.
—Sir Thomas Fitzosborne

There are no two people on earth who could not be turned into deadly enemies by a devilishly contrived indiscretion.
—Hugo von Hofmannstahl

Nothing is more certain of destroying any good feeling that may be cherished towards us than to show distrust. To be suspected as an enemy is often enough to make a man become so; the whole matter is over, there is no further use of guarding against it. On the contrary, confidence leads us naturally to act kindly, we are affected by the good opinion which others entertain of us, and we are not easily induced to lose it.
—Madame Marie de Sévigné

A man cannot be too careful in his choice of his enemies.
—Oscar Wilde

An enemy is anyone who tells the truth about you.
—Elbert Hubbard

Our enemy's opinion of us comes closer to the truth than our own.
—François de La Rochefoucauld

Our friends abandon us only too easily, and our enemies are implacable.
—François Marie de Voltaire

Experience dreads an enemy however humble.
—Publilius Syrus

There is no little enemy.
—Benjamin Franklin

It is a general mistake to think the men we like are good for everything, and those we do not, good for nothing.
—Lord Halifax

Nothing would more contribute to make a man wise than to have always an enemy in his view.
—Lord Halifax

Everyone needs a warm personal enemy or two to keep him free from rust in the movable parts of his mind.
—Gene Fowler

The wise learn many things from their foes.
—Aristophanes

He that wrestles with us strengthens our nerves, and sharpens our skill. Our antagonist is our helper.
—Edmund Burke

Pay attention to your enemies, for they are the first to discover your mistakes.
—Antisthenes

You can discover what your enemy fears most by observing the means he uses to frighten you.
—Eric Hoffer

One must destroy one's adversaries' seriousness with laughter, and their laughter with seriousness.
—Gorgias of Leontini

For every man there is something in the vocabulary that would stick to him like a second skin. His enemies have only to find it.
—Ambrose Bierce

Love comes from blindness, friendship from knowledge.
—Comte Roger de Bussy-Rasbutin

Your friend is the man who knows all about you and still likes you.
—Elbert Hubbard

It is one of blessings of old friends that you can afford to be stupid with them.
—Ralph Waldo Emerson

Friendship is one mind in two bodies.
—Mencius

So long as we love we serve; so long as we are loved by others, I would say that we are almost indispensable; and no man is useless while he has a friend.
—Robert Louis Stevenson

The only way to have a friend is to be one.
—Ralph Waldo Emerson

Friendship is like money, easier made than kept.
—Samuel Butler (II)

Life without a friend is death without a witness.
—George Herbert

If a man does not make new acquaintances as he advances through life, he will soon find himself left alone; one should keep his friendships in constant repair.
—Samuel Johnson

Develop the art of friendliness. One can experience a variety of emotions staying home and reading or watching television; one will be alive but hardly living. Most of the meaningful aspects of life are closely associated with people. Even the dictionary definition of life involves people.
—William L. Abbott

It brings comfort and encouragement to have companions in whatever happens.
—St. John Chrysostom

That's what friendship means: sharing the prejudice of experience.
—Charles Bukowski

A friend who cannot at a pinch remember a thing or two that never happened is as bad as one who does not know how to forget.
—Samuel Butler (II)

While love lasts, it subsists on itself, and sometimes thrives on those very things which seem likely to kill it, on caprice, unkindness, distance or jealousy. Friendship on the contrary needs help: lacking care, mutual trust and kindness, it withers away.
—Jean de La Bruyère

To have a true friendship, you have to do more than exchange Christmas cards or call each other once a year. There has to be some continued support and attention; otherwise the relationship is a sentimental attachment rather than a true friendship.
—Dr. Dolores Kreisman

To let friendship die away by negligence and silence is certainly not wise. It is voluntarily to throw away one of the greatest comforts of this weary pilgrimage.
—Samuel Johnson

If you have one true friend you have more than your share.
—Thomas Fuller (II)

If you have a friend worth loving,
   Love him. Yes, and let him know
That you love him, ere life's evening
   Tinge his brow with sunset glow.
Why should good words never be said
   Of a friend till he is dead?
—Daniel W. Hoyt

We have fewer friends than we imagine, but more than we know.
—Hugo von Hofmannsthal

PART 6

MATURITY

Maturity is the capacity
to endure uncertainty.
—John Finley

Such Is Life

The Death of Youth is a Shipwreck.
—Thomas Fuller (II)

Ah, what shall I be at fifty
Should nature keep me alive,
If I find the world so bitter
When I am but twenty-five.
—Alfred, Lord Tennyson

Is life so wretched? Isn't it rather your hands which are too small, your vision which is muddied? You are the one who must grow up.
—Dag Hammarskjöld

Do not think that years leave us and find us the same!
—Lord Lytton

Anybody who is 25 or 30 years old has physical scars from all sorts of things, from tuberculosis to polio. It's the same with the mind.
—Moses R. Kaufman

All growth is a leap in the dark, a spontaneous, unpremeditated act without benefit of experience.
—Henry Miller

One of the signs of passing youth is the birth of a sense of fellowship with other human beings as we take our place among them.
—Virginia Woolf

It is a sign of passing youth when man begins to check up on his illusions.
—Author Unknown

To live with fear and not be afraid is the final test of maturity.
—Edward Weeks

A man's maturity consists of having found again the seriousness one had as a child, at play.
—Friedrich Wilhelm Nietzsche

All of us, who are worth anything, spend our manhood in unlearning the follies, or expiating the mistakes of our youth.
—Percy Bysshe Shelley

We have not passed that subtle line between childhood and adulthood until we move from the passive voice to the active voice—that is, until we have stopped saying "It got lost," and say, "I lost it."
—Sydney J. Harris

Youth ends when we perceive that no one wants our gay abandon. And the end may come in two ways: the realization that other people dislike it, or that we ourselves cannot continue with it. Weak men grow older in the first way, strong men in the second.
—Cesare Pavese

The knell of my thirtieth year has sounded; and in three or four years my youth will be as a faint haze on the sea, an illusive recollection.
—George Moore

PART 7

THE PASSIONS

Passion is a sort of fever in the mind, which ever
leaves us weaker than it found us. It, more than
anything, deprives us the use of our judgment;
for it raises a dust very hard to see through.
It may not unfitly be termed the mob of man,
that commits a riot upon his reason.
—William Penn

Such Is Life

There are moments in life when the heart is so full of emotion
That if by chance it be shaken, or into its depths like a pebble
Drops some careless word, it overflows, and its secret,
Spilt on the ground like water, can never be gathered together.
—Henry Wadsworth Longfellow

He submits to be seen through a microscope, who suffers himself
to be caught in a fit of passion.
—Johann Kaspar Lavater

We ride through life on the beast within us. Beat the animal but
you can't make it think.
—Luigi Pirandello

In the human heart there is a perpetual generation of passions, so
that the overthrow of one is almost always the establishment of
another.
—François de La Rochefoucauld

The passions do not die out; they burn out.
—Ninon de Lenclos

The duration of our passions is no more dependent upon us than
the duration of our life.
—François de La Rochefoucauld

It is difficult to overcome one's passions, and impossible to
satisfy them.
—Marguerite de La Sablière

If we resist our passions, it is more from their weakness than
from our strength.
—François de La Rochefoucauld

Such Is Life

The ruling passion, be it what it will,
The ruling passion conquers reason still.
—Alexander Pope

Passion is the drunkenness of the mind.
—Robert South

Passion often renders the most clever man a fool, and even sometimes renders the most foolish man clever.
—François de La Rochefoucauld

When you have found out the prevailing passion of any man, remember never to trust him where that passion is concerned.
—Lord Chesterfield

Passions make us feel, but never see clearly.
—Charles de Secondat Montesquieu

There are moments when our passions speak and decide for us, and we seem to stand by and wonder.
—George Eliot

There is no secret of the heart which our actions do not disclose.
—Molière

Nothing is less in our power than the heart, and far from commanding we are forced to obey it.
—Jean Jacques Rousseau

The heart has reasons that reason does not understand.
—Jacques Bénigne Bossuet

Nine times in ten, the heart governs the understanding.
—Lord Chesterfield

The head is ever the dupe of the heart.
—François de La Rochefoucauld

The head learns new things, but the heart forever more practices old experiences.
—Henry Ward Beecher

The logic of the heart is absurd.
—Julie de Lespinasse

It is said that passion makes one think in a circle.
—Oscar Wilde

The most sober men, when they walk alone without care and employment of the mind, would be unwilling the vanity and extravagance of their thoughts should be publicly seen: which is a confession that passions unguided are for the most part mere madness.
—Thomas Hobbes

All passions exaggerate: it is only because they exaggerate that they are passions.
—Sébastien R. Nicholas Chamfort

No man can guess in cold blood what he may do in a passion.
—H. G. Bohn

Guard thy sail from passion's sudden blast.
—Charles Simmons

A man in a passion rides a horse that runs away with him.
—Thomas Fuller (I)

Man's chief merit consists in resisting the impulses of his nature.
—Samuel Johnson

How many of our daydreams would darken into nightmares were there any danger of their coming true.
—Logan Pearsall Smith

All men that are ruined, are ruined on the side of their natural propensities.
—Edmund Burke

I conceive that the great part of the miseries of mankind are brought upon them by false estimates they have made of the value of things.
—Benjamin Franklin

Our visions begin with our desires.
—Audre Lorde

As long as we live in this world we cannot be without tribulation and temptation.
—Thomas á Kempis

All men are tempted. There is no man that lives that can't be broken down, provided it is the right temptation, put in the right spot.
—Henry Ward Beecher

For to tempt and to be tempted are things very nearly allied, and in spite of the finest maxims of morality impressed upon the mind, whenever feeling has anything to do in the matter, no sooner is it excited than we have already gone vastly farther than we are aware of.
—Catherine the Great

You know, humanly speaking, there is a certain degree of temptation which will overcome any virtue.
—Samuel Johnson

Better shun the bait than struggle in the snare.
—John Dryden

It is easier to stay out than get out.
—Mark Twain

Every temptation is great or small according as the man is.
—Jeremy Taylor

Temptation rarely comes in working hours. It is in their leisure time that men are made or marred.
—William Mackergo Taylor

The difference between those whom the world esteems as good and those whom it condemns as bad, is in many cases little else than that the former have been better sheltered from temptation.
—Augustus and Julius Hare

It is not from nature, but from education and habits, that our wants are chiefly derived.
—Henry Fielding

Some desire is necessary to keep life in motion.
—Samuel Johnson

All human activity is prompted by desire.
—Bertrand Russell

Desire is the essence of a man.
—Benedict Baruch Spinoza

It is the nature of man to long after things forbidden and to desire what is denied us.
—François Rabelais

Desire is the uneasiness a man finds in himself upon the absence of anything whose present enjoyment carries the idea of delight with it.
—Johann Kaspar Lavater

Our desires always increase with our possessions. The knowledge that something remains yet unenjoyed impairs our enjoyment of the good before us.
—Samuel Johnson

The thing that you can't get is the thing that you want, mainly.
—Mark Twain

The more anybody wants a thing, the more they do think others want it.
—Mary Webb

Man is the only animal whose desires increase as they are fed; the only animal that is never satisfied.
—Henry George

The thirst of desire is never filled, nor fully satisfied.
—Cicero

We are far from knowing all our desires.
—François de La Rochefoucauld

It is much easier to suppress a first desire than to satisfy those that follow.
—François de La Rochefoucauld

If your desires be endless, your cares and fears will be so too.
—Thomas Fuller (I)

The true way to gain much, is never to desire to gain too much. He is not rich that possesses much, but he that covets no more; and he is not poor that enjoys little, but he that wants too much.
—Francis Beaumont

We should aim rather at leveling down our desires than leveling up our means.
—Aristotle

It is not the greatness of a man's means that makes him independent, so much as the smallness of his wants.
—William Cobbett

One-half of knowing what you want is knowing what you must give up before you get it.
—Sidney Howard

There are two tragedies in life. One is not to get your heart's desire. The other is to get it.
—George Bernard Shaw

When our desires are fulfilled, we never fail to realize the wealth of imagination and the paucity of reality.
—Ninon de Lenclos

Nothing is as good as it seems before hand.
—George Eliot

Desires are nourished by delay.
—John Ray

We do not succeed in changing things according to our desire, but gradually our desires change.
—Marcel Proust

What is not ours charms more than our own.
—Ovid

People often grudge others what they cannot enjoy themselves.
—Æsop

This is the greatest of all punishments, to be made unhappy by another's happiness.
—Baltasar Grácian

Oh, how bitter a thing it is to look into happiness through another man's eyes.
—William Shakespeare

Nothing sharpens sight like envy.
—Thomas Fuller (I)

Envy speaks of what she sees, not of what is beneath the surface.
—Publilius Syrus

We spend our time envying people whom we wouldn't wish to be.
—Jean Rostand

Our envy always outlives the happiness of those we envy.
—François de La Rochefoucauld

One of envy's favorite stratagems is the attempt to provoke envy in the envied one.
—Leslie Farber

People are often proud of their passions, even of the worst, but envy is a passion so timid and shame-faced that no one ever dare acknowledge it.
—François de La Rochefoucauld

A show of envy is an insult to oneself.
—Yevgeny Yevtushenko

Envy is the deformed and distorted offspring of egotism; and when we reflect on the strange and disproportioned character of the parent, we cannot wonder at the perversity and waywardness of the child.
—William Hazlitt

We ought to be guarded against every appearance of envy, as a passion that always implies inferiority wherever it resides.
—Pliny the Elder

Envy is a blemish of the mind; it is to the mind what disease is to the body.
—Salomon Ibn Gabirol

If envy were a fever, all mankind would be ill.
—Danish Proverb

Envy makes strange bed-fellows.
—Norman Douglas

Never trust anyone who wants what you've got. Friend or no, envy is an overwhelming emotion.
—Blythe Holbrooke

There is more venom than truth in the words of envy.
—Publilius Syrus

Envy which talks and cries out is always maladroit; it is the envy which keeps silent that one ought to fear.
—Antoine Rivarol

Hatred is active and envy passive dislike; there is but one step from envy to hate.
—Johann Wolfgang von Goethe

Malice may be sometimes out of breath, envy never.
—Lord Halifax

Men always hate most what they envy most.
—H. L. Mencken

Envy is more irreconcilable than hatred.
—François de La Rochefoucauld

Few men have the strength of character to rejoice in a friend's success without a touch of envy.
—Æschylus

Whenever a friend succeeds, a little something in me dies.
—Gore Vidal

Envy is admiration in despair.
—Author Unknown

One likes people much better when they're battered down by a prodigious siege of misfortune than when they triumph.
—Virginia Woolf

It is usually the case with most men that their nature is so constituted that they pity those who fare badly and envy those who fare well.
—Benedict Baruch Spinoza

Pity is often a reflection of our own evils in the ills of others. It is a delicate foresight of the troubles into which we may fall.
—François de La Rochefoucauld

He that pities another, remembers himself.
—George Herbert

We are so fond of one another, because our ailments are the same.
—Jonathan Swift

All feel pity for those like themselves.
—Claudian

Pity cureth envy.
—Thomas Fuller (II)

Pity is best taught by fellowship in woe.
—Samuel Taylor Coleridge

Pity is not natural to man. Children and savages are always cruel. Pity is acquired and improved by the cultivation of reason. We may have uneasy sensations from seeing a creature in distress, without pity; but we have not pity unless we wish to relieve him.
—Samuel Johnson

The response man has the greatest difficulty in tolerating is pity, especially when he warrants it. Hatred is a tonic, it makes one live, it inspires vengeance, but pity kills, it makes our weakness weaker.
—Honoré de Balzac

No one wishes to be pitied for his mistakes.
—Luc de Clapiers de Vauvenargues

I seem to be the only person in the world who doesn't mind being pitied. If you love me, pity me. The human state is pitiable: born to die, capable of so much, accomplishing so little; killing instead of creating, destroying instead of building, hating instead of loving. Pitiful, pitiful.
—Jessamyn West

One cannot weep for the entire world. It is beyond human strength. One must choose.
—Jean Anouilh

In women pity begets love, in men love begets pity.
—John Churton Collins

We feel a sort of bitter-sweet pricking of malicious delight in contemplating the misfortunes of others.
—Michel de Montaigne

If some great catastrophe is not announced every morning, we feel a certain void. "Nothing in the paper today," we sigh.
—Paul Valéry

Comfort: A state of mind produced by contemplation of a neighbor's uneasiness.
—Ambrose Bierce

We grow tired of everything but turning others into ridicule, and congratulating ourselves on their defects.
—William Hazlitt

Man's life is a warfare against the malice of men.
—Baltasar Grácian

We are more inclined to hate one another for points on which we differ, than to love one another for points on which we agree. The reason perhaps is this: when we find others that agree with us, we seldom trouble ourselves to confirm that agreement; but when we chance on those who differ from us, we are zealous both to convince and to convert them. Our pride is hurt by the failure, and disappointed pride engenders hatred.
—Charles Caleb Colton

When we feel that we lack whatever is needed to secure someone else's esteem, we are very close to hating him.
—Luc de Clapiers de Vauvenargues

Love, friendship, respect, do not unite people as much as a common hatred of something.
—Anton Chekhov

People hate, as they love, unreasoningly.
—William Makepeace Thackeray

Thousands are hated, while none are loved, without a real cause.
—Johann Kaspar Lavater

We hate some persons because we do not know them; and will not know them because we hate them.
—Charles Caleb Colton

Folks never understand the folks they hate.
—James Russell Lowell

Pure good soon grows insipid, wants variety and spirit. Pain is bitter-sweet, which never surfeits. Love turns, with a little indulgence, to indifference or disgust; hatred alone is immortal.
—William Hazlitt

Malice drinks one half of its own poison.
—Seneca

Hatred is the madness of the heart.
—Lord Byron

Hatred is self-punishment.
—Hosea Ballou

The price of hating other human beings is loving oneself less.
—Eldridge Cleaver

The hatred we bear our enemies injures their happiness less than our own.
—Jean-Antoine Petit-Senn

If you hate a person, you hate something in him that is part of yourself. What isn't part of ourselves doesn't disturb us.
—Hermann Hesse

Hate is the consequence of fear; we fear something before we hate it; a child who fears noises becomes a man who hates noise.
—Cyril Connolly

Hatred rarely does any harm to its object. It is the hater who suffers. His soul is warped and his life poisoned by dwelling on past injuries or projecting schemes of revenge. Rancour in the bosom is the foe of personal happiness.
—Lord Beaverbrook

Bad temper is its own scourge. Few things are more bitter than to feel bitter. A man's venom poisons himself more than his victim.
—Charles Buxton

Do not trust a malicious man because you have long been intimate with him. A serpent will still bite, though it may have been kept and tended a long time.
—Panchatantra

The intention to injure can always find a reason.
—Publilius Syrus

Malice will always find bad motives for good actions.
—Thomas Jefferson

If you're out to beat a dog, you're sure to find a stick.
—Yiddish Proverb

There is nobody who is not dangerous for someone.
—Madame Marie de Sévigné

The worst, the least curable hatred is that which has superseded deep love.
—Euripides

Hatred is blind, as well as love.
—Thomas Fuller (II)

'Tis a human trait to hate one you have wronged.
—Seneca

To have done more hurt to a man than he can, or is willing to expiate, inclineth the doer to hate the sufferer. For he must expect revenge, or forgiveness; both of which are hateful.
—Thomas Hobbes

Hatred is so durable and obstinate, that Reconciliation on a sick Bed is the greatest sign of death.
—Jean de La Bruyère

Enmity is anger watching the opportunity for revenge.
—Cicero

This is certain, that a man that studieth revenge keeps his wounds green, which otherwise would heal and do well.
—Francis Bacon

Contempt will sooner kill an injury than revenge.
—H. G. Bohn

Revenge is the poor delight of little minds.
—Juvenal

Vengeance has no foresight.
—Napoleon Bonaparte

In revenges men look not at the greatness of the evil past, but the greatness of the good to follow.
—Thomas Hobbes

Revenge is a much more punctual paymaster than gratitude.
—Charles Caleb Colton

Take care that no one hate you justly.
—Publilius Syrus

Nobody ever forgets where he buried the hatchet.
—Kin Hubbard

The bare recollection of anger kindles anger.
—Publilius Syrus

Nothing on earth consumes a man more quickly than the passion of resentment.
—Friedrich Wilhelm Nietzsche

Anger as soon as fed is dead
'Tis starving makes it fat.
—Emily Dickinson

Anger ventilated often hurries towards forgiveness; anger concealed often hardens into revenge.
—Edward G. Bulwer-Lytton

Anger is hard to combat because it is willing to buy revenge with life.
—Heraclitus

To be furious
Is to be frightened out of fear.
—William Shakespeare

Anger makes any coward brave.
—Cato

Anger always thinks it has power beyond its power.
—Publilius Syrus

Violence in the voice is only the death rattle of reason in the throat.
—John Frederick Boyes

Anger blows out the lamp of the mind.
—Robert Green Ingersoll

Anger turns the mind out of doors and bolts the entrance.
—Plutarch

The angry man never wanted woe.
—Thomas Drake

'Tis said that wrath is the last thing in a man to grow old.
—Alcaeus

A tart temper never mellows with age; and a sharp tongue is the only edged tool that grows keener with constant use.
—Washington Irving

There is nothing that so much gratifies an ill tongue as when it finds an angry heart.
—Thomas Fuller (II)

If your body were to be put at the disposal of a stranger, you would certainly be indignant. Then aren't you ashamed of putting your mind at the disposal of chance acquaintance, by allowing yourself to be upset if he happens to abuse you?
—Epictetus

To be angry is to revenge the faults of others upon yourself.
—Alexander Pope

Anger is a blind thing: often it prevents our seeing obvious matters, or obscures matters already understood.
—Chrysippus

We are told, "Let not the sun go down on your wrath," but I would add, never act or write till it has done so. This rule has saved me from many an act of folly. It is wonderful what a different view we take of the same event four-and-twenty hours after it has happened.
—Sydney Smith

The greatest remedy for anger is delay.
—Seneca

He who can suppress a moment's anger may prevent a day of sorrow.
—Author Unknown

Men who have had a great deal of experience learn not to lose their temper.
—Charles Victor Cherbuliez

He who can command his temper and his countenance the best, will always have an infinite advantage over the other.
—Lord Chesterfield

The happiness and misery of men depend no less on temper than fortune.
—François de La Rochefoucauld

By controlling the anger of a minute, you may avoid the remorse of a lifetime.
—Selwyn Gurney Champion

People hardly do anything in anger, of which they do not repent.
—Samuel Richardson

When anger rises, think of the consequences.
—Confucious

Anybody can become angry—that is easy; but to be angry with the right person, and to the right degree, and at the right time, and for the right purpose, and in the right way—that is not within everybody's power and is not easy.
—Aristotle

Whenever you are angry, be assured that it is not only a present evil, but that you have increased a habit.
—Epictetus

Anger is a spender—few indulge it without cost.
—Seneca

An angry man is again angry with himself when he returns to reason.
—Publilius Syrus

The intoxication of anger, like that of the grape, shows us to others, but hides us from ourselves. We injure our own cause in the opinion of the world when we too passionately defend it.
—Charles Caleb Colton

When a man is wrong and won't admit it, he always gets angry.
—Thomas C. Haliburton

When a man fights it means a fool has lost his argument.
—Chinese Proverb

I learned long ago never to wrestle with a pig. You get dirty, and besides, the pig likes it.
—Cyrus Ching

People in a temper often say a lot of terrible, silly things they mean.
—Penelope Gilliat

Never forget what a man says to you when he is angry.
—Henry Ward Beecher

We judge ourselves by our motives and others by their actions.
—Dwight Morris

Suspicions amongst thoughts are like bats amongst the birds, they ever fly by twilight.
—Francis Bacon

Nothing can happen but the suspicious man believes that somebody did it on purpose.
—Robert Lynd

Suspicion is far more apt to be wrong than right; oftener unjust than just. It is no friend to virtue, and always an enemy to happiness.
—Hosea Ballou

Suspicion is very often a useless pain.
—Samuel Johnson

Suspicion is a thing very few people can entertain without letting the hypothesis turn, in their minds, to fact.
—David Cort

The less we know the more we suspect.
—Josh Billings

There is no rule more invariable than that we are paid for our suspicions by finding what we suspected.
—Henry David Thoreau

No innocence can stand up under suspicion, if it is conscious of being suspected.
—Henry David Thoreau

It is only too easy to compel a sensitive human being to feel guilty about anything.
—Morton Irving Selden

Our distrust of another justifies his deceit.
—François de La Rochefoucauld

Suspicion always haunts the guilty mind.
—William Shakespeare

From the body of one guilty deed a thousand ghostly fears and haunting thoughts proceed.
—William Wordsworth

Guilt has very quick ears to an accusation.
—Henry Fielding

The guilty think all talk is of themselves.
—Geoffrey Chaucer

Alas! how difficult it is not to betray guilt by our countenance.
—Ovid

Everyone in daily life carries such a heavy burden on his own conscience that he is reluctant to penalize those who have been caught.
—Brooks Atkinson

There is a sort of man who pays no attention to his good actions, but is tormented by his bad ones.
—W. Somerset Maugham

Every man is guilty of all the good he didn't do.
—François Marie de Voltaire

A wise man rules his passions, a fool obeys them.
—Publilius Syrus

Such Is Life

When the passions become masters, they are vices.
—Blaise Pascal

Strong as our passions are, they may be starved into submission, and conquered, without being killed.
—Charles Caleb Colton

A man who has not passed through the inferno of his passions has never overcome them.
—Carl Jung

Act nothing in a furious passion. It's putting to sea in a storm.
—Thomas Fuller (I)

The end of passion is the beginning of repentance.
—Owen Feltham

We should employ our passions in the service of life, not spend life in the service of our passions.
—Sir Richard Steele

To know your ruling passion, examine your castles in the air.
—Richard Whately

PART 8

LOVE

A kiss, when all is said, what is it?
An oath that's given closer than before;
A promise more precise; the sealing of
Confessions that till then were barely breathed;
A rosy dot placed on the "i" in loving;
'Tis a secret told to the mouth instead of the ear.
—Edmond Rostand

Such Is Life

Man is the hunter; woman is his game.
The sleek and shining creatures of the chase,
We hunt them for the beauty of their skins;
They love us for it, and we ride them down.
—Alfred, Lord Tennyson

O' she is the antidote to desire.
—William Congreve

And with a velvet lip, print on his brow such language as tongue
hath never spoken.
—Lydia H. Sigourney

Once he drew, with one long kiss, my whole soul through my lips.
—Alfred, Lord Tennyson

There's nothing half so sweet in life as love's young dream.
—Thomas Moore

Love is the most terrible, and also the most generous, of the
passions; it is the only one which includes in its dreams the
happiness of someone else.
—Alphonse Karr

Our feelings were given us to excite to action, and when they end
in themselves, they are cherished to no good purpose.
—Daniel Sanford

Our affections are our life. We live by them; they supply our
warmth.
—William Ellery Channing

Love is the outreach of self toward completion.
—Ralph W. Sockman

Love is the word used to label the sexual excitement of the young, the habituation of the middle-aged, and the mutual dependence of the old.
—John Ciardi

Love is something far more than desire for sexual intercourse; it is the principle means of escape from the loneliness which afflicts men and women throughout the greater part of their lives.
—Bertrand Russell

Loving can cost a lot but not loving always costs more, and those who fear to love often find that want of love is an emptiness that robs the joy from life.
—Merle Shain

Love is all we have, the only way that each can help the other.
—Euripides

Love opens the doors into everything, as far as I can see, including and perhaps most of all, the door into one's own secret, and often terrible and frightening, real self.
—May Sarton

Love is an orgy of emotions.
—Author Unknown

We are shaped and fashioned by what we love.
—Johann Wolfgang von Goethe

The affections are like lightning: you cannot tell where they will strike till they have fallen.
—Jean Baptiste Lacordaire

If it is your time love will track you down like a cruise missile. If you say, "No! I don't want it right now," that's when you'll get it for sure. Love will make a way out of no way. Love is an exploding cigar which we willingly smoke.
—Lynda Barry

Love is born suddenly, without further thought, as result of one's temperament or one's weakness: a single trait of beauty can hold one fast, can settle one's fate. Friendship on the contrary grows up gradually, in course of time, through association, through long familiarity. How much wit, goodness of heart, loyalty, kindness and consideration one's friends need to achieve, over a number of years, far less than is sometimes done in one instant by a fair face or a fair hand.
—Jean de La Bruyère

There is nothing holier in this life of ours than the first consciousness of love—the first fluttering of its silken wings—the first rising sound and breath of that wind which is so soon to sweep through the soul, to purify or to destroy.
—Henry Wadsworth Longfellow

Oh, love is real enough; you will find it someday, but it has one archenemy—and that is life.
—Jean Anouilh

    Each time we love,
We turn a nearer and broader mark
To that keen archer, sorrow, and he strikes.
—Alexander Smith

Love and sorrow twins are born.
—Thomas Blacklock

Anyone beginning to love must prepare to suffer.
—Chevalier de Méré

He who wants a rose must respect the thorn.
—Persian Proverb

To love is to deprive someone of the right to make us suffer and at the same time to put the power to do so in his hands.
—Comtesse Diane

Cupid is a traitor who scratches even when one plays with him.
—Ninon de Lenclos

Love is an emotion experienced by the many and enjoyed by the few.
—Jean Anouilh

There is hardly any activity, any enterprise, which is started with such tremendous hopes and expectations and yet which fails so regularly as love.
—Erich Fromm

Romance is very pretty in novels, but the romance of a life is always a melancholy matter.
—Anthony Trollope

It is impossible to love and be wise.
—Francis Bacon

The first sigh of love is the last of wisdom.
—Antoine Bret

Love is like an hourglass, with the heart filling up as the brain empties.
—Jules Renard

In love we never think of moral qualities, and scarcely of intellectual ones. Temperament and manners alone, with beauty, excite love.
—William Hazlitt

In every man's heart there is a secret nerve that answers to the vibrations of beauty.
—Christopher Morley

There is hardly a human life which would not have been different if the idea of beauty in the mind of the man who had lived it had been different.
—Walter Bagehot

Beauty is power; a smile is its sword.
—Charles Reade

Love is the harvest of beauty.
—Author Unknown

Beauty: The power by which a woman charms a lover and terrifies a husband.
—Ambrose Bierce

Tell a woman she's a Beauty, and the Devil will tell her so ten times.
—Thomas Fuller (II)

Beauty may have fair leaves, yet bitter fruit.
—Author Unknown

Love built on beauty, soon as beauty, dies.
—John Donne

There should be as little merit in loving a woman for her beauty, as a man for his prosperity, both being equally subject to change.
—Alexander Pope

Beauty is the first present nature gives to women and the first it takes away.
—George Brossin Méré

Beauty soon grows familiar to the lover,
Fades in his eye, and palls upon the sense.
—Joseph Addison

The hues of the opal, the light of the diamond, are not to be seen if the eye is too near.
—Ralph Waldo Emerson

Familiarity is a magician that is cruel to beauty but kind to ugliness.
—Ouida

Kindness in women, not their beauteous looks,
Shall win my love.
—William Shakespeare

Who has not experienced how, on near acquaintance, plainness becomes beautified, and beauty loses its charm, exactly according to the quality of the heart and mind? And from this cause am I of the opinion that the want of outward beauty never disquiets a noble nature or will be regarded as a misfortune. It never can prevent people from being amiable and beloved in the highest degree.
—Fredrika Bremer

Love covers a multitude of sins. When a scar cannot be taken away, the next kind office is to hide it. Love is never so blind as when it is to spy faults. It is like the painter, who, being to draw the picture of a friend having a blemish in one eye, would picture only the other side of his face.
—Robert South

Love is a great beautifier.
—Louisa May Alcott

Men and women seldom agree in their opinion of a woman's qualities; their interests are too diverse. The feminine charms that delight men have no attraction for other women: the countless ways by which women arouse strong passions in men give rise to aversion and antipathy in their own sex.
—Jean de La Bruyère

The epithet beautiful is used by surgeons to describe operations which their patients describe as ghastly, by physicists to describe methods of measurement which leave sentimentalists cold, by lawyers to describe cases which ruin all the parties to them, and by lovers to describe the objects of their infatuation, however unattractive they may appear to the unaffected spectators.
—George Bernard Shaw

Nobody's sweetheart is ugly.
—J. J. Vadé

Inasmuch as love grows in you, so in you beauty grows.
—Saint Augustine

Beauty is the lover's gift.
—William Congreve

Where the mouth is sweet and the eyes intelligent, there is always the look of beauty, with a right heart.
—Leigh Hunt

Women need not be beautiful every day of their lives; it is sufficient that they have moments which one does not forget and the return of which one expects.
—Charles Victor Cherbuliez

Women wish to be loved without a why or wherefore—not because they are pretty or good, or well-bred, or graceful, or intelligent, but because they are themselves.
—Henri Frédéric Amiel

Whatever makes an impression on the heart seems lovely in the eye.
—Saadi

It is the heart always that sees, before the head can see.
—Thomas Carlyle

The eyes are the pioneers that first announce the soft tale of love.
—Sextus Propertius

Love's tongue is in the eyes.
—Phineas Fletcher

Love enters a man through his eyes; a woman, through her ears.
—Polish Proverb

There is no disguise which can hide love where it exists, nor feign it where it does not.
—François de La Rochefoucauld

When the heart is a-fire, some sparks will fly out of the mouth.
—Thomas Fuller (II)

Love is a child that speaks in broken language, yet then he speaks most plain.
—John Dryden

There is nothing like desire for preventing the things one says from bearing any resemblance to what one has in one's mind.
—Marcel Proust

Love teaches even asses to dance.
—French Proverb

Human love is often but the encounter of two weaknesses.
—François Mauriac

A mixture of admiration and pity is one of the surest recipes for affection.
—André Maurois

The lover is made happier by his love than the object of his affection.
—Ralph Waldo Emerson

Love is a canvas furnished by Nature and embroidered by imagination.
—François Marie de Voltaire

The emotion of love gives all of us a misleading illusion of knowing the other.
—Milan Kundera

Love is merely the exchange of two fantasies and the contact of two skins.
—Sébastien R. Nicholas Chamfort

Love is the child of illusion and the parent of disillusion.
—Miguel de Unamuno

Love is an affair of credulity.
—Ovid

One is easily fooled by that which one loves.
—Molière

The mind naturally believes and the will naturally loves, so that when there are no true objects for them they necessarily become attached to false ones.
—Blaise Pascal

We attract hearts by the qualities we display: we retain them by the qualities we possess.
—Jean Baptiste Antoine Suard

Love is not love
Which alters when it alteration finds,
Or bends with the remover to remove:
O, no! It is an ever fixed mark
That looks on tempests and is never shaken.
—William Shakespeare

You learn to love by loving—by paying attention and doing what one thereby discovers has to be done.
—Aldous Huxley

The one who will be found in trial capable of great acts of love is ever the one who is always doing considerate small ones.
—Frederick William Robertson

A true lover always feels in debt to the one he loves.
—Ralph W. Sockman

If there is anything better than to be loved it is loving.
—Author Unknown

Caresses, expressions of one sort or another, are necessary to the life of the affections as leaves are to the life of a tree. If they are wholly restrained, love will die at the roots.
—Nathaniel Hawthorne

Love does not consist in gazing at each other but in looking outward together in the same direction.
—Antoine de Saint-Exupéry

To love is to place our happiness in the happiness of another.
—Gottfried Wilhelm von Leibnitz

Love . . . consists in this, that two solitudes protect and limit and greet each other.
—Rainer Maria Rilke

We cannot really love anybody with whom we never laugh.
—Agnes Repplier

Love vanquishes time. To lovers, a moment can be eternity, eternity can be the tick of a clock.
—Mary Parrish

It is a certain sign of love to want to know, to relive, the childhood of the other.
—Cesare Pavese

The first duty of love is to listen.
—Paul Tillich

The reason that lovers never weary each other is because they are always talking about themselves.
—François de La Rochefoucauld

Love is a constant interrogation.
—Milan Kundera

To conceal anything from those to whom I am attached, is not in my nature. I can never close my lips where I have opened my heart.
—Charles Dickens

The pleasantest part of a man's life is generally that which passes in courtship, provided his passion be sincere, and the party beloved kind with discretion. Love, desire, hope, all the pleasing emotions of the soul, rise in the pursuit.
—Joseph Addison

Courtship: The timid sipping of two thirsty souls from a goblet which both can easily drain but neither replenish.
—Ambrose Bierce

When one feels oneself smitten by love for a woman, one should say to oneself, "Who are the people around her, What kind of life has she led?" All one's future happiness lies in the answer.
—Alfred de Vigny

Love is an ideal thing, marriage a real thing; a confusion of the real with the ideal never goes unpunished.
—Johann Wolfgang von Goethe

In love, there is always the one who kisses and one who offers the cheek.
—French Proverb

Judgment of beauty can err, what with the wine and the dark.
—Ovid

Love: the delusion that one woman differs from another.
—H. L. Mencken

Women are like dreams—they are never the way you would like to have them.
—Luigi Pirandello

Women are happier in the love they inspire than in that they feel; men are just the contrary.
—Edme Pierre Chanvot de Beauchêne

Open and obvious devotion from any sort of man is always pleasant to any sort of woman.
—Rudyard Kipling

A woman . . . always feels herself complimented by love, though it may be from a man incapable of winning her heart, or perhaps even her esteem.
—Abel Stevens

Love is stronger than self-love, since we can love a woman who scorns us.
—Luc de Clapiers de Vauvenargues

Women often think they love when they do not love. The business of a love affair, the emotion of mind that sentiment induces, the natural bias towards the pleasure of being loved, the difficulty of refusing, persuades them that they have real passion when they have but flirtation.
—François de La Rochefoucauld

The man's desire is for the woman; but the woman's desire is rarely other than for the desire of the man.
—Samuel Taylor Coleridge

Women are always eagerly on the lookout for any emotion.
—Stendhal

What lies lurk in a kiss.
—Heinrich Heine

A kiss can be a comma, a question mark or an exclamation point. That's a basic spelling that every woman should know.
—Mistinguette

There is the kiss of welcome and of parting; the long, lingering, loving, present one; the stolen, or the mutual one; the kiss of love, of joy, and of sorrow; the seal of promise and receipt of fulfillment. It is strange, therefore, that a woman is invincible whose army consists of kisses, smiles, sighs, and tears?
—Thomas C. Haliburton

To inspire love is a woman's greatest ambition, believe me. It's the one thing women care about and there's no woman so proud that she doesn't rejoice at heart in her conquests.
—Molière

Women are like death: they pursue those who flee from them, and flee from those who pursue them.
—German Proverb

The fickleness of the woman I love is only equaled by the infernal constancy of the women who love me.
—George Bernard Shaw

Woman would be more charming if one could fall into her arms without falling into her hands.
—Ambrose Bierce

Woman begins by resisting man's advances and ends by blocking his retreat.
—Author Unknown

The desire of a man for a woman is not directed at her because she is a human being, but because she is a woman. That she is a human being is of no concern to him.
—Immanuel Kant

It never displeases a woman to make love to her.
—Miguel de Cervantes

Most females will forgive a liberty rather than a slight.
—Charles Caleb Colton

Whether a pretty woman grants or withholds her favors, she always likes to be asked for them.
—Ovid

Women sometimes forgive a man who forces the opportunity, but never a man who misses one.
—Charles de Talleyrand-Périgord

If men knew all that women think, they would be twenty times more audacious.
—Alphonse Karr

A man is as good as he has to be, and a woman is as bad as she dares.
—Elbert Hubbard

The safety of women consists in one circumstance: Men do not possess at the same time the knowledge of thirty-five and the blood of seventeen.
—William Maginn

The sex instinct is one of the three or four prime movers of all that we do and are and dream, both individually and collectively.
—Philip Wylie

The absolute yearning of one human body for another particular one and its indifference to substitutes is one of life's major mysteries.
—Iris Murdoch

Love in young men: for the most part is not love but sexual desire, and its accomplishment is the end.
—Miguel de Cervantes

Love is the history of a woman's life; it is an episode in a man's.
—Madame Germaine de Staël

To a woman the first kiss is just the end of the beginning but to a man it is the beginning of the end.
—Helen Rowland

(Virtue:) Our vocabulary is defective; we give the same name to woman's lack of temptation and man's lack of opportunity.
—Ambrose Bierce

None are more struck with the charms of virtue in the fair sex than those who, by their very admiration of it, are carried to a desire of ruining it.
—Joseph Addison

Virtue and love are two ogres: one must eat the other.
—Comtesse d'Houdetot

Modesty does not long survive innocence.
—Edmund Burke

Once gone, modesty never returns.
—Publilius Syrus

The daughter-in-law of Pythagoras said that a woman who goes to bed with a man ought to lay aside her modesty with her skirt, and put it on again with her petticoat.
—Michel de Montaigne

Men always want to be a woman's first love. That is there clumsy vanity. We women have a more subtle instinct about things. What we like is to be a man's last romance.
—Oscar Wilde

What most men desire is a virgin who is a whore.
—Edward Dahlberg

There can be no peace of mind in love, since the advantage one has secured is never anything but a fresh starting-point for further desires.
—Marcel Proust

Love is a thirst that is never slaked.
—Henry David Thoreau

After a man finds out that the woman is no angel, he tries to ascertain to what extent she isn't.
—Author Unknown

Virtue which parleys, is near surrender.
—Author Unknown

The duration of passion is proportionate with the original resistance of the woman.
—Honoré de Balzac

We never attach ourselves lastingly to anything that has not cost us care, labor and longing.
—Honoré de Balzac

The beauty of novelty is to love as flower to the fruit: it lends a lustre which is easily lost and which never returns.
—François de La Rochefoucauld

A feast is more fatal to love than a fast.
—Charles Caleb Colton

One must cease letting oneself be eaten when one tastes best: that is known to those who want to be loved long.
—Friedrich Wilhelm Nietzsche

As bees their sting, so the promiscuous leave behind them in each encounter something of themselves by which they are made to suffer.
—Cyril Connolly

Do not exploit. Do not be exploited. Remember that sex is not out there, but in here, in the deepest layer of your own being. There is not only a morning after—there are also lots of days and years after.
—Jacob Neusner

It is better to desire than to enjoy, to love than to be loved.
—William Hazlitt

Love without desire is a delusion; it does not exist in nature.
—Ninon de Lenclos

A man and a woman make far better friendships than can exist between two of the same sex; but with this condition, that they never have made, or are to make, love with each other.
—Lord Byron

Friendship may, and often does, grow into love, but love never subsides into friendship.
—Lord Byron

There is no word in the Latin language that signifies a female friend. *Amica* means a mistress: and perhaps there is no friendship betwixt the sexes wholly disunited from a degree of love.
—William Shenstone

Platonic Love: the interval between events.
—Author Unknown

Show me a genuine case of platonic friendship, and I shall show you two old or homely faces.
—Austin O'Malley

Of course a platonic relationship is possible—but only between husband and wife.
—Author Unknown

As there is no love without desire, there is none without hope.
—Author Unknown

Love can hope, where reason would despair.
—Lord George Lyttelton

He alone knows what love is who loves without hope.
—Johann Friedrich von Schiller

Where we really love, we often dread more than we desire the solemn moment that exchanges hope for certainty.
—Madame Germaine de Staël

Who's not sat tense before his own heart's curtain?
—Rainer Maria Rilke

Love is a springtime plant that perfumes everything with its hope, even the ruins to which it clings.
—Gustave Flaubert

We ought not to complain if someone we dearly love behaves now and then in ways we find distasteful, nerve-wracking or hurtful. Instead of grumbling we should avidly horde up our feelings of irritation and bitterness: they will serve to alleviate our grief on the day when she is gone and we will miss her.
—Cesare Pavese

Whoever said love conquers all was a fool. Because almost everything conquers love—or tries to.
—Edna Ferber

It may sound shocking, yet I must say it: we can even love several individuals at one time, with nearly equal tenderness, and we need not lie when we assure each of our passion.
—Max Nordau

Of all the plagues a lover bears,
Sure rivals are the worst.
—William Walsh

An angry lover tells himself many lies.
—Publilius Syrus

Love tells us many things that are not so.
—Ukranian Proverb

And oft, my jealousy shapes faults that are not.
—William Shakespeare

When one love one doubts even what one most believes.
—François de La Rochefoucauld

A jealous man always finds more than he looks for.
—Madeleine de Scudéry

What frenzy dictates, jealousy believes.
—John Gay

It is not love that is blind, but jealousy.
—Lawrence Durrell

Jealousy is that pain which a man feels from the apprehension
that he is not equally beloved by the person he entirely loves.
—Joseph Addison

Doubt of the reality of love ends by making us doubt everything.
—Henri Frédéric Amiel

Jealousy lives upon doubts. It becomes madness or ceases
entirely as soon as we pass from doubt to certainty.
—François de La Rochefoucauld

Jealousy sees things always with magnifying glasses which make
little things large.
—Miguel de Cervantes

Trifles light as air
Are to the jealous confirmations strong
As proofs of holy writ.
—William Shakespeare

Jealousy is the great exaggerator.
—Johann Friedrich von Schiller

O, beware, my lord, of jealousy;
It is the green-eyed monster which doth mock
The meat it feeds on.
—William Shakespeare

The jealous man poisons his own banquet, and then eats it.
—Author Unknown

Jealousy is . . . a tiger that tears not only its prey but also its own raging heart.
—Michael Beer

Jealousy is said to be the offspring of love. Yet, unless the parent makes haste to strangle the child, the child will not rest till it has poisoned the parent.
—Augustus and Julius Hare

Jealousy, that dragon which slays love under the pretense of keeping it alive.
—Havelock Ellis

Though jealousy be produced by love, as ashes are by fire, yet jealousy extinguishes love as ashes smother the flame.
—Margaret de Navarre

Doubts and jealousies often beget the facts they fear.
—Thomas Jefferson

At the gate where suspicion enters, love goes out.
—Thomas Fuller (I)

Confidence, like the soul, never returns whence it has once departed.
—Publilius Syrus

Neither reproaches nor encouragements are able to revive a faith that is waning.
—Nathalie Sarraute

The great unhappiness of this passion (jealousy) is that it naturally tends to alienate the affection which it is so solicitous to engross: and that for these two reasons: because it lays too great a constraint on the words and actions of the suspect person; and, at the same time, shows you have no honorable opinion of her; both of which are strong motives to aversion.
—Joseph Addison

A jealous man merely makes himself ridiculous; he should surely remember that when another man admires his wife's charms, it is only a tribute to his judgment and should be accepted accordingly.
—B. de Mesquita

Jealousy is the greatest of all evils, and that which awakens least pity in those who cause it.
—François de La Rochefoucauld

The jealous are troublesome to others, but a torment to themselves.
—William Penn

To jealousy, nothing is more frightful than laughter.
—François Sagan

Jealousy dislikes the world to know it.
—Lord Byron

Jealousy is not love, but self-love.
—François de La Rochefoucauld

There is no passion in which the love of self reigns so powerfully as in love; and we are always more ready to sacrifice the peace of the person we love, than to lose our own.
—François de La Rochefoucauld

The deepest and most passionate love is that which survives the death of esteem.
—Ouida

Love is not always blind and there are few things that cause greater wretchedness than to love with all your heart someone who you know is unworthy of love.
—W. Somerset Maugham

Love without esteem cannot reach far or rise high; it is an angel with but one wing.
—Alexander Dumas *fils*

Time, which strengthens friendship, weakens love.
—Jean de La Bruyère

When a man becomes familiar with his goddess, she quickly sinks into a woman.
—Joseph Addison

Familiarities are the aphides that imperceptibly suck out the juices intended for the germ of love.
— Walter Savage Landor

Can we possibly imagine love without anxiously following our image in the mind of the beloved? When we are no longer interested in how we are seen by the person we love, it means we no longer love.
—Milan Kundera

Habit is the chloroform of love.
—Geneviève Antoine-Dariaux

Love comes unseen; we only see it go.
—Austin Dobson

It is almost always the fault of the lover not to know when he ceases to be loved.
—François de La Rochefoucauld

Ever has it been that love knows not its own depth until the hour of separation.
—Kahlil Gibran

Would that the thorns did not outlive the rose.
—Jean Paul Richter

Nothing is so embarrassing as the first *tête-à-tête*, when there is everything to say, unless it be the last, when everything has been said.
—Nestor Roqueplan

We always deceive ourselves twice about the people we love—first to their advantage, then to their disadvantage.
—Albert Camus

I hate and I love. You may ask why I do so. I do not know, but I feel it and am in torment.
—Catullus

Love commingled with hate is more powerful than love. Or hate.
—Joyce Carol Oates

When love is concerned, it is easier to renounce a feeling than to give up a habit.
—Marcel Proust

It is impossible to love a second time what one has really ceased to love.
—François de La Rochefoucauld

There is always something ridiculous about the passions of people whom one has ceased to love.
—Oscar Wilde

Women hope that dead love may revive, but men know that of all dead things, none are so past recall as a dead passion.
—Ouida

Love and regret go hand in hand in this world of changes swifter than the shifting of the clouds reflected in the mirror of the sea.
—Joseph Conrad

It is folly to pretend that one ever wholly recovers from a disappointed passion. Such wounds always leave a scar. There are faces I can never look upon without emotion; there are names I can never hear spoken without almost starting.
—Henry Wadsworth Longfellow

One loves more the first time, better the second.
—Rochepedre

No one has ever loved anyone the way everyone wants to be loved.
—Mignon McLaughlin

The way to love anything is to realize that it might be lost.
—G. K. Chesterton

The story of a love is not important—what is important is that one is capable of love. It's perhaps the only glimpse we are permitted of eternity.
—Helen Hayes

Talk not of wasted affection; affection never was wasted.
—Henry Wadsworth Longfellow

No matter how you look at it, all the emotions connected with love are not really immortal; like all other passions in life, they are bound to fade at some point. The trick is to convert love into some lasting friendship that overcomes the fading of passion. But that requires effort and an honest attitude on all parts. . . .
—Harold Pinter

It is as absurd to pretend that one cannot love the same woman always as to pretend that a good artist needs several violins to execute a piece of music.
—Honoré de Balzac

Be not in haste to marry, nor to engage your affections, where there is no probability of a return. Do not fancy every woman you see the heroine of a romance. . . . Avoid this error as you would shrink back from a precipice. All your fine sentiments and romantic notions will (of themselves) make no more impression on one of these delicate creatures, than on a piece of marble. Their soft bosoms are steel to your amorous refinements, if you have no other pretensions. It is not what you think of them that determines their choice, but what they think of you.
—William Hazlitt

That you may be loved, be lovable.
—Ovid

When you fish for love, bait with your heart, not your brain.
—Mark Twain

We cease loving ourselves if no one loves us.
—Madame Germaine de Staël

If nobody loves you, be sure it is your own fault.
—Phillip Doddridge

He that shuts Love out, in turn shall be
Shut out from Love, and on her threshold lie
Howling in the outer darkness.
—Alfred, Lord Tennyson

PART 9

THE FAMILY

I would like to have engraved inside every wedding band
BE KIND TO ONE ANOTHER.
This is the Golden Rule of marriage and the secret
of making love last through the years.
—Randolph Ray

Such Is Life

Taught by care, the patient man and wife
Agree to share the bitter-sweet of life.
—George Crabbe

   For what thou art is mine:
Our state cannot be sever'd; we are one,
One flesh; to lose thee were to lose myself.
—John Milton

They dream in courtship, but in wedlock wake.
—Alexander Pope

Matrimony—the high sea for which
no compass has ever been invented.
—Heinrich Heine

In courtship everything is regarded as provisional and preliminary, and the smallest sample of virtue or accomplishment is taken to guarantee delightful stores which the broad leisure of marriage will reveal. But the door-sill of marriage once crossed, expectation is concentrated on the present. Having once embarked on your marital voyage, it is impossible not to be aware that you make no way and that the sea is not within sight—that, in fact, you are exploring an enclosed basin.
—George Eliot

They perceived that the love, unceasing and ecstatic, of which they had dreamt before their union, was a chimera existing only in the imagination; and they awoke, with sobered feelings, to seek content in rational affection . . . : each acknowledging, with a sigh, that even in a marriage of love, the brilliant anticipations of

imagination are never realized; that disappointment awaits poor mortals even in that brightest portion of existence—The Honey-Moon.
—Countess of Blessington

Honeymoons are the beginning of wisdom—but the beginning of wisdom is the end of romance.
—Helen Rowland

Love is blind, but marriage restores its sight.
—George C. Lichtenberg

It doesn't much signify whom one marries, for one is sure to find out next morning that it was someone else.
—Samuel Rogers

Marriage is a book of which the first chapter is written in poetry and the remaining chapters in prose.
—Beverly Nichols

The days just prior to marriage are like a snappy introduction to a tedious book.
—Wilson Mizner

Marriage is a feast where the grace is sometimes better than the dinner.
—Charles Caleb Colton

Marriage is a covered dish.
—Swiss Proverb

There is a French saying: "Love is the dawn of marriage, and marriage is the sunset of love."
—J. de Finod

Marriage means expectations and expectations mean conflict.
—Anthony Clare

Love in marriage should be the accomplishment of a beautiful dream, and not, as it too often is, the end.
—Alphonse Karr

Those marriages generally abound most with love and constancy that are preceded by a long courtship. The passion should strike root and gather strength before marriage be grafted on it.
—Joseph Addison

Marry in haste, repent at leisure.
—English Proverb

Only choose in marriage a woman whom you would choose as a friend if she were a man.
—Joseph Joubert

It is not lack of love but lack of friendship that makes unhappy marriages.
—Friedrich Wilhelm Nietzsche

She is but half a wife that is not, nor is capable of being, a friend.
—William Penn

Choose a wife rather by your ear than by your eye.
—English Proverb

In marriage do thou be wise; prefer the person before money; virtue before beauty; the mind before the body.
—William Penn

I chose my wife, as she did her wedding gown, for qualities that would wear well.
—Oliver Goldsmith

Many a man in love with a dimple makes the mistake of marrying the whole girl.
—Stephen Leacock

Men are always to be duped. . . . They are always wooing goddesses and marrying mere mortals.
—Washington Irving

There is not one in a hundred of either sex who is not taken in when they marry. Look where I will, I see that it *is* so; and I feel

that it *must* be so, when I consider that it is, of all transactions, the one in which people expect the most from others, and are least honest themselves.
—Jane Austen

The difficulty with marriage is that we fall in love with a personality, but must live with a character.
—Peter De Vries

When men marry they think they are marrying a particular girl with a particular character, and they don't seem to realize that it will change. . . . It is not so much the girl's character that matters as all the influences she undergoes during her early married life.
—Countess Sophie Tolstoy

A girl becomes a wife with her eyes wide open. She knows that those sweetest words, "I take thee to be my wedded husband," really mean, "I promise thee to cook three meals a day for 60 years; thee will I clean up after; thee will I talk to even when thou art not listening; thee will I worry about, cry over and take all manner of hurts from."
—Alan Beck

It is better for a woman to marry a man who loves her than a man she loves.
—Arabian Proverb

A woman's lot is made for her by the love she accepts.
—George Eliot

A woman, let her be as good as she may, has got to put up with the life her husband makes for her.
—George Eliot

I had often wondered why young women should marry, as they have so much more freedom, and so much more attention paid to them while unmarried, than when married.
—Samuel Johnson

If you want to sacrifice the admiration of many men for the criticism of one, go ahead, get married.
—Katherine Hepburn

Marriage is a lottery in which men stake their liberty and women their happiness.
—Madame de Rieux

Being asked whether it was better to marry or not, he (Socrates) replied, "Whichever you do you will repent of it."
—Diogenes Laertius

Marriage may often be a stormy lake, but celibacy is almost always a muddy horse-pond.
—Thomas Love Peacock

Marriage has many pains, but celibacy has no pleasures.
—Samuel Johnson

A wife is essential to great longevity; she is the receptacle of half a man's cares, and two-thirds of his ill-humor.
—Charles Reade

Wives are young men's mistresses, companions for middle age, and old men's nurses.
—Francis Bacon

Marriage enlarges the scene of our happiness and miseries. A marriage of love is pleasant; a marriage of interest easy; and a marriage where both meet happy. A happy marriage has in it all the pleasures of friendship, all the enjoyments of sense and reason; and indeed all the sweets of life.
—Joseph Addison

Marriage hath in it less of beauty, but more of safety than the single life; it hath more care, but less danger; it is more merry, and more sad; is fuller of sorrows, and fuller of joys: it lies under

more burdens, but is supported by all the strengths of love and charity, and those burdens are delightful.
—Jeremy Taylor

Marriage is that relation between man and woman in which the independence is equal, the dependence mutual, and the obligation reciprocal.
—Louis K. Anspacher

A successful marriage is an edifice that must be rebuilt every day.
—André Maurois

More things belong (to marriage) than four bare legs in a bed.
—John Heywood

You mustn't force sex to do the work of love or love to do the work of sex.
—Mary McCarthy

The happiness of married life depends upon making small sacrifices with readiness and cheerfulness.
—John Selden

It usually takes some time for the husband and the wife to know each other's humours and habits, and to find what surrender of their own they can make with the least reluctance for their mutual good.
—Amelia Opie

What counts in making a happy marriage is not so much how compatible you are, but how you deal with incompatibility.
—George Levinger

I have known many happy marriages, but never a compatible one. The whole aim of marriage is to fight through and survive the instant when incompatibility becomes unquestionable. For a man and a woman, as such, are incompatible.
—G. K. Chesterton

In marriage, for a man, in order to get the precise thing or things that he wants, he has to take a lot of other things that he does not want.
—H. L. Mencken

Success in marriage does not come merely through finding the right mate, but through being the right mate.
—Barnett Brickner

The bonds of matrimony are like any other bonds—they mature slowly.
—Peter De Vries

It takes a long time to be really married. One marries many times at many levels within a marriage. If you have more marriages than you have divorces within the marriage, you're lucky and you stick it out.
—Ruby Dee

A successful marriage requires falling in love many times, always with the same person.
—Mignon McLaughlin

One advantage of marriage, it seems to me, is that when you fall out of love with him, or he falls out of love with you, it keeps you together until you maybe fall in again.
—Judith Viorst

It is a lovely thing to have a husband and wife developing together and having the feeling of falling in love again. That is what marriage really means: helping one another to reach the full status of being persons, responsible and autonomous beings who do not run away from life.
—Paul Tournier

I think a man and a woman should choose each other for life, for the simple reason that a long life with all its accidents is barely enough for a man and a woman to understand each other; and in this case to understand is to love.
—John Butler Yeats

Marriage is three parts love and seven parts forgiveness of sins.
—Langdon Mitchell

Keep thy eyes wide open before marriage; and half shut afterwards.
—Thomas Fuller (II)

The long-term accommodation that protects marriage and other such relationships is . . . forgetfulness.
—Alice Walker

There is probably nothing like living together for blinding people to each other.
—Ivy Compton-Burnett

Marriage should war incessantly with that monster that is the ruin of everything. This is the monster of habit.
—Honoré de Balzac

A marriage where not only esteem, but passion is kept awake, is, I am convinced, the most perfect state of sublunary happiness: but it requires great care to keep this tender plant alive.
—Frances Brooke

Men and women, in marrying, make a vow to love one another. Would it not be better for their happiness if they made a vow to please one another?
—Stanislaus Leszcynski

Kindness is the life's blood, the elixir of marriage. Kindness makes the difference between passion and caring. Kindness is tenderness. Kindness is love, but perhaps greater than love. . . . Kindness is good will. Kindness says, "I want you to be happy." Kindness comes very close to the benevolence of God.
—Randolph Ray

It was the opinion of I know not what sage that there was but one good woman in the world, and his advice was, that every man should think and believe that this one good woman was his own wife, and in this way he would live happy.
—Miguel de Cervantes

How much the wife is dearer than the bride.
—George Lyttelton

Her husband's eye . . . , the truest mirror that an honest wife can see her beauty in.
—John Tobin

A man likes his wife to be just clever enough to comprehend his cleverness, and just stupid enough to admire it.
—Israel Zangwill

Everybody all over the world takes a wife's estimate into account in forming an opinion of a man.
—Honoré de Balzac

Husband: what is left of the lover after the nerve has been extracted.
—Helen Rowland

Husbands never become good; they merely become proficient.
—H. L. Mencken

A married man forms married habits and becomes dependent on marriage as a sailor becomes dependent on the sea.
—George Bernard Shaw

Love makes marriage possible; habit makes it endurable.
—Author Unknown

Marriage is the hospital of love.
—German Proverb

Marriage is a good deal like the circus: there is not as much in it as is represented in the advertising.
—Edgar Watson Howe

Marriage is based on the theory that when a man discovers a brand of beer exactly to his taste he should at once throw up his job and go to work in the brewery.
—George Jean Nathan

Marriage: The state or condition of a community consisting of a master, a mistress and two slaves, making in all, two.
—Ambrose Bierce

The most happy marriage I can picture . . . would be the union of a deaf man to a blind woman.
—Samuel Taylor Coleridge

There never was a wife that liked her lot.
—John Davies

The land of marriage has this peculiarity: the strangers are desirous of inhabiting it, while its natural inhabitants would willingly be banished from thence.
—Michel de Montaigne

Unlived life is a destructive and irresistible force working quietly but relentlessly. The result is that the married woman begins to doubt marriage. The unmarried woman believes in it, because she desires marriage.
—Carl Jung

Marriage is an arrangement by which two people start by getting the best out of each other and often end by getting the worst.
—Gerald Brenan

People who marry tease Fate.
—Author Unknown

Oh, how many torments lie in the small circle of a wedding ring.
—Colley Cibber

I suspect that in every good marriage there are times when love seems to be over.
—Madeleine L'Engle

The first sign that things are amiss between the two who thought they were entering paradise together, is generally a sense of loneliness, a feeling that the one who was expected to have all in common is outside some experience, some subtle delight, and fails to understand the needs of the loved one. Trivialities are

often the first indicators of something which takes its roots unseen in the profoundest depths.
—Marie Stopes

If you are afraid of loneliness, don't marry.
—Anton Chekhov

To marry is to learn to be alone.
—French Proverb

Loneliness is never more cruel than when it is felt in close propinquity with someone who has ceased to communicate.
—Germaine Greer

The silken texture of the marriage tie bears a daily strain of wrong and insult to which no other human relation can be subjected without lesion.
—William Dean Howells

There are couples who dislike one another furiously for several hours at a time; there are couples who dislike one another permanently; and there are couples who never dislike one another; but these last are people who are incapable of disliking anybody.
—George Bernard Shaw

The love of some men for their wives is like that of Alfieri for his horse. "My attachment for him," said he, "went so far as to destroy my peace every time that he had the least ailment; but my love for him did not prevent me from fretting and chafing him whenever he did not wish to go my way."
—Christian Nestell Bovee

Marriage is one long conversation checkered by disputes.
—Robert Louis Stevenson

During a long and varied career as a bachelor, I have noticed that marriage is the death of politeness between a man and a woman.
—Arnold Bennett

For every quarrel a man and a wife have before others, they have a hundred when alone.
—Edgar Watson Howe

Even the God of Calvin never judged anyone as harshly as married couples judge each other.
—Wilfrid Sheed

In all matrimonial associations there is, I believe, one constant factor—a desire to deceive the person with whom one lives as to some weak spot in one's character or in one's career. For it is intolerable to live constantly with one human being who perceives one's small meannesses. It is really death to do so—that is why so many marriages turn out unhappily.
—Ford Madox Ford

Marriage is good for nothing but to make friends fall out.
—Thomas Shadwell

A man may be a fool and not know it—but not if he is married.
—H. L. Mencken

A wife is to thank God her husband has faults; a husband without faults is a dangerous observer.
—Lord Halifax

Never feel remorse for what you have thought about your wife; she has thought much worse things about you.
—Jean Rostand

Marriage is a bargain, and somebody has to get the worst of the bargain.
—Helen Rowland

Marriage is like life in this—that it is a field of battle, and not a bed of roses.
—Robert Louis Stevenson

Marriage, in life, is like a duel in the midst of a battle.
—Edmund About

Marriage with a good woman is a harbour in the tempest of life; with a bad woman, it is a tempest in the harbour.
—Jean-Antoine Petit-Senn

Wedlock is hell if at least one side does not love.
—Sir Richard Steele

We perceive when love begins and when it declines by our embarrassment when alone together.
—Jean de La Bruyère

There are few people who are not ashamed of being loved when they love no longer.
—François de La Rochefoucauld

Mourning the loss of someone we love is happiness compared with having to live with someone we hate.
—Jean de La Bruyère

Heaven has no rage like love to hatred turned.
—William Congreve

It is hard to fight an enemy who has outposts in your head.
—Sally Kempton

It takes two to make a marriage a success and only one a failure.
—Herbert Samuel

It is not marriage that fails; it is people that fail. All that marriage does is to show people up.
—Harry Emerson Fosdick

We bury love;
Forgetfulness grows over it like grass:
That is a thing to weep for, not the dead.
—Alexander Smith

The chains of matrimony are so heavy that it takes two to bear
them, and sometimes three.
—Alexander Dumas *père*

They that marry where they do not love, will love where they do
not marry.
—Thomas Fuller (I)

Ah, the relationships we get into just to get out of the ones we are
not brave enough to say are over.
—Julia Phillips

One always likes to daydream about people one didn't get to
know very well, and about affairs that were not destined to last.
—Milán Füst

No matter how happily a woman may be married, it always
pleases her to discover that there is a nice man who wishes that
she were not.
—H. L. Mencken

Who hath a fair wife needs more than two eyes.
—John Ray

A lover tells a woman all that a husband hides from her.
—Honoré de Balzac

It is easier to be a lover than a husband, for the reason that it is
harder to be witty every day than to say pretty things now and
then.
—Honoré de Balzac

Monogamy is like good crystal—beautiful—but once you get it, all
it takes is one chip and it's never the same again.
—Fred Barton

No adultery is bloodless.
—Natalia Ginzburg

When cheated, wife or husband feels the same.
—Euripides

The double standard of morality will survive in this world so long as the woman whose husband has been lured away is favored with the sympathetic tears of other women, and a man whose wife has made off is laughed at by other men.
—H. L. Mencken

It is the fear of middle-age in the young, of old-age in the middle-aged, which is the prime cause of infidelity, that infallible rejuvenator.
—Cyril Connolly

How desperately we wish to maintain our trust in those we love! In the face of everything, we try to find reasons to trust. Because losing faith is worse than falling out of love.
—Sonia Johnson

When something like this happens, you suddenly have no sense of reality at all. You have lost a piece of your past. The infidelity itself is small potatoes compared to the low-level brain damage that results when a whole chunk of your life turns out to be completely different from what you thought it was. It becomes impossible to look back at anything that's happened . . . without wondering what was really going on.
—Nora Ephron

As a rule the person found out in a betrayal of love holds, all the same, the superior position of the two. It is the betrayed one who is humiliated.
—Ada Leverson

Traditionally, sex has been a very private, secretive activity. Herein perhaps lies its powerful force for uniting people in a strong bond. As we make sex less secretive, we may rob it of its power to hold men and women together.
—Thomas Szasz

Americans, who make more of marrying for love than any other people, also break up more of their marriages, but the figure reflects not so much the failure of love as the determination of people not to live without it.
—Morton Hunt

It is seldom indeed that one parts on good terms, because if one were on good terms one would not part.
—Marcel Proust

When we two parted,
in silence and tears,
half broken-hearted
to sever for years,
pale grew thy cheek and cold,
colder thy kiss.
—Lord Byron

There are four stages in a marriage. First there's the affair, then the marriage, then children and finally the fourth stage, without which you cannot know a woman, the divorce.
—Norman Mailer

Divorce: A bugle blast that separates the combatants and makes them fight at long range.
—Ambrose Bierce

To deny divorce to persons who unfortunately need it, is to lock the door after love has fled.
—B. B. Lindsay

Divorce and suicide have many characteristics in common and one crucial difference: although both are devastatingly public admissions of failure, divorce, unlike suicide, has to be lived through.
—A. Alvarez

I doubt if there is one married person on earth who can be objective about divorce. It is always a threat, admittedly or not, and such a dire threat that it is almost a dirty word.
—Nora Johnson

However often marriage is dissolved, it remains indissoluble. Real divorce, the divorce of heart and nerve and fiber, does not exist, since there is no divorce from memory.
—Virgilia Peterson

Divorce is the psychological equivalent of a triple coronary by-pass. After such a monumental assault on the heart, it takes years to amend all the habits and attitudes that led up to it.
—Mary Kay Blakely

A divorce is like an amputation; you survive, but there's less of you.
—Margaret Atwood

Divorce is defeat.
—Lucille Ball

And love, grown faint and fretful,
With lips but half regretful,
Sighs, and with eyes forgetful
Weeps that no loves endure.
—Algernon Charles Swinburne

It is difficult suddenly to put aside a long-standing love; it is difficult, but somehow you must do it.
—Catullus

There is a time for departure even when there's no certain place to go.
—Tennessee Williams

All changes, even the most longed for, have their melancholy: for what we leave behind us is a part of ourselves; we must die to one life before we can enter another!
—Anatole France

Nobody told me how hard and lonely change is.
—Joan Gilbertson

Divorces as well as marriages can fail.
—Maurice Merleau-Ponty

The best proof that experience is useless is that the end of one love does not disgust us from beginning another.
—Paul Bourget

To marry a second time represents the triumph of hope over experience.
—Samuel Johnson

Love seems the swiftest, but it is the slowest of all growths. No man or woman really knows what perfect love is until they have been married a quarter of a century.
—Mark Twain

The love we have in youth is superficial compared to the love that an old man has for his old wife.
—Will Durant

A long-term marriage has to move beyond chemistry to compatibility, to friendship, to companionship. It is certainly not that passion disappears, but that it is conjoined with other ways of love.
—Madeleine L'Engle

In love's old age, as in that of life itself, we are still alive for the suffering but no longer for the pleasures.
—François de La Rochefoucauld

At the end of what is called the "sexual life" the only love which has lasted is the love which has everything, every disappointment, every failure and every betrayal, which has accepted even the sad fact that in the end there is no desire so deep as the simple desire for companionship.
—Graham Greene

The quiet mutual gaze of a trusting husband and wife is like the first moment of rest or refuge from a great weariness or a great danger.
—George Eliot

A lady of 47 who has been married 27 years and has 6 children knows what love really is and once described it for me like this: "Love is what you've been through with somebody."
—James Thurber

Marriage is our last, best chance to grow up.
—Joseph Barth

Who of us is mature enough for offspring before the offspring themselves arrive? The value of marriage is not that adults produce children but that children produce adults.
—Peter De Vries

Most of us become parents long before we have stopped being children.
—Mignon McLaughlin

All the time a person is a child he is both a child and learning to be a parent. After he becomes a parent he becomes predominantly a parent reliving childhood.
—Dr. Benjamin Spock

Parenthood remains the greatest single preserve of the amateur.
—Alvin Toffler

Making a decision to have a child—it's momentous. It is to decide forever to have your heart go walking around outside your body.
—Elizabeth Stone

Having a family is like having a bowling alley installed in your brain.
—Martin Mull

He that raises a large family does, indeed, while he lives to observe them, stand a broader mark for sorrow; but then he stands a broader mark for pleasure too.
—Benjamin Franklin

Families with babies and families without babies are sorry for each other.
—Edgar Watson Howe

Children are horribly insecure; the life of a parent is the life of a gambler.
—Sydney Smith

Children blessings seem, but torments are.
—Thomas Otway

Children sweeten labours; but they make misfortunes more bitter.
—Francis Bacon

Children are poor men's riches.
—English Proverb

Every child born into the world is a new thought of God, an ever-fresh and radiant possibility.
—Kate Douglas Wiggin

I love little children, and it is not a slight thing when they, who are fresh from God, love us.
—Charles Dickens

When a healthy three-year-old child says "I love you" there is meaning in it like that between men and women who love and are in love.
—D. W. Winnicott

A child's hand in yours—what tenderness it arouses, what power it conjures. You are instantly the very touchstone of wisdom and strength.
—Marjorie Holmes

Women make us poets, children make us philosophers.
—Malcolm de Chazal

What in us the women leave uncultivated, children cultivate when we retain them near us.
—Johann Wolfgang von Goethe

Romance fails us and so do friendships, but the relationship of parent and child, less noisy than all others, remains indelible and indestructible, the strongest relationship on earth.
—Theodor Reik

There is no friendship, no love, like that of the parent for the child.
—Henry Ward Beecher

He that has no children knows not what is love.
—H. G. Bohn

How many hopes and fears, how many ardent wishes and anxious apprehensions are twisted together in the threads that connect the parent with the child!
—Samuel Griswold Goodrich

The potential possibilities of any child are the most intriguing and stimulating in all creation.
—Ray L. Wilbur

Every beetle is a gazelle in the eyes of its mother.
—Moorish Proverb

I discovered when I had a child of my own that I had become a biased observer of small children. Instead of looking at them with affectionate but nonpartisan eyes, I saw each of them as older or younger, bigger or smaller, more or less graceful, intelligent, or skilled than my own child.
—Margaret Mead

The boy is the man in miniature: and the distinguishing characteristics of the individual are the same through the whole course of life.
—James Boswell

A girl is Innocence playing in the mud, Beauty standing on its head, and Motherhood dragging a doll by the foot.
—Alan Beck

Life . . . would give her everything of consequence, life would shape her, not we. All we were good for was to make the introductions.
—Helen Hayes

The least and most imperceptible impressions received in our infancy have consequences very important, and of a long duration. It is with these first impressions, as with a river whose waters we can easily turn, by different canals, in quite opposite courses, so that from the insensible direction the stream receives at its source, it takes different directions, and at last arrives at places far distant from each other; and with the same facility we may, I think, turn the minds of children to what direction we please.
—John Locke

Begin to instruct as soon as a child has any notion of the difference between good and evil. And this is as soon as he knows your smile from your frown.
—Samuel Palmer

Judicious mothers will always keep in mind, that they are the first book read, and the last put aside, in every child's library.
—C. Lennox Remond

What the mother sings to the cradle goes all the way down to the coffin.
—Henry Ward Beecher

The mother's heart is the child's schoolroom.
—Henry Ward Beecher

Men are what their mother's make them.
—Ralph Waldo Emerson

Education commences at the mothers knee, and every word spoken within the hearing of little children tends toward the formation of character.
—Hosea Ballou

Before the child even gets to school it will have received crucial, almost irrevocable sex education and this will have been taught by the parents, who are not aware of what they are doing.
—Mary S. Calderone

Parents think their children should keep their innocence as long as possible. The world doesn't work that way. If parents ever have a choice between mentioning something to children or not mentioning something to children, they should mention it. If there's a choice between talking and not talking, always choose talking, even if it is more difficult.
—Grace Hechinger

Home is the chief school of human virtue.
—William Ellery Channing

The only moral lesson that is suited for a child—the most important lesson for every time of life—is this: "Never hurt anybody."
—Jean Jacques Rousseau

To make your children capable of honesty is the beginning of education.
—John Ruskin

The conscience of children is formed by the influences that surround them; their notions of good and evil are the result of the moral atmosphere they breathe.
—Jean Paul Richter

What's done to children, they will do to society.
—Karl A. Menninger

The hearts of small children are delicate organs. A cruel beginning in this world can twist them into curious shapes.
—Carson McCullers

The sower may mistake and sow his peas crookedly: the peas make no mistake, but come up and show his line.
—Ralph Waldo Emerson

Parents wonder why the streams are bitter, when they themselves have poisoned the fountain.
—John Locke

Whatever you would have your children become, strive to exhibit in your own lives and conversation.
—Lydia H. Sigourney

Thou canst not rebuke in children what they see practiced in thee. Till reason be ripe, examples direct more than precepts. Such as is thy behavior before thy children's faces, such is theirs behind thy back.
—Frances Quarles

The talk of a child in the street is that of his father and mother.
—Babylonian Talmud

Children have never been very good at listening to their elders, but they have never failed to imitate them.
—James Baldwin

What the child imitates he is trying to understand.
—Friedrich W. A. Froebel

The words that a father speaks to his children in the privacy of home are not heard by the world, but, as in whispering galleries, they are clearly heard at the end, and by posterity.
—Jean Paul Richter

The popular idea that a child forgets easily is not an accurate one. Many people go right through life in the grip of an idea which has been impressed on them in very tender years.
—Agatha Christie

Oh, what a tangled web do parents weave
When they think their children are naïve.
—Ogden Nash

Children, like dogs, have so sharp and fine a scent that they detect and hunt out everything—the bad before all the rest. They also know well enough how this or that friend stands with their parents; and as they practice no dissimulation whatever, they serve as excellent barometers by which to observe the degree of favor or disfavor at which we stand with their parents.
—Johann Wolfgang von Goethe

Children are very nice observers, and they will often perceive your slightest defects. In general, those who govern children forgive nothing in them, but everything in themselves.
—François de Fénelon

Conceal your weakness from your child, lest he despise your instruction, and be hardened in his folly; for he who sees your folly, will scarce be ashamed of his own.
—George Shelley

Children have more need of models than of critics.
—Joseph Joubert

I hardly know so melancholy a reflection as that parents are necessarily the sole directors of the management of children, whether they have or have not judgment, penetration or taste to perform the task.
—Lord Fulke Gréville

Till society is very differently constituted, parents, I fear, will still insist on being obeyed because they will be obeyed, and constantly endeavor to settle that power on a divine right which will not bear the investigation of reason.
—Mary Wollstonecraft

There should be no enforced respect for grown-ups. We cannot prevent children from thinking us fools by merely forbidding

them to utter their thoughts; in fact, they are more likely to think ill of us if they dare not say so.
—Bertrand Russell

Don't demand respect, as a parent. Demand civility and insist on honesty. But respect is something you must earn—with kids as well as with adults.
—William Attwood

It is better to keep children to their duty by a sense of honor and by kindness than by fear.
—Terence

I do not like punishments. You will never torture a child into duty; but a sensible child will dread the frown of a judicious mother more than all the rods, dark rooms, and scolding school-mistresses in the universe.
—H. K. White

A torn jacket is soon mended, but hard words bruise the heart of a child.
—Henry Wadsworth Longfellow

Feel the dignity of a child. Do not feel superior to him, for you are not.
—Robert Henri

Don't set your wit against a child.
—Jonathan Swift

It is a shameful thing to insult a little child. It has its feelings, it has its small dignity; and since it cannot defend them, it is surely an ignoble act to injure them.
—Mark Twain

If a child tells a lie, tell him that he has told a lie, but don't call him a liar. If you define him as a liar, you break down his confidence in his own character.
—Jean Paul Richter

A suspicious parent makes an artful child.
—Thomas C. Haliburton

What children expect from parents is not to be "understood," but only to be loved, even though this love may be expressed clumsily or in sternness. Intimacy does not exist between generations— only trust.
—Carl Zucker

The most important thing a father can do for his children is to love their mother.
—Theodore M. Hesburgh

Be ever gentle with the children God has given you, watch over them constantly; reprove them earnestly, but not in anger. In the forcible language of Scripture, "Be not bitter against them." I once heard a kind father say; "I talk to them very much, but do not like to beat my children—the world will beat them." It was a beautiful thought, though not elegantly expressed. Yes: there is not one child in the circle round the table, healthful and happy as they look now, on whose head, if long enough spared, the storm will not beat. Adversity may wither them, sickness may fade, a cold world may frown on them, but amidst all let memory carry them back to a home where the law of kindness reigned, where the mother's reproving eye was moistened with a tear, and the father frowned "more in sorrow than in anger."
—Elihu Burrit

Love your children with all your hearts, love them enough to discipline them before it is too late. . . . Praise them for important things, even if you have to stretch them a bit. Praise them alot. They live on it like bread and butter and they need it more than bread and butter.
—Lavina Christensen Fugal

Words of praise, indeed, are almost as necessary to warm a child into a congenial life as acts of kindness and affection. Judicious praise is to children what the sun is to flowers.
—Christian Nestell Bovee

In praising a child, we love and praise not that which is, but that which we hope for.
—Johann Wolfgang von Goethe

We can't form our children on our own concepts; we must take them and love them as God gives them to us.
—Johann Wolfgang von Goethe

Your children are not your children. They are the sons and daughters of Life's longing for itself.
—Kahlil Gibran

You may give them your love but not your thoughts,
For they have their own thoughts.
You may house their bodies but not their souls,
For their souls dwell in the house of tomorrow, which you cannot visit, not even in your dreams.
You may strive to be like them, but seek not to make them like you,
For life goes not backward nor tarries with yesterday.
You are the bows from which your children as living arrows are sent forth.
—Kahlil Gibran

Children need love, especially when they do not deserve it.
—Harold S. Hulbert

Loving a child doesn't mean giving in to all his whims; to love him is to bring out the best in him, to teach him to love what is difficult.
—Nadia Boulanger

Direct your efforts more to preparing youth for the path and less to preparing the path for the youth.
—Ben Lindsey

A man who gives his children habits of industry provides for them better than by giving them a fortune.
—Richard Whately

You cannot teach a child to take care of himself unless you will let him try to take care of himself. He will make mistakes; and out of these mistakes will come his wisdom.
—Henry Ward Beecher

Parents learn a lot from their children about coping with life.
—Muriel Spark

All children must look after their own upbringing. Parents can only give good advice or put them on the right paths, but the final forming of a person's character lies in their own hands.
—Anne Frank

Be aware that young people have to be able to make their own mistakes and that times change.
—Gina Shapira

Children are like grown people; the experience of others is never of any use to them.
—Alphonse Daudet

It always grieves me to contemplate the initiation of children into the ways of life when they are scarcely more than infants. It checks their confidence and simplicity, two of the best qualities that Heaven gives them, and demands that they share our sorrows before they are capable of entering into our entertainments.
—Charles Dickens

We should treat children as God does us, who makes us happiest when He leaves us under the influence of innocent delusions.
—Johann Wolfgang von Goethe

The future is always a fairy land to the young.
—George Augustus Sala

Children have neither past nor future; and unlike ourselves, they enjoy the present.
—Jean de La Bruyère

The business of being a child interests the child not at all. Children very rarely play at being other children.
—David Holloway

It should be noted that children at play are not playing about; their games should be seen as their most serious-minded activity.
—Michel de Montaigne

Idleness, indolence, and laziness, vices so natural to children, disappear as soon as they begin to play; they are then lively, attentive, exact observers of rule and order, never pardon the least slip, and several times begin again one and the same thing, in which they failed; these are sure forebodings that they may, hereafter, neglect their duties, but will forget nothing that can promote their pleasures.
—Jean de La Bruyère

There are no end to the violations committed by children on children, quietly talking alone.
—Elizabeth Bowen

What is more enchanting than the voices of young people when you can't hear what they say?
—Logan Pearsall Smith

Children are overbearing, supercilious, passionate, envious, inquisitive, egotistical, idle, fickle, timid, intemperate, liars, and dissemblers; they laugh and weep easily, are excessive in their joys and sorrows, and that about the most trifling objects; they bear no pain, but like to inflict it on others; they are men already.
—Jean de La Bruyère

God knows that a mother needs fortitude and courage and tolerance and flexibility and patience and firmness and nearly every other brave aspect of the human soul. But because I happen to be a parent of almost fiercely maternal nature, I praise casualness. It seems to me the rarest of virtues. It is useful enough when children are small. It is important to the point of necessity when they are adolescents.
—Phyllis McGinley

Adolescence is a twentieth-century invention most parents approach with dread and look back on with the relief of survivors.
—Faye Moskowitz

Children in a family are like flowers in a bouquet: there's always one determined to face in an opposite direction from the way the arranger desires.
—Marcelene Cox

To be a good parent, you have to put yourself second, to recognize that the child has feelings and needs separate from yours, and fulfill those needs without expecting anything in return.
—Howard Kogan

Parents are the bones on which children sharpen their teeth.
—Peter Ustinov

There are times when parenthood seems nothing more than feeding the hand that bites you.
—Peter De Vries

The most hateful, and yet the commonest and oldest, sort of ingratitude is that of children towards their parents.
—Luc de Clapiers de Vauvenargues

Children begin by loving their parents. After a time they judge them. Rarely, if ever, do they forgive them.
—Oscar Wilde

Parents—especially step-parents—are sometimes a bit of a disappointment to their children. They don't fulfill the promise of the early years.
—Anthony Powell

A king, recognizing his incompetence, can either delegate or abdicate his duties. A father can do neither. If only sons could see the paradox, they would understand the dilemma.
—Marlene Dietrich

The mother—daughter relationship is paradoxical and, in a sense, tragic. It requires the most intense love on the mother's side, yet this very love must help the child grow away from the mother and to become fully independent.
—Erich Fromm

The most important thing that parents can teach their children is how to get along without them.
—Frank Clark

Children do not know how their parents love them, and they never will till the grave closes over those parents, or till they have children of their own.
—P. Cooke

A father's love is for his children, and the children's love for their children.
—Babylonian Talmud

The family you come from isn't as important as the family you're going to have.
—Ring Lardner

Our children are here to stay, but our babies and toddlers and preschoolers are gone as fast as they can grow up—and we have only a short moment with each. When you see a grandfather take a baby in his arms, you see that the moment hasn't always been long enough.
—St. Clair Adams Sullivan

PART 10

THE ARENA

The way to gain a good reputation is to
endeavor to be what you desire to appear.
—Socrates

Such Is Life

It is not the critic who counts; not the man who points out how the strong man stumbles, or where the doer of deeds could have done them better. The credit belongs to the man who is actually in the arena, whose face is marred by dust and sweat and blood, who strives valiantly, who errs and comes short again and again because there is no effort without error and shortcomings, who knows the great devotion, who spends himself in a worthy cause, who at best knows in the end the high achievement of triumph and who at worst, if he fails while daring greatly, knows his place shall never be with those timid and cold souls who know neither victory nor defeat.
—Theodore Roosevelt

Indolence is a delightful but distressing state; we must be doing something to be happy. Action is no less necessary than thought to the instinctive tendencies of the human frame.
—Mohandas K. Gandhi

The need for devotion to something outside ourselves is even more profound than the need for companionship. If we are not to go to pieces or whither away, we all must have some purpose in life; for no man can live for himself alone.
—Ross Parmenter

Life, to be worthy of a rational being, must be always in progression; we must always propose to do more or better than in time past. The mind is enlarged and elevated by mere purposes, though they end as they begin by airy contemplation.
—Samuel Johnson

I find the great thing in this world is not so much where we stand, as in what direction we are moving: To reach the port of heaven, we must sail sometimes with the wind and sometimes against it, but we must sail, and not drift, nor lie at anchor.
—Oliver Wendell Holmes, Sr.

A ship in port is safe, but that's not what ships are built for.
—Grace Murray Hopper

Every human being has a work to carry on within, duties to perform abroad, influence to exert, which are peculiarly his, and which no conscience but his own can teach.
—William Ellery Channing

He that embarks in the voyage of life will always wish to advance rather by the impulse of the wind than the strokes of the oar; and many founder in their passage, while they lie waiting for the gale.
—Samuel Johnson

A great deal of talent is lost in the world for want of a little courage. Every day sends to their graves a number of obscure men who have only remained in obscurity because their timidity has prevented them from making a first effort.
—Sydney Smith

Men are often capable of greater things than they perform. They are sent into the world with bills of credit, and seldom draw to their full extent.
—Horace Walpole

We judge ourselves by what we feel capable of doing; others judge us by what we have done.
—Henry Wadsworth Longfellow

It is a mortifying reflection for a man to consider what he has done, compared with what he might have done.
—Samuel Johnson

People wish to learn to swim and at the same time to keep one foot on the ground.
—Marcel Proust

The fact is, that to do anything in this world worth doing, we must not stand back shivering and thinking of the cold and danger, but jump right in and scramble through as well as we can.
—Sydney Smith

You can't cross the sea merely by standing and staring at the water.
—Sir Rabindranath Tagore

He that leaveth nothing to chance will do few things ill, but he will do very few things.
—Lord Halifax

Who waits until circumstances completely favor his undertaking, will never accomplish anything.
—Martin Luther

It had long since come to my attention that people of accomplishment rarely sat back and let things happen to them. They went out and happened to things.
—Elinor Smith

I do not believe in a fate that falls on men however they act; but I do believe in a fate that falls on men unless they act.
—G. K. Chesterton

Who dares nothing, need hope for nothing.
—Johann Friedrich von Schiller

We live in a wonderful world that is full of beauty, charm and adventure. There is no end to the adventures that we can have if only we seek them with our eyes open.
—Jawaharlal Nehru

Adventure is not outside a man; it is within.
—David Grayson

Life shrinks or expands in proportion to one's courage.
—Anaïs Nin

Thoughts are but dreams until their effects be tried.
—William Shakespeare

Our deeds determine us, as much as we determine our deeds.
—George Eliot

Every action of our lives touches on some chord that will vibrate in eternity.
—Edwin Hubbell Chapin

Nothing ever happens but once in this world. What I do now I do once for all. It is over and gone, with all its eternity of solemn meaning.
—Thomas Carlyle

Action may not always bring happiness; but there is no happiness without action.
—Benjamin Disraeli

From the moment of birth we are immersed in action, and can only fitfully guide it by taking thought.
—Alfred North Whitehead

Life is made up of constant calls to action, and we seldom have time for more than hastily contrived answers.
—Learned Hands

Impulse has more effect than conscious purpose in molding men's lives.
—Bertrand Russell

Thought is the blossom; language the bud; action the fruit behind it.
—Ralph Waldo Emerson

Think like a man of action and act like a man of thought.
—Henri Bergson

Part of having a strong sense of self is to be accountable for one's actions. No matter how much we explore motives or lack of motives, we are what we do.
—Janet Geringer Woititz

The actions of men are the best interpreters of their thoughts.
—John Locke

What a man believes may be ascertained, not from his creed, but from the assumptions on which he habitually acts.
—George Bernard Shaw

There is no action so slight, nor so mean, but it may be done to a great purpose, and ennobled therefore; nor is any purpose so great but that slight actions may help it, and may be so done as to help it much.
—John Ruskin

When we cannot act as we wish, we must act as we can.
—Terence

Do what you can, with what you have, where you are.
—Theodore Roosevelt

We do not choose our own parts in life, and have nothing to do with selecting those parts. Our simple duty is confined to playing them well.
—Epictetus

To be a man is, precisely, to be responsible.
—Antoine de Saint-Exupéry

Our duty is to be useful, not according to our desires but according to our powers.
—Henri Frédéric Amiel

What, then, is your duty? What the day demands.
—Johann Wolfgang von Goethe

Our grand business is not to see what lies dimly at a distance, but to do what lies clearly at hand.
—Thomas Carlyle

Such Is Life

Do something every day that you don't want to do; this is the golden rule for acquiring the habit of doing your duty without pain.
—Mark Twain

The reward of one duty done is the power to fulfill another.
—George Eliot

When you have a number of disagreeable duties to perform always do the most disagreeable first.
—Josiah Quincy

The wise man does at once what the fool does finally.
—Baltasar Grácian

No task is a long one but the task on which one dare not start. It becomes a nightmare.
—Charles Baudelaire

There is nothing so easy but that it becomes difficult when you do it with reluctance.
—Terence

To think we are able is almost to be so.
—Samuel Smiles

When Duty comes a-knocking at your gate,
Welcome him in; for if you bid him wait,
He will depart only to come once more
And bring seven other duties to your door.
—Edwin Markham

A duty dodged is like a debt unpaid; it is only deferred, and we must come back and settle the account at last.
—Joseph F. Newton

He who is false in present duty breaks a thread in the loom, and will find the flaw when he may have forgotten its cause.
—Henry Ward Beecher

Hell is truth seen too late—duty neglected in its season.
—Tryon Edwards

Our greatest weariness comes from work not done.
—Eric Hoffer

Can anything be sadder than work left unfinished? Yes; work never begun.
—Christina Rossetti

Better do it than wish it done.
—Author Unknown

You cannot plow a field by turning it over in your mind.
—Author Unknown

No man's spirits were ever hurt by doing his duty; on the contrary, one good action, one temptation resisted and overcome, one sacrifice of desire or interest, purely for conscience' sake, will prove a cordial for weak and low spirits, far beyond what either indulgence or diversion or company can do for them.
—William Paley

Accustom yourself to submit on all and every occasion, and on the most minute, no less than on the most important circumstances of life, to a small and present evil, to obtain a greater distant good. This will give decision, tone and energy to the mind, which, thus disciplined, will often reap victory from defeat, and honor from repulse.
—Charles Caleb Colton

The reward of a thing well done is to have done it.
—Ralph Waldo Emerson

The best way out is always through.
—Robert Frost

That kind of life is most happy which affords us most opportunities of gaining our own esteem.
—Samuel Johnson

No man who is occupied in doing a very difficult thing, and doing it very well, ever loses his self-respect.
—George Bernard Shaw

Occupation is the necessary basis of all enjoyment.
—Leigh Hunt

The more we do, the more we can do.
—William Hazlitt

No thoroughly occupied man was ever yet very miserable.
—Letitia Landon

Work spares us from three great evils: boredom, vice, and need.
—François Marie de Voltaire

We work not only to produce but to give value to time.
—Eugène Delacroix

We always have time enough, if we will but use it aright.
—Johann Wolfgang von Goethe

Few things are impossible to diligence and skill. . . . Great works are performed, not by strength, but perseverance.
—Samuel Johnson

Skill and confidence are an unconquered army.
—George Herbert

If little labor, little are our gains;
Man's fortunes are according to his pains.
—Robert Herrick

I look on that man as happy, who, when there is a question of success, looks into his work for a reply.
—Ralph Waldo Emerson

What men want is not talent, it is purpose; in other words, not the power to achieve, but will to labor. I believe that labor judiciously and continuously applied becomes genius.
—Edward G. Bulwer-Lytton

If you have great talents, industry will improve them; if moderate abilities, industry will supply their deficiencies. Nothing is denied to well-directed labor; nothing is ever to be attained without it.
—Sir Joshua Reynolds

What we hope ever to do with ease, we must learn first to do with diligence.
—Samuel Johnson

The indefatigable pursuit of an unattainable perfection, even though it consist in nothing more than in the pounding of an old piano, is what alone gives meaning to our life on this unavailing star.
—Logan Pearsall Smith

Ideals are like the stars: you will not succeed in touching them with your hands, but like the seafaring man on the desert of waters, you choose them as your guide, and following them, you reach your destiny.
—Carl Schurz

Every artist was first an amateur.
—Ralph Waldo Emerson

There is probably no man living, though ever so great a fool, that cannot do something or other well.
—Samuel Warren

Each man has an aptitude born with him.
—Ralph Waldo Emerson

It is a pleasant fact that you will know no man long, however low in the social scale, however poor, miserable, intemperate, and worthless he may appear to be, a mere burden to society, but you will find at last that there is something which he understands and can do better than any other.
—Henry David Thoreau

There is none who cannot teach somebody something, and there is none so excellent but he is excelled.
—Baltasar Grácian

Every man loves what he is good at.
—Thomas Shadwell

The test of a vocation is the love of the drudgery it involves.
—Logan Pearsall Smith

Repetition is reality, and it is the seriousness of life.
—Sören Kierkegaard

One is often kept in the right road by a rut.
—Gustave Droz

Nothing is really work unless you would rather be doing something else.
—Sir James Matthew Barrie

Few enterprises of great labor or hazard would be undertaken if we had not the power of magnifying the advantages we expect from them.
—Samuel Johnson

Most people spend most of their days doing what they do not want to do in order to earn the right, at times, to do what they may desire.
—John Mason Brown

Work is the meat of life, pleasure the dessert.
—Bertie Charles Forbes

God gives every bird its food, but he does not throw it into the nest.
—Josiah Gilbert Holland

Heaven ne'er helps the man who will not help himself.
—Sophocles

We all find time to do what we really want to do.
—William Feather

Don't yield to that alluring witch, Laziness, or else be prepared to surrender all that you have won in your better moments.
—Horace

Shun idleness, it is the rust that attaches itself to the most brilliant metals.
—François Marie de Voltaire

Sloth, like rust, consumes faster than labor wears, while the used key is always bright.
—Benjamin Franklin

Laziness grows on people; it begins in cobwebs and ends in iron chains.
—Thomas Fowell Buxton

We make a mistake if we believe that only the violent passions like ambition and love can subdue the others. Laziness, for all her languor, is nevertheless often mistress: she permeates every aim and action in life and imperceptibly eats away and destroys passions and virtues alike.
—François de La Rochefoucauld

Laziness travels so slowly that poverty soon overtakes him.
—Benjamin Franklin

In the prospect of poverty there is nothing but gloom and melancholy; the mind and the body suffer together; its miseries bring no alleviations; it is a state in which every virtue is obscured, and in which no conduct can avoid reproach; a state in which cheerfulness is insensibility, and dejection sullenness, of which the hardships are without honor, and the labors without reward.
—Samuel Johnson

Poverty destroys pride. It is difficult for an empty bag to stand upright.
—Alexander Dumas *fils*

The misfortunes of poverty carry with them nothing harder to bear than it exposes men to ridicule.
—Juvenal

Nature magically suits a man to his fortunes, by making them the fruit of his character.
—Ralph Waldo Emerson

It never occurs to fools that merit and good fortune are closely united.
—Johann Wolfgang von Goethe

Self-distrust is the cause of most of our failures. In the assurance of strength there is strength, and they are the weakest, however strong, who have no faith in themselves or their powers.
—Christian Nestell Bovee

The greatest mistake you can make in life is to be continually fearing that you may make one.
—Elbert Hubbard

They are able because they think they are able.
—Virgil

Great souls have wills; feeble ones have wishes.
—Chinese Proverb

Will is character in action.
—William McDougall

No one knows what he can do till he tries.
—Publilius Syrus

The mere aspiration is partial realization.
—Anna Cora Mowatt

A successful individual sets his next goal somewhat but not too much above his last achievement. In this way he steadily raises his level of aspiration.
—Kurt Lewin

Most people would succeed in small things if they were not troubled with great ambitions.
—Henry Wadsworth Longfellow

Ambition is the mind's immodesty.
—Sir William Davenant

Ambition is not a vice of little people.
—Michel de Montaigne

Keep away from people who try to belittle your ambitions. Small people always do that, but the really great make you feel that you, too, can become great.
—Mark Twain

When one is trying to do something beyond his known powers it is useless to seek the approval of friends. Friends are at their best in moments of defeat.
—Henry Miller

When a man succeeds, he does it in spite of everybody, not with the assistance of everybody.
—Edgar Watson Howe

Men, on the average, will be kindly or hostile in their feelings toward each other in proportion as they feel their lives unsuccessful or successful.
—Bertrand Russell

A successful man cannot realize how hard an unsuccessful man finds life.
—Edgar Watson Howe

Nothing is more humiliating than to see idiots succeed in enterprises we have failed in.
—Gustave Flaubert

There is nothing more disappointing than failing to accomplish a thing, unless it is to see somebody else accomplish it.
—Henry S. Haskins

Defeat should never be a source of discouragement, but rather a fresh stimulus.
—Robert South

Never confuse a single defeat with a final defeat.
—F. Scott Fitzgerald

There is no failure except in no longer trying. There is no defeat except from within, no really insurmountable barrier save our own inherent weakness of purpose.
—Kin Hubbard

Defeat never comes to any man until he admits it.
—Josephus Daniels

Failure is often God's own tool for carving some of the finest outlines in the character of his children; and, even in this life, bitter and crushing failures have often in them the germs of new and quite unimagined happiness.
—Thomas Hodgkin

Failure is instructive. The person who really thinks learns quite as much from his failures as from his successes.
—John Dewey

What is defeat? Nothing but education, nothing but the first step to something better.
—Wendell Phillips

A failure establishes only this, that our determination to succeed was not strong enough.
—Christian Nestell Bovee

No man succeeds in everything he undertakes. In that sense we are all failures. The great point is not to fail in ordering and sustaining the effort of your life. In this matter vanity is what leads us astray. He hurries us into situations from which we must come out damaged; whereas pride is our safeguard, by the reserve it imposes on the choice of our endeavor as much as by the virtue of its sustaining power.
—Joseph Conrad

If you have made mistakes, even serious ones, there is always another chance for you. What we call failure is not the falling down, but the staying down.
—Mary Pickford

Meet success like a gentleman and disaster like a man.
—Lord Birkenhead

Always imitate the behavior of winners when you lose.
—George Meredith

A man's life is interesting primarily when he has failed—I well know. For it's a sign that he tried to surpass himself.
—Georges Clemenceau

The line between failure and success is so fine that we scarcely know when we pass it: so fine that we are often on the line and do not know it.
—Elbert Hubbard

Success is relative: it is what we can make of the mess we have made of things.
—T. S. Eliot

The man who seeks one, and but one, thing in life may hope to achieve it; but he who seeks all things, wherever he goes, only reaps, from the hopes which he sows, a harvest of barren regrets.
—Edward G. Bulwer-Lytton

Many do with opportunities as children do at the seashore; they fill their little hands with sand, and then let the grains fall through, one by one, till all are gone.
—Thomas R. Jones

You must train your intuition—you must trust that small voice inside you which tells you exactly what to say, what to decide. Your intuition is your instrument. If you can imagine, I throw a

spear into the dark. That is my intuition, and then I have to send an expedition into the jungle to find the spear and to find a way to the spear. And that is absolutely another process. That is my intellect.
—Ingmar Bergman

A wise man will make more opportunities than he finds.
—Francis Bacon

Do not suppose opportunity will knock twice at your door.
—Sébastien R. Nicholas Chamfort

"Be bold!" first gate; "Be bold, be bold, and evermore be bold!" second gate; "Be not too bold!" third gate.
—Inscription on the Gates of Busyrane

We make way for the man who boldly pushes past us.
—Christian Nestell Bovee

Vanity is often the unseen spur.
—William Makepeace Thackeray

In great attempts it is glorious even to fail.
—Cassius

The only people who never fail are those who never try.
—Ilka Chase

Fortune knocks at least once at every man's door.
—English Proverb

Fortune gives to many too much, but none enough.
—Martial

No one is satisfied with his fortune, nor dissatisfied with his intellect.
—Madame Antoinette Deshoulières

The power of fortune is confessed only by the miserable, for the happy impute all their success to prudence or merit.
—Jonathan Swift

Not only is fortune blind herself, but as a rule she even blinds those whom she has embraced.
—Cicero

Fortune is a great deceiver. She sells very dear the things she seems to give us.
—Vincent Voiture

Let none be over-confident when fortune smiles; let none despair of better things when fortune fails.
—Seneca

We feel good fortune and bad only in proportion to our self-love.
—François de La Rochefoucauld

Fortune can take from us nothing but what she gave us.
—Thomas Fuller (II)

Fortune always leaves a door open in disasters, whereby to find a remedy.
—Miguel de Cervantes

The tallest trees are most in the power of the winds, and ambitious men of the blasts of fortune.
—William Penn

Let everyone witness how many different cards fortune has up her sleeve when she wants to ruin a man.
—Benvenuto Cellini

The road to ruin is always kept in good repair.
—Author Unknown

Ovid finely compares a man of broken fortune to a falling column; the lower it sinks, the greater weight it is obliged to sustain.
—Oliver Goldsmith

That great baby, the world, however it may cry up and pretend to admire its idols, is just like the little girl who, after dressing up

her doll in all its finery, and caressing it till she is tired, is not easy till she has pulled it to pieces again and reduced it to its original rags and wool.
—William Hazlitt

A reputation once broken may possibly be repaired, but the world will always keep their eyes on the spot where the crack was.
—Bishop Joseph Hall

Men are seldom underrated; the mercury in a man finds its true level in the eyes of the world just as certainly as it does in the glass of a thermometer.
—Josh Billings

Posterity gives every man his true value.
—Tacitus

The reputation of a thousand years may be determined by the conduct of one hour.
—Japanese Proverb

Good will, like a good name, is got by many actions, and lost by one.
—Lord Francis Jeffrey

Men are rewarded and punished not for what they do, but rather for how their acts are defined. This is why men are most interested in better justifying themselves than in better behaving themselves.
—Thomas Szasz

We do not content ourselves with the life we have in ourselves and in our own being; we desire to live an imaginary life in the mind of others, and for this purpose we endeavor to shine.
—Blaise Pascal

The short and true way to reputation is to take care to be in truth what we would have others think us to be.
—Author Unknown

It is better to be hated for what you are than to be loved for what you are not.
—André Gide

It is better to deserve honors and not have them than to have them and not deserve them.
—Mark Twain

If you wish your merit to be known, acknowledge that of other people.
—Oriental Proverb

Be nice to people on your way up because you'll meet them on your way down.
—Wilson Mizner

If you want people to think well of you, do not speak well of yourself.
—Blaise Pascal

A man's accusations of himself are always believed; his praises of self never.
—Michel de Montaigne

When someone sings his own praises, he always gets the tune too high.
—Mary H. Waldrip

Modesty is the only sure bait when you angle for praise.
—Lord Chesterfield

Get someone else to blow your horn and the sound will carry twice as far.
—Will Rogers

When someone praises you, be judge alone:
Trust not men's judgment of you, but your own.
—Cato

Praise is always pleasing, let it come from whom, or upon what account it will.
—Michel de Montaigne

What is it that we all live upon but self-esteem? When we want praise it is only because praise enables us to think well of ourselves. Every one to himself is the centre and pivot of all the world.
—Anthony Trollope

How a little praise warms out of a man the good that is in him, as the sneer of contempt which he feels is unjust chills the ardor to excel.
—Edward G. Bulwer-Lytton

The applause of a single human being is of great consequence.
—Samuel Johnson

We begin to praise when we begin to see a thing needs our assistance.
—Henry David Thoreau

One good deed, dying tongueless,
Slaughters a thousand waiting upon that.
Our praises are our wages.
—William Shakespeare

The praises of others may be of use in teaching us, not what we are, but what we ought to be.
—Augustus and Julius Hare

Even the praises we do not think honest are sometimes dear to us.
—Luc de Clapiers de Vauvenargues

The modesty that shrinks from praise is really only desire to have it more delicately expressed.
—François de La Rochefoucauld

We bestow on others praise in which we do not believe, on condition that in return they bestow upon us praise in which we do.
—Jean Rostand

We dislike praising, and never praise anybody except out of self-interest. Praise is a subtle, concealed, and delicate form of flattery which gratifies giver and receiver in different ways: the latter accepts it as the due reward of his merit, the former bestows it so as to draw attention to his own fairness and discrimination.
—François de La Rochefoucauld

True merit, like a river, the deeper it is, the less noise it makes.
—Lord Halifax

There's a lot to be said for the fellow who doesn't say it himself.
—Maurice Switzer

True modesty does not consist in an ignorance of our merits, but in a due estimate of them.
—Augustus and Julius Hare

There is scarce any man who cannot persuade himself of his own merit. Has he common sense, he prefers it to genius, has he some diminutive virtues, he prefers them to great talents.
—Sewall

Great merit, or great failings, will make you respected or despised; but trifles, little attentions, mere nothings, either done or neglected, will make you either liked or disliked in the general run of the world.
—Lord Chesterfield

When dealing with people, remember you are not dealing with creatures of logic, but with creatures of emotion, creatures bristling with prejudice, and motivated by pride and vanity.
—Dale Carnegie

If thou art a master, be sometimes blind; if a servant, sometimes deaf.
—Thomas Fuller (I)

Any fault in a superior is found out by his inferior.
—Publilius Syrus

Nothing, indeed, but the possession of some power can with any certainty discover what at the bottom is the true characteristic of any man.
—Edmund Burke

If you wish to know what a man is, place him in authority.
—Yugoslav Proverb

Hateful is the power, and pitiable is the life, of those who wish to be feared rather than to be loved.
—Cornelius Nepos

Much misconstruction and bitterness are spared to him who thinks naturally upon what he owes to others rather than what he ought to expect from them.
—Madame François Guizot

Watch out for the fellow who talks about putting things in order! Putting things in order always means getting other people under your control.
—Denis Diderot

Distrust all in whom the impulse to punish is powerful.
—Friedrich Wilhelm Nietzsche

Those see nothing but faults that seek nothing else.
—Thomas Fuller (II)

He that most curteisly commandeth, to him men most obeyen.
—Geoffrey Chaucer

If you would be important, let it be through the excellence of your talents, rather than through your position.
—Baltasar Grácian

The superior man thinks of his character, the inferior man of his position.
—Confucius

Let us never forget that every station in life is necessary; that each deserves our respect; that not the station itself, but the worthy fulfillment of its duties does honor to man.
—Author Unknown

True dignity is never gained by place, and never lost when honours are withdrawn.
—Philip Massinger

So much is a man worth as he esteems himself.
—François Rabelais

Every man believes that he has a greater possibility.
—Ralph Waldo Emerson

No road is too long to the man who advances deliberately and without undue haste; and no honors are too distant for the man who prepares himself for them with patience.
—Jean de La Bruyère

Life affords no higher pleasure than that of surmounting difficulties, passing from one step of success to another, forming new wishes and seeing them gratified.
—Samuel Johnson

If one advances confidently in the directions of his dreams, and endeavors to live the life which he has imagined, he will meet with a success unexpected in common hours.
—Henry David Thoreau

There is no such thing as a great man or a great woman. People believe in them just as they used to believe in unicorns or dragons. The greatest man or woman is 99 per cent just like yourself.
—George Bernard Shaw

The real difference between men is energy. A strong will, a settled purpose, an invincible determination, can accomplish almost anything; and in this lies the distinction between great men and little men.
—Thomas Fuller (I)

Everyone has a fair turn to be as great as he pleases.
—Jeremy Collier

First, when everybody tells you that you are being idealistic or impractical, consider the possibility that everybody could be wrong about what is right for you. Look inside yourself the way nobody else can. Will the pursuit of your dream hurt anybody? Do you stand at least a fair chance of success? If you fail, will you be seriously damaged or merely embarrassed? If you succeed, will it change your life for the better? When you can persuade yourself that your dream is worthwhile and achievable—then say thank you to the doubters and take the plunge. . . . How much better to know that we have dared to live our dreams than to live our lives in a lethargy of regret.
—Gilbert E. Kaplan

The secret of success is constancy to purpose.
—Benjamin Disraeli

Never think that you're not good enough yourself. A man should never think that. My belief is that in life people will take you very much at your own reckoning.
—Anthony Trollope

Excessive forethought and too great solicitude for the future are often productive of misfortune; for the affairs of the world are subject to so many accidents that seldom do things turn out as even the wisest predicted; and whoever refuses to take advantage of present good from fear of future danger, provided the danger be not certain and near, often discovers to his annoyance and disgrace that he has lost opportunities full of profit and glory, from dread of dangers which have turned out to be wholly imaginary.
—Francesco Guicciardini

There is an hour in each man's life appointed
To make his happiness, if then he seize it.
—John Fletcher

Nothing is impossible; there are ways that lead to everything, and if we had sufficient will we should always have sufficient means. It is often merely for an excuse that we say things are impossible.
—François de La Rochefoucauld

To believe a business impossible is the way to make it so. How many feasible projects have miscarried through despondency, and been strangled in their birth by a cowardly imagination.
—Jeremy Collier

Do not attempt to do a thing unless you are sure of yourself; but do not relinquish it simply because someone else is not sure of you.
—Stewart E. White

Our doubts are traitors,
and make us lose the good we oft might win,
by fearing to attempt.
—William Shakespeare

Were the diver to think on the jaws of the shark he would never lay hands on the precious pearl.
—Saadi

Half the failures of life arise from pulling in one's horse as he is leaping.
—Augustus and Julius Hare

Think you can, think you can't, either way you're right.
—Henry Ford

He is not worthy of the honeycomb
That shuns the hive because the bees have stings.
—William Shakespeare

Aim at the sun, and you may not reach it; but your arrow will fly far higher than if aimed at an object on a level with yourself.
—Joel Hawes

Not failure, but low aim, is crime.
—James Russell Lowell

Our greatest glory is not in never falling but in rising every time we fall.
—Confucius

It is hard to fail, but it is worse never to have tried to succeed.
—Theodore Roosevelt

A useless life is early death.
—Johann Wolfgang von Goethe

Lack of something to feel important about is almost the greatest tragedy a man may have.
—Arthur E. Morgan

Every individual has a place to fill in the world, and is important in some respect, whether he chooses to be so or not.
—Nathaniel Hawthorne

It is right to be contented with what we have, never with what we are.
—James Mackintosh

Our accepting what we are must always inhibit our being what we ought to be.
—John Fowles

First say to yourself what you would be; and then do what you have to do.
—Epictetus

God gives us the nuts, but he does not crack them.
—German Proverb

Every man is the architect of his own fortune.
—Appius Claudius Caecus

The creation of a thousand forests is in one acorn.
—Ralph Waldo Emerson

Such Is Life

PART 11

THE MIND

A mind forever
Voyaging through strange seas of thought alone.
—William Wordsworth

Such Is Life

Minds differ still more than faces.
—François Marie de Voltaire

What a wee little part of a person's life are his acts and his words!
His real life is led in his head, and is known to none but himself.
—Mark Twain

It is the habitual thought that frames itself into our life. It affects
us even more than our intimate social relations do. Our
confidential friends have not so much to do in shaping our lives
as thoughts have which we harbor.
—John William Teal

All that we are is the result of what we have thought.
—Dhammapada

It is the mind which creates the world about us, and even though
we stand side by side in the same meadow, my eyes will never see
what is beheld by yours, my heart will never stir to the emotions
with which yours is touched.
—George Gissing

The mind of man may be compared to a musical instrument with
a certain range of tones, beyond which in both directions we have
an infinitude of silence.
—John Tyndall

Every man takes the limits of his own field of vision for the limits
of the world.
—Arthur Schopenhauer

The human understanding is like a false mirror, which, receiving
rays irregularly, distorts and discolors the nature of things by
mingling its own nature with it.
—Francis Bacon

We perceive and are affected by changes too subtle to be
described.
—Henry David Thoreau

There's nothing of so infinite vexation
As man's own thoughts.
—John Webster

The secret thoughts of a man run over all things, holy, profane, clean, obscene, grave, and light, without shame or blame.
—Thomas Hobbes

Our thoughts are often worse than we are.
—George Eliot

Man's great misfortune is that he has no organ, no kind of eyelid or brake, to mask or block a thought, or all thought, when he wants to.
—Paul Valéry

It is sometimes better to slip over thoughts and not go to the bottom of them.
—Madame Marie de Sévigné

Thinking is, or ought to be, a coolness and a calmness; and our poor brains beat too much for that.
—Herman Melville

Only in quiet waters things mirror themselves undistorted. Only in a quiet mind is adequate perception of the world.
—Hans Margolius

When the eye is cleared of obstacles it sees sharply. When the ear is cleared of obstacles it hears well. When the nose is not blocked up, it smells well. When the mouth is cleared, it tastes well. When the mind is clear, it thinks well.
—Chuang-Tse

Our most important thoughts are those which contradict our emotions.
—Paul Valéry

Anger and worry are the enemies of clear thought.
—Madeleine Brent

Some act first and think afterwards, which means they must concern themselves more with the excuses for, than the consequences of their acts: others think neither before, nor after, when all should be continuous thinking.
—Baltasar Grácian

It is for want of thinking, that most Men are undone.
—Thomas Fuller (II)

The worth of the mind consisteth not in going high, but in marching orderly.
—Michel de Montaigne

Every situation in life provides us ready-made with the outfit of thoughts and ways of behaving which perfectly fit it.
—Logan Pearsall Smith

It is by presence of mind in untried emergencies that the native metal of man is tested.
—James Russell Lowell

Intelligence is quickness in seeing things as they are.
—George Santayana

Intelligence is quickness to apprehend as distinct from ability, which is capacity to act wisely on the thing apprehended.
—Alfred North Whitehead

The proportion of those who think is extremely small; yet every individual flatters himself that he is one of the number.
—Charles Caleb Colton

Common sense is the most fairly distributed thing in the world, for each one thinks he is so well-endowed with it that even those who are the hardest to satisfy in all other matters are not in the habit of desiring more of it than they already have.
—René Descartes

Such is the nature of men that however they may acknowledge many others to be more witty, or more eloquent, or more learned, yet they will hardly believe there may be many so wise as themselves.
—Thomas Hobbes

Many complain of their looks, but none of their brains.
—Yiddish Proverb

Intellect is invisible to the man who has none.
—Arthur Schopenhauer

Many persons might have attained to wisdom had they not assumed that they already possessed it.
—Seneca

One can render the mind more active and supple, the same as the body; it is only necessary to exercise the one as we exercise the other.
—Luc de Clapiers de Vauvenargues

Our minds are like our stomachs; they are whetted by the change of their food, and variety supplies both with fresh appetite.
—Quintilian

The mind is like the stomach. It is not how much you put into it that counts, but how much it digests.
—Albert Jay Nock

The mind is but a barren soil—a soil which is soon exhausted, and will produce no crop, or only one, unless it be continually fertilized and enriched with foreign matter.
—Sir Joshua Reynolds

The human mind cannot create anything. It produces nothing until after having been fertilized by experience and meditation; its acquisitions are the germs of its production.
—Comte de Buffon

Minds, like bodies, will often fall into a pimpled, ill-conditioned state from mere excess of comfort.
—Charles Dickens

Few minds wear out; more rust out.
—Christian Nestell Bovee

Wise men become wiser as they grow older, ignorant men more ignorant.
—Babylonian Talmud

Ignorance is a voluntary misfortune.
—Nicholas Ling

To be ignorant of one's ignorance is the malady of the ignorant.
—Amos Bronson Alcott

You'd go wrong less often if you knew your ignorance.
—Publilius Syrus

Everybody is ignorant only on different subjects.
—Will Rogers

Most ignorance is vincible ignorance. We don't know because we don't want to know.
—Aldous Huxley

A man only becomes wise when he begins to calculate the approximate depth of his ignorance.
—Gian Carlo Menotti

Every man's follies are the caricature resemblances of his wisdom.
—John Sterling

Our chief wisdom consists in knowing our follies and faults, that we may correct them.
—Author Unknown

It is never too late to grow wise.
—Henry Fielding

The doors of wisdom are never shut.
—Benjamin Franklin

Perfect wisdom hath four equal parts, *viz.*, wisdom, the principle of doing things aright; justice, the principle of doing things equally in public and private; fortitude, the principle of not flying danger, but meeting it; and temperance, the principle of subduing desires and living moderately.
—Plato

We do not receive wisdom, we must discover it for ourselves, after a journey through the wilderness which no-one else can make for us, which no-one can spare us, for our wisdom is the point of view from which we come at last to regard the world.
—Marcel Proust

No man was ever wise by chance.
—Seneca

It takes a great deal of elevation of thought to produce a very little elevation of life.
—Ralph Waldo Emerson

The mind's direction is more important than its progress.
—Joseph Joubert

All truly wise thoughts have been thought already thousands of times; but to make them truly ours, we must think them over again honestly, till they take root in our personal experience.
—Johann Wolfgang von Goethe

A thought is often original though you have uttered it a hundred times. It has come to you over a new route, by a new and express train of association.
—Oliver Wendell Holmes, Sr.

The thoughts that are unsought for are commonly the most valuable, and should be secured, because they seldom return.
—Francis Bacon

A moment's insight is sometimes worth a life's experience.
—Oliver Wendell Holmes, Sr.

The voice of the intellect is a soft one, but it does not rest until it has gained a hearing. This is one of the few points in which one may be optimistic about the future of mankind.
—Sigmund Freud

Our thoughts are epochs in our lives; all else is but a journal of the winds that blow while we are here.
—Henry David Thoreau

Thinking is the talking of the soul with itself.
—Plato

A man's private thought can never be a lie; what he thinks, is to him the truth, always.
—Mark Twain

Most of our so-called reasoning consists in finding arguments for going on believing as we already do.
—James Robinson

A narrow mind begets obstinacy, and we do not easily believe what we cannot see.
—François de La Rochefoucauld

Man is made by his belief. As he believes, so he is.
—Bhagavadgita

We are born believing. A man bears beliefs, as a tree bears apples.
—Ralph Waldo Emerson

We are all tattooed in our cradles with the beliefs of our tribe.
—Oliver Wendell Holmes, Sr.

The confirmed prejudices of a thoughtful life, are as hard to change as the confirmed habits of an indolent life: and as some must trifle away age, because they trifled away youth, others must labor on in a maze or error, because they have wandered there too long to find their way out.
—Lord Bolingbroke

Change of opinion is often only the progress of sound thought and growing knowledge.
—Tryon Edwards

We can believe what we choose. We are answerable for what we choose to believe.
—Cardinal Newman

Man is a reasoning rather than a reasonable animal.
—Alexander Hamilton

Every man hears only what he understands.
—Johann Wolfgang von Goethe

Every man regards a subject as it affects him.
—Baltasar Grácian

A man, to be greatly good, must imagine intensely and comprehensively; he must put himself in the place of another and of many others; the pains and pleasures of his species must become his own.
—Percy Bysshe Shelley

Nine-tenths of the serious controversies which arise in life result from misunderstanding, result from one man not knowing the facts which to the other man seem important, or otherwise failing to appreciate his point of view.
—Louis D. Brandeis

The recognition of personal separateness—of others having their own concepts, different from his, because they see things from their position and condition as individuals and not from his own—is not ordinarily possible before a child is seven. Immaturity in adults reveals itself clearly in the retention of this infantile orientation.
—Miriam Lindstrom

The motto should not be: Forgive one another; rather, Understand one another.
—Emma Goldman

To understand everything makes one very tolerant.
—Madame Germaine de Staël

The trouble with most people is that they think with their hopes or fears or wishes rather than with their minds.
—Will Durant

Imagination and fiction make up more than three quarters of our real life.
—Simone Weil

No man will be found in whose mind airy notions do not sometimes tyrannize, and force him to hope or fear beyond the limits of sober probability.
—Samuel Johnson

The mind is ever ingenious in making its own distress.
—Author Unknown

Our griefs, as well as our joys, owe their strongest colors to our imaginations. There is nothing so grievous to be borne that pondering upon it will not make it heavier; and there is no pleasure so vivid that the animation of fancy cannot enliven it.
—Jane Porter

My imagination longs to dash ahead and plan developments; but I have noticed that when things happen in one's imaginings, they never happen in one's life, so I am curbing myself.
—Dodie Smith

Imagination is too often accompanied by somewhat irregular logic.
—Benjamin Disraeli

Illusions commend themselves to us because they save us pain and allow us to enjoy pleasure instead. We must therefore accept it without complaint when they sometimes collide with a bit of reality against which they are dashed to pieces.
—Sigmund Freud

No man is happy without a delusion of some kind. Delusions are as necessary to our happiness as realities.
—Christian Nestell Bovee

Imagination was given to man to compensate him for what he is not; a sense of humor to console him for what he is.
—Francis Bacon

Rob the average man of his life-illusion and you rob him of his happiness at one stroke.
—Henrik Ibsen

Every age is fed on illusions, lest men should renounce life early and the human race come to an end.
—Joseph Conrad

Imagination grows by exercise and contrary to common belief is more powerful in the mature than in the young.
—W. Somerset Maugham

The notion that as a man grows older his illusions leave him is not quite true. What is true is that his early illusions are supplanted by new and, to him, equally convincing illusions.
—George Jean Nathan

We wake from one dream into another.
—Ralph Waldo Emerson

As long as the heart preserves desire, the mind preserves illusion.
—François de Chateaubriand

Better a dish of illusion and a hearty appetite for life, than a feast of reality and indigestion therewith.
—Harry A. Overstreet

Life is the art of being well deceived; and in order that the deception may succeed it must be habitual and uninterrupted.
—William Hazlitt

Fancy rules over two thirds of the universe, the past and the future, while reality is confined to the present.
—Jean Paul Richter

A pleasant illusion is better than a harsh reality.
—Christian Nestell Bovee

We must select the illusion which appeals to our temperament, and embrace it with passion, if we want to be happy.
—Cyril Connolly

Happiness, that grand mistress of the ceremonies in the dance of life, impels us through all its mazes and meanderings, but leads none of us by the same route.
—Charles Caleb Colton

Happiness is not an ideal of reason but of imagination.
—Immanuel Kant

Man's real life is happy, chiefly because he is ever expecting that it soon will be so.
—Edgar Allan Poe

Happiness is an imaginary condition formerly often attributed by the living to the dead, now usually attributed by adults to children, and by children to adults.
—Thomas Szasz

Happiness isn't something you experience; it's something you remember.
—Oscar Levant

We are never happy: we can only remember that we were so once.
—Alexander Smith

Ask yourself whether you are happy, and you will cease to be so.
—John Stuart Mill

We never enjoy perfect happiness; our most fortunate successes are mingled with sadness; some anxieties always perplex the reality of our satisfaction.
—Pierre Corneille

Happiness is like a sunbeam, which the least shadow intercepts, while adversity is often as the rain of spring.
—Chinese Proverb

There is not a string attuned to mirth but has its chord of melancholy.
—Thomas Hood

What is happiness? A shaft of light cutting through heavy fog.
—Milán Füst

To be stupid, selfish, and have good health are three requirements for happiness, though if stupidity is lacking, all is lost.
—Gustave Flaubert

A person is never happy except at the price of some ignorance.
—Anatole France

Happiness is the perpetual possession of being well deceived.
—Jonathan Swift

We rarely can find anyone who can say he has lived a happy life, and who, content with his life, can retire from the world like a satisfied guest.
—Horace

I have now reigned above fifty years in victory or peace, beloved by my subjects, dreaded by my enemies, and respected by my allies. Riches and honors, power and pleasure, have waited on my call, nor does any earthly blessing appear to have been wanting to my felicity. In this situation, I have diligently numbered the days of pure and genuine happiness which have fallen to my lot; they amount to fourteen. O man, place not thy confidence in this present world!
—The Caliph Abd-El-Raham

We are long before we are convinced that happiness is never to be found, and each believes it possessed by others, to keep alive the hope of obtaining it for himself.
—Samuel Johnson

If we only wanted to be happy it would be easy; but we want to be happier than other people, which is almost always difficult, since we think them happier than they are.
—Charles de Secondat Montesquieu

Over there, where you are not—there is happiness.
—G. P. Schmidt Von Lübeck

Our happiness is but an unhappiness more or less consoled.
—Jean-François Ducis

Hardly a man, whatever his circumstances and situation, but if you get his confidence, will tell you that he is not happy. It is, however, certain that all men are not unhappy in the same degree, though by these accounts we might also be tempted to think so. Is not this to be accounted for by supposing that all men measure the happiness they possess by the happiness they desire, or think they deserve?
—Lord Fulke Gréville

Our aches and pains conform to opinion. A man's as miserable as he thinks he is.
—Seneca

No man is happy who does not think himself so.
— Publilius Syrus

Misery is almost always the result of thinking.
—Joseph Joubert

Few habits are more injurious than musing, which differs from thinking as pacing one's chamber does from walking abroad. The mind learns nothing, returning perpetually over the same barren track. Where the thoughts are sombre, the evil is doubly great, and not only time and vigor are squandered, but melancholy becomes fixed. It is really a disease, and the question how it should be treated is one of the most important in anthropology.
—James W. Alexander

To be melancholy is to be forever thinking of oneself.
—Comtesse Diane

Gaiety is forgetfulness of the self, melancholy is memory of the self: in that state the soul feels all the power of its roots, nothing distracts it from its profound homeland and the look that it casts upon the outer world is gently dismayed.
—Adrienne Monnier

When any fit of gloominess, or perversion of mind, lays hold upon you, make it a rule not to publish it by complaints, but exert your whole care to hide it. By endeavoring to hide it you will drive it away.
—Samuel Johnson

Life is so full of miseries, minor and major; they pass so close upon us at every step of the way, that it is hardly worthwhile to call one another's attention to their presence.
—Agnes Repplier

If you are melancholy for the first time, you will find upon a little inquiry, that others have been melancholy many times, and yet are cheerful now. If you have been melancholy many times, recollect that you have got over those times; and try if you cannot find means of getting over them better.
—Leigh Hunt

When it has happened to thee to be unfortunate, master, remember the sayings of Euripides and then wilt thou be more easy—"There is no man who is happy in every way." Then imagine thyself to be one of the great crowd of mankind.
—Philippides

Unquestionably, it is possible to do without happiness; it is done involuntarily by nineteen-twentieths of mankind.
—John Stuart Mill

Just try to be happy. Unhappiness starts with wanting to be happier.
—Sam Levenson

Happiness is a ball after which we run wherever it rolls, and we push it with our feet when it stops.
—Johann Wolfgang von Goethe

We are never so happy or so unhappy as we suppose.
—François de La Rochefoucauld

A man should always consider how much he has more than he wants, and how much more unhappy he might be than he really is.
—Joseph Addison

Do not indulge in dreams of having what you have not, but reckon up the chief of the blessings you do possess, and then thankfully remember how you would crave for them if they were not yours.
—Marcus Aurelius Antoninus

The secret of contentment is knowing how to enjoy what you have, and to be able to lose all desire for things beyond your reach.
—Lin Yutang

Contentment is a pearl of great price, and whoever procures it at the expense of ten thousand desires makes a wise and a happy purchase.
—John Balguy

Man is fond of counting his troubles, but he does not count his joys. If he counted them up as he ought to, he would see that every lot has enough happiness provided for it.
—Fyodor Mikhailovich Dostoevsky

A prudent man will think more important what fate has conceded to him than what it has denied.
—Baltasar Grácian

Do not spoil what you have by desiring what you have not; but remember that what you now have was once among the things only hoped for.
—Epicurus

There are two things to aim at in life: first, to get what you want; and, after that, to enjoy it. Only the wisest of mankind achieve the second.
—Logan Pearsall Smith

To be without some of the things you want is an indispensable part of happiness.
—Bertrand Russell

When one door of happiness closes, another opens; but often we look so long at the closed door that we do not see the one which has been opened for us.
—Helen Keller

Joy is not in things; it is in us.
—Author Unknown

Happiness is not a state to arrive at, but a manner of traveling.
—Margaret Lee Runbeck

Happiness is not a destination. It is a method of life.
—Burton Hills

Human felicity is produced not so much by great pieces of good fortune that seldom happen, as by little advantages that occur every day.
—Benjamin Franklin

The happiness of life is made up of minute fractions—the little soon forgotten charities of a kiss or smile, a kind look, a heartfelt compliment, and the countless infinitesimals of pleasurable and genial feeling.
—Samuel Taylor Coleridge

The best things . . . are put together of a night and vanish with the morning.
—Kazuo Ishiguro

True happiness is of a retired nature, and an enemy to pomp and noise; it arises, in the first place, from the enjoyment of one's self; and, in the next, from the friendship and conversation of a few select companions.
—Joseph Addison

Happiness is not given but exchanged.
—Comtesse Diane

Occasionally in life there are those moments of unutterable
fulfillment which cannot be completely explained by those
symbols called words. Their meanings can only be articulated by
the inaudible language of the heart.
—Martin Luther King, Jr.

The greatest happiness of life is the conviction that we are loved,
loved for ourselves, or rather loved in spite of ourselves.
—Victor Hugo

The man who has so little knowledge of human nature as to seek
happiness by changing anything but his own dispositions, will
waste his life in fruitless efforts, and multiply the griefs which he
proposes to remove.
—Charles Caleb Colton

Happiness depends upon ourselves.
—Aristotle

Happiness is a butterfly, which, when pursued, is always just
beyond your grasp, but which, if you will sit down quietly, may
alight upon you.
—Author Unknown

The foolish man seeks happiness in the distance, the wise grows
it under his feet.
—James Oppenheim

Eden is that old-fashioned House
We dwell in every day
Without suspecting our abode
Until we drive away.
—Emily Dickinson

So long as we can lose any happiness, we possess some.
—Booth Tarkington

Every joy is gain
And gain is gain, however small.
—Robert Browning

Happiness is like a cat. If you try to coax it or call it, it will avoid you. It will never come. But if you pay no attention to it and go about your business, you'll find it rubbing against your legs and jumping into your lap. So forget pursuing happiness. Pin your hopes on work, on family, on learning, on knowing, on loving. Forget pursuing happiness, pursue these other things, and with luck happiness will come.
—William Bennett

Happiness is the only sanction of life; where happiness fails, existence remains a mad and lamentable experiment.
—George Santayana

The grand essentials of happiness are: something to do, something to love, and something to hope for.
—Allan K. Chalmers

Hope is itself a species of happiness, and perhaps the chief happiness which this world affords.
—Samuel Johnson

Hope is the best possession. None are completely wretched but those who are without hope, and few are reduced so low as that.
—William Hazlitt

Hope is the only good thing that disillusion respects.
—Luc de Clapiers de Vauvenargues

If it were not for hopes, the heart would break.
—Thomas Fuller (II)

Hope is the last thing that dies in a man.
—François de La Rochefoucauld

Hope inspires the wise, and deludes the indolent.
—Luc de Clapiers de Vauvenargues

You believe easily that which you hope for earnestly.
—Terence

He who expects much will be often disappointed; yet disappointment seldom cures us of expectation.
—Samuel Johnson

No day is without its innocent hope.
—John Ruskin

Hope is but the dream of those that wake.
—Matthew Prior

"Hope" is the thing with feathers -
    That perches in the soul -
    And sings the tune without the words -
    And never stops—at all.
—Emily Dickinson

Hope springs eternal in the human breast;
Man never is, but always to be, blest.
—Alexander Pope

Hope, like the gleaming taper's light
Adorns and cheers our way;
And still, as dark grows the night,
Emits a brighter ray.
—Oliver Goldsmith

The natural flights of the human mind are not from pleasure to
pleasure, but from hope to hope.
—Samuel Johnson

The best part of our lives we pass in counting on what is to come.
—William Hazlitt

Anticipation and Hope are born twins.
—Jean Jacques Rosseau

Such are the vicissitudes of the world through all its parts, that day and night, labor and rest, hurry and retirement, endear each other; such are the changes that keep the mind in action: we desire, we pursue, we obtain, we are satisfied; we desire something else and begin a new pursuit.
—Samuel Johnson

We love to expect, and when expectation is either disappointed or gratified, we want to be again expecting.
—Samuel Johnson

Man is a wanting animal—as soon as one of his needs is satisfied, another appears in its place. This process is unending. It continues from birth to death.
—Douglas McGregor

We part more easily with what we possess than with our expectations of what we hope for.
—Henry Home

A man's delight in looking forward to and hoping for some particular satisfaction is a part of the pleasure flowing out of it, enjoyed in advance. But this is afterward deducted, for the more we look forward to anything the less we enjoy it when it comes.
—Arthur Schopenhauer

Everyone is dragged on by their favorite pleasure.
—Virgil

The love of pleasure is universal, though every face does not show it.
—Publilius Syrus

No man is a hypocrite in his pleasures.
—Samuel Johnson

Pleasure is nothing else but the intermission of pain, the enjoying of something I am in great trouble for till I have it.
—John Selden

There is no harbor of peace
From the changing waves of joy and desire.
—Euripides

We long passionately for certain things, the very thought of
which excites and transports us: if we happen to obtain them, we
appreciate them more calmly than we had expected, and our
enjoyment of them is less than our desire for something even
better.
—Jean de La Bruyère

It is not only old and early impressions that deceive us; the
charms of novelty have the same power.
—Blaise Pascal

The power of habit and the charm of novelty are the two adverse
forces which explain most of the follies of mankind.
—Comtesse Diane

Novelty is the great parent of pleasure.
—Robert South

Variety's the very spice of life, that gives it all its flavor.
—William Cowper

The most delightful pleasures cloy without variety.
—Publilius Syrus

Things forbidden have a secret charm.
—Tacitus

A sense of wrongdoing is an enhancement of pleasure.
—Oliver Wendell Holmes, Jr.

Whatever is guarded we desire the more; few love what they may
have.
—Ovid

The expectation of pleasures hoped for is combined with the
recollection of pleasures past.
—Cicero

In our pursuit of the things of this world, we usually prevent enjoyment by expectation; we anticipate our happiness, and eat out the heart and sweetness of worldly pleasures by delightful forethoughts of them; they do not answer the expectation, or satisfy the desires which were raised about them, and they vanish into nothing.
—John Tillotson

Expectation: The state or condition of mind which in the procession of human emotions is preceded by hope and followed by despair.
—Ambrose Bierce

The act of longing for something will always be more intense than the requiting of it.
—Gail Godwin

Nothing is so good as it seems beforehand.
—George Eliot

The hours we pass with happy prospects in view are more pleasing than those crowded with fruition. In the first instance, we cook the dish to our own appetite; in the latter, Nature cooks for us.
—Oliver Goldsmith

Do not bite at the bait of pleasure till you know there is no hook beneath it.
—Thomas Jefferson

Laughing, if loud, ends in a deep sigh; and all pleasures have a sting in the tail, though they carry beauty on the face.
—Jeremy Taylor

There is no such thing as pure pleasure; some anxiety always goes with it.
—Ovid

Experience finds few of the scenes that lively hope designs.
—George Crabbe

In diving to the bottom of pleasure we bring up more gravel than pearls.
—Honoré de Balzac

Most pleasures, like flowers, when gathered, die.
—Edward Young

Pleasure is very seldom found where it is sought. Our brightest blazes of gladness are commonly kindled by unexpected sparks.
—Samuel Johnson

What we anticipate seldom occurs; what we least expect generally happens.
—Benjamin Disraeli

Hope is generally a wrong guide, though it is very good company by the way.
—Lord Halifax

The things we have most longed for never happen; or if they do, it is never at the time nor under the circumstances when they could have made us happiest.
—Jean de La Bruyère

The slow compromise, or even surrender, of our fondest hopes is a regular feature of normal human life.
—Leston L. Havens

The old hope is the hardest to be lost.
—Elizabeth Barrett Browning

The setting of a great hope is like the setting of the sun. The brightness of our life is gone.
—Henry Wadsworth Longfellow

It would be well if Hopes carried Men only to the top of the hill, without throwing them afterwards down the precipice.
—Lord Halifax

The sudden disappointment of a hope leaves a scar which the ultimate fulfillment of that hope never removes.
—Thomas Hardy

Hope is the only universal liar who never loses his reputation for veracity.
—Robert Green Ingersoll

Hope is the great falsifier of truth.
—Baltasar Grácian

A ship ought not to be held by one anchor, nor life by a single hope.
—Epictetus

Men should do with their hopes as they do with tame fowl: cut their wings that they may not fly over the wall.
—Lord Halifax

If we hope for what we are not likely to possess, we act and think in vain, and make life a greater dream and shadow than it really is.
—Joseph Addison

One of the best safeguards of our hopes . . . is to be able to mark off the areas of hopelessness and to acknowledge them, to face them directly, not with despair but with the creative intent of keeping them from polluting all the areas of possibility.
—William F. Lynch

Everyone believes very easily whatever he fears or desires.
—Jean de La Fontaine

Fear cannot be without hope nor hope without fear.
—Benedict Baruch Spinoza

The thing I fear most is fear.
—Michel de Montaigne

There is little peace or comfort in life if we are always anxious as to future events. He that worries himself with the dread of possible contingencies will never be at rest.
—Samuel Johnson

There is often less danger in the things we fear than in the things we desire.
—John Churton Collins

It's on the path you do not fear that the wild beast catches you.
—African Proverb

Nothing happens in life either as it is feared or as it is hoped.
—Alphonse Karr

The joys we expect are not so bright, nor the troubles so dark as we fancy they will be.
—Charles Reade

Nothing in life is more remarkable than the unnecessary anxiety which we endure, and generally occasion ourselves.
—Benjamin Disraeli

Our worst misfortunes never happen, and most miseries lie in anticipation.
—Honoré de Balzac

The horror of every agony is in its anticipation.
—Anthony Trollope

Nothing is so wretched or foolish as to anticipate misfortunes. What madness is it to be expecting evil before it comes.
—Seneca

Present fears
Are less than horrible imaginings.
—William Shakespeare

We are more often frightened than hurt: we suffer more in imagination than in reality.
—Seneca

Fancy tortures more people than does reality.
—Ouida

Real and imaginary evils have the same effect on the human mind.
—Author Unknown

Everybody is afraid for himself, and everybody thinks his neighbor's fears are ridiculous, as they generally are.
—J. A. Spender

Fear is implanted in us as a preservative from evil; but its duty, like that of other passions, is not to overbear reason, but to assist it. It should not be suffered to tyrannize in the imagination, to raise phantoms of horror, or to beset life with supernumerary distresses.
—Samuel Johnson

No passion so effectually robs the mind of all its power of acting and reasoning as fear.
—Edmund Burke

"The trouble is, Sancho," said Don Quixote, "you are so afraid that you cannot see or hear properly: for one of the effects of fear is to disturb the senses and cause things to appear other than what they are."
—Miguel de Cervantes

Of all the passions, fear weakens judgment most.
—Cardinal de Retz

A panic is a sudden desertion of us, and a going over to the enemy of our imagination.
—Christian Nestell Bovee

Worry gives a small thing a big shadow.
—Swedish Proverb

It is not work that kills men; it is worry. Worry is rust upon the blade.
—Henry Ward Beecher

The reason why worry kills more people than work is that more people worry than work.
—Robert Frost

It is not the cares of today, but the cares of tomorrow that weigh a man down.
—George MacDonald

No man ever sank under the burden of the day. It is when tomorrow's burden is added to the burden of today, that the weight is more than a man can bear.
—George MacDonald

Concern should drive us into action and not into depression.
—Karen Horney

If pleasures are greatest in anticipation, just remember that this is also true of trouble.
—Elbert Hubbard

There is great beauty in going through life fearlessly. Half our fears are baseless, the other half discreditable.
—Christian Nestell Bovee

You gain strength, courage and confidence by every experience in which you really stop to look fear in the face. You are able to say to yourself, "I lived through this horror. I can take the next thing that comes along." . . . You must do the thing you think you cannot do.
—Anna Eleanor Roosevelt

A person afraid all the time must need an awful amount of courage to get through each day.
—Richard Bausch

Fear never robs tomorrow of its sorrow—it only robs today of its strength.
—Author Unknown

Let us be of good cheer, however, remembering that the misfortunes hardest to bear are those which never come.
—James Russell Lowell

Keep cool: it will be all one a hundred years hence.
—Ralph Waldo Emerson

Hope is as cheap as despair.
—Thomas Fuller (II)

In all things it is better to hope than to despair.
—Johann Wolfgang von Goethe

Despair is a greater deceiver than hope.
—Luc de Clapiers de Vauvenargues

The mass of men lead lives of quiet desperation. What is called resignation is confirmed desperation. . . . A stereotyped but unconscious despair is concealed even under what are called the games and amusements of mankind.
—Henry David Thoreau

It is not impossibilities which fill us with the deepest despair, but possibilities which we have failed to realize.
—Robert Mallet

Despair exaggerates not only our misery but also our weakness.
—Luc de Clapiers de Vauvenargues

Self-pity is easily the most destructive of the non-pharmaceutical narcotics; it is addictive, gives momentary pleasure and separates the victim from reality.
—John W. Gardner

Despair would not be so anguished a condition as it is were it as wholly and hopelessly estranged as it believes itself to be.
—Leslie Farber

There is no despair so absolute as that which comes with the first moments of our first great sorrow, when we have not yet known what it is to have suffered and be healed, to have despaired and recovered hope.
—George Eliot

Who falls from all he knows of bliss,
Cares little into what abyss.
—Lord Byron

I can't tell if a straw ever saved a drowning man, but I know that a mere glance is enough to make despair pause. For in truth we who are creatures of impulse are not creatures of despair. Suicide, I suspect, is very often the outcome of mere mental weariness—not an act of savage energy, but the final symptom of complete collapse.
—Joseph Conrad

A still small voice spake unto me,
"Thou art so full of misery,
Were it not better not to be?"
—Alfred, Lord Tennyson

Nowadays not even a suicide kills himself in desperation. Before taking the step he deliberates so long and so carefully that he literally chokes with thought. It is even questionable whether he should be called a suicide, since it is really thought which takes his life. He does not die *with* deliberation, but *from* deliberation.
—Sören Kierkegaard

It takes so little, so infinitely little, for a person to cross the border beyond which everything loses meaning: love, convictions, faith, history. Human life—and herein lies its secret—takes place in the immediate proximity of that border, even in direct contact with it; it is not miles away, but a fraction of an inch.
—Milan Kundera

Probably no one commits suicide without thinking about it much of his life.
—Alfred Kazin

Every suicide is an awful poem of sorrow!
—Honoré de Balzac

If this life be not a real fight, in which something is eternally gained for the universe by success, it is no better than a game of private theatricals from which one may withdraw at will.
—William James

Many are of the opinion that we should not desert from the world's garrison, without the express command of him who has placed us here.
—Michel de Montaigne

The wish for death is a coward's part.
—Ovid

Suicide sometimes proceeds from cowardice, but not always; for cowardice sometimes prevents it; since as many live because they are afraid to die, as die because they are afraid to live.
—Charles Caleb Colton

The thought of suicide is a great consolation: with the help of it one has got through many a bad night.
—Friedrich Wilhelm Nietzsche

It requires more courage to suffer than to die.
—Napoleon Bonaparte

When all the blandishments of life are gone,
The coward sneaks to death, the brave lives on.
—Martial

Sometimes even to live is an act of courage.
—Seneca

To die, and thus avoid poverty of love, or anything painful, is not the part of a brave man, but rather of a coward. The runaway from trouble is a form of cowardice and, while it is true that the suicide braves death, he does it not for some noble object but to escape some ill.
—Aristotle

Contempt for life is easy in distress; he is truly brave who can endure a wretched life.
—Martial

True heroism consists in being superior to the ills of life in whatever shape they may challenge him to combat.
—Napoleon Bonaparte

It is a brave act of valor to contemn death; but where life is more terrible than death it is then the truest valor to dare to live.
—Sir Thomas Browne

He
That kills himself to avoid misery, fears it,
And, at the best, shows but a bastard valor.
This life's a fort committed to my trust,
Which I must not yield up, till it be forced:
Nor will I. He's not valiant that dares die,
But he that boldly bears calamity.
—Phillip Massinger

It takes far less courage to kill yourself than it takes to make yourself wake up one more time.
—Judith Rossner

The man who, in a fit of melancholy, kills himself today, would have wished to live had he waited a week.
—François Marie de Voltaire

Beware of desperate steps; the darkest day, live till tomorrow, will have passed away.
—William Cowper

When we pray for death we really desire a fuller life.
—Author Unknown

Each of us bears his own hell.
—Virgil

Every man has a rainy corner in his life, from which bad weather besets him.
—Jean Paul Richter

Fate finds for every man
His share of misery.
—Euripides

If misery loves company, misery has company enough.
—Henry David Thoreau

Every heart has its secret sorrows, which the world knows not; and oftentimes we call a man cold when he is only sad.
—Henry Wadsworth Longfellow

Never morning wore to evening, but some heart did break.
—Alfred, Lord Tennyson

A moment of time may make us unhappy for ever.
—John Gay

At certain periods of life, we live years of emotion in a few weeks, and look back on those times as on great gaps between the old life and the new.
—William Makepeace Thackeray

By sorrow of the heart the spirit is broken.
—Proverbs

The more a man loves, the more he suffers. The sum of possible grief for each soul is in proportion to its degree of perfection.
—Henry Frédéric Amiel

To spare oneself from grief at all cost can be achieved only at the price of total detachment, which excludes the ability to experience happiness.
—Erich Fromm

No greater grief than to remember days of gladness when sorrow is at hand.
—Johann Friedrich von Schiller

Joy and grief are never far apart. In the same street the shutters of one house are closed while the curtains of the next are brushed by the shadows of the dance. A wedding party returns from the church; and a funeral winds to its door. The smiles and sadness of life are the tragi-comedy of Shakespeare. Gladness and sighs brighten the dim mirror he beholds.
—Robert Eldridge Willmott

The rose and the thorn, and sorrow and gladness are linked together.
—Saadi

Pleasure is frail like a dew-drop, while it laughs it dies. But sorrow is strong and abiding.
—Sir Rabindranath Tagore

At certain moments a single almost insignificant sorrow may, by association, bring together all the little relicts of pain and discomfort, bodily and mental, that we have endured even from infancy.
—Samuel Taylor Coleridge

New grief awakens old.
—Thomas Fuller (II)

When sorrows come, they come not single spies,
But in battalions!
—William Shakespeare

There is no sorrow which length of time does not diminish and soften.
—Cicero

One often calms one's grief by recounting it.
—Pierre Corneille

While grief is fresh, every attempt to divert only irritates. You must wait till it be digested, and then amusement will dissipate the remains of it.
—Samuel Johnson

The ocean has her ebbings—so has grief.
—Thomas Campbell

On the wings of Time grief flies away.
—Jean de La Fontaine

Weeping is perhaps the most human and universal of all relief measures.
—Karl A. Menninger

Tears are the silent language of grief.
—François Marie de Voltaire

It is some relief to weep; grief is satisfied and carried off by tears.
—Ovid

Tears are the safety-valves of the heart when too much pressure is laid on it.
—Albert Smith

To weep is to make less the depth of grief.
—William Shakespeare

Tearless grief bleeds inwardly.
—Christian Nestell Bovee

Some tears belong to us because we are unfortunate: others because we are humane: many because we are mortal. But most are caused by being unwise. It is these last, only, that of necessity produce more.
—Leigh Hunt

The greatest griefs are those we cause ourselves.
—Sophocles

We are all the same—the fools of our own woes!
—Matthew Arnold

It is impossible to resign ourselves to the misery of which we ourselves have been the cause.
—Comtesse Diane

Only one-fourth of the sorrow in each man's life is caused by outside uncontrollable elements, the rest is self-imposed by failing to analyze and act with calmness.
—George Jackson

Much unhappiness has come into the world because of bewilderment and things left unsaid.
—Fyodor Mikhailovich Dostoevsky

The violence done us by others is often less painful than that which we do to ourselves.
—François de La Rochefoucauld

Suffering is the surest means of making us truthful to ourselves.
—Jean Charles de Sismondi

Sorrows are our best educators. A man can see further through a tear than a telescope.
—Author Unknown

Certain thoughts are prayers. There are moments when, whatever be the attitude of the body, the soul is on its knees.
—Victor Hugo

Sorrow makes men sincere.
—Henry Ward Beecher

Man never reasons so much and becomes so introspective as when he suffers; since he is anxious to get at the cause of his sufferings, to learn who has produced them, and whether it is just or unjust that he should have to bear them.
—Luigi Pirandello

I do not believe that sheer suffering teaches. If suffering alone taught, all the world would be wise, since everyone suffers. To suffering must be added mourning, understanding, patience, love, openness and the willingness to remain vulnerable.
—Anne Morrow Lindbergh

By suffering willingly what we cannot avoid, we secure ourselves from vain and immoderate disquiet; we preserve for better purposes that strength which would be unprofitably wasted in wild efforts of desperation, and maintain that circumspection which may enable us to seize every support, and improve every alleviation.
—Samuel Johnson

Although the world is full of suffering, it is full also of the overcoming of it.
—Helen Keller

Only your own hands can wipe your tears away.
—Egyptian Proverb

Such Is Life

Sorrow is a disease in which every patient must treat himself.
—François Marie de Voltaire

If you expect to be cured, you must uncover your wound.
—Boethius

Wounds heal and become scars. But scars grow with us.
—Stanislaus I

What deep wounds ever closed without a scar?
The heart bleeds longest, and but heals to wear
That which disfigures it.
—Lord Byron

On the sands of life sorrow treads heavily, and leaves a print time cannot wash away.
—Henry Neele

We are healed of a suffering only by experiencing it to the full.
—Marcel Proust

We do not die of anguish, we live on. We continue to suffer, we drink the cup drop by drop.
—George Sand

You may break your heart, but men will still go on as before.
—Marcus Aurelius Antoninus

The only cure for grief is action.
—George Henry Lewes

Never despair; but if you do, work on in despair.
—Edmund Burke

So long as you wear this mortal body, you will be subject to weariness and sadness of heart. . . . When this happens, you will be wise to resort to humble, exterior tasks, and restore yourself by good works.
—Thomas á Kempis

Sorrow preys upon its solitude, and nothing more diverts it from its sad visions of the other world, then calling it at moments back to this. The busy have no time for tears.
—Lord Byron

Emotion turned back on itself, and not leading on to thought or action, is the element of madness.
—John Sterling

Today I felt pass over me
A breath of wind from the wings of madness.
—Charles Baudelaire

It is not the one thing nor the other that leads to madness, but the space in between them.
—Jeanette Winterson

Insanity is not a distinct and separate empire; our ordinary life borders upon it, and we cross the frontier in some part of our nature. The aim should not be to run away, but only to keep from falling in altogether.
—Hippolyte A. Taine

Sanity is a madness put to good uses; waking life is a dream controlled.
—George Santayana

A man who is "sound of mind" is one who keeps the inner madman under lock and key.
—Paul Valéry

It is a common calamity; at some one time we have all been mad.
—J. Baptista Mantuanus

Sanity is very rare: every man almost, and every woman, has a dash of madness.
—Ralph Waldo Emerson

Every man is mad, but in a different manner, and upon some particular objects.
—Matthew Prior

The human race consists of the dangerously insane and such as are not.
—Mark Twain

We do not have to visit a madhouse to find disordered minds; our planet is the mental institution of the universe.
—Johann Wolfgang von Goethe

The way it is now, the asylums can hold the sane people, but if we tried to shut up the insane we should run out of building materials.
—Mark Twain

We are all born mad. Some remain so.
—Samuel Beckett

We all seem a little mad to each other; an excellent arrangement for the bulk of humanity which finds in it an easy motive of forgiveness.
—Joseph Conrad

Madness is always fascinating, for it reveals the ungluing we all secretly fear: the mind taking off from the body, the possibility that the magnet that attaches us to a context in the world can lose its grip.
—Molly Haskell

Most men are within a finger's breadth of being mad.
—Diogenes Laertius

Of course, no man is entirely in his right mind at any time.
—Mark Twain

When we remember we are all mad, the mysteries disappear and life stands explained.
—Mark Twain

There is no genius free from some tincture of madness.
—Seneca

Insanity is often the logic of an accurate mind overtaxed.
—Oliver Wendell Holmes, Sr.

A man may dwell so long upon a thought that it may take him prisoner.
—Lord Halifax

The mind is a dangerous weapon, even to the possessor, if he knows not discreetly how to use it.
—Michel de Montaigne

Happiness or misery is in the mind. It is the mind that lives.
—William Cobbett

The mind is its own place, and in itself
Can make a heaven of Hell, a hell of Heaven.
—John Milton

Make not your thoughts your prison.
—William Shakespeare

Such Is Life

PART 12

THE SELF

You are only what you are
when no one is looking.
—Robert C. Edwards

Such Is Life

From childhood's hour I have not been
As others were—I have not seen
As others saw.
—Edgar Allan Poe

When I say "I," I mean a thing absolutely unique, not to be confused with any other.
—Ugo Betti

A desire to be observed, considered, esteemed, praised, beloved, and admired by his fellows is one of the earliest as well as the keenest dispositions discovered in the heart of man.
—John Adams

We feel that we are greater than we know.
—William Wordsworth

The greatest magnifying glasses in the world are a man's own eyes when they look upon his own person.
—Alexander Pope

We believe, first and foremost, what makes us feel we are fine fellows.
—Bertrand Russell

We measure the excellency of other men, by some excellency we conceive to be in ourselves.
—John Selden

We prefer ourselves to others, only because we have a more intimate consciousness and confirmed opinion of our own claims and merits than of any other person's.
—William Hazlitt

Every man is prompted by the love of himself to imagine that he possesses some qualities, superior, either in kind or degree, to those which he sees allotted to the rest of the world; and, whatever apparent disadvantage he may suffer in comparison with others, he has some invisible distinctions, some latent reserve of excellence, which he throws into the balance, and by which he generally fancies that it is turned in his favour.
—Samuel Johnson

Humility is the most difficult of all virtues to achieve, nothing dies harder than the desire to think well of ourselves.
—T. S. Eliot

It is easy for every man, whatever be his character with others, to find reasons for esteeming himself.
—Samuel Johnson

Every man, however little, makes a figure in his own eyes.
—Henry Home

What hypocrites we seem to be whenever we talk of ourselves! Our words are so humble, while our hearts are so proud.
—Augustus and Julius Hare

Few people are modest enough to be content to be estimated at their true worth.
—Luc de Clapiers de Vauvenargues

It is an error to suppose that no man understands his own character. Most people know even their failings very well, only they persist in giving them names different from those usually assigned by the rest of the world.
—Sir Arthur Helps

Many a man has a kind of kaleidoscope, where the broken bits of glass are his merits and fortunes; and they fall into harmonious arrangements and delight him, often most mischievously, and to his ultimate detriment; but they are a present pleasure.
—Sir Arthur Helps

We all wear some disguise, make some professions, use some artifice, to set ourselves off as being better than we are; and yet it is not denied that we have some good intentions and praiseworthy qualities at bottom.
—William Hazlitt

Many an honest man practices upon himself an amount of deceit sufficient, if practiced upon another, and in a little different way, to send him to the state prison.
—Christian Nestell Bovee

It is not in human nature to deceive others, for any long time, without, in a measure, deceiving ourselves.
—Cardinal Newman

Nothing is so easy as to deceive one's self, as our affections are subtle persuaders; but such illusions are often inconsistent with the reality of things.
—Demosthenes

It is as hard to see one's self as to look backwards without turning round.
—Henry David Thoreau

Other men's sins are before our eyes; our own are behind our backs.
—Seneca

Lying to ourselves is more deeply ingrained than lying to others.
—Fyodor Mikhailovich Dostoevsky

We discover in ourselves what others hide from us, and we recognize in others what we hide from ourselves.
—Luc de Clapiers de Vauvenargues

The best of lessons, for a good many people, would be to listen at a keyhole. It is a pity for such that the practice is dishonorable.
—Madame Anne Sophie Swetchine

There's nothing like eavesdropping to show you that the world outside your head is different from the world inside your head.
—Thornton Wilder

We all think we are exceptional, and are surprised to find ourselves criticized just like anyone else.
—Comtesse Diane

The very purpose of existence is to reconcile the glowing opinion we hold of ourselves with the appalling things that other people think about us.
—Quentin Crisp

What others think of us would be of little moment did it not, when known, so deeply tinge what we think of ourselves.
—George Santayana

It is thus with most of us: we are what other people say we are. We know ourselves chiefly by hearsay.
—Eric Hoffer

We are all apt to believe what the world believes about us.
—George Eliot

Every man values himself more than all the rest of men, but he always values other's opinion of himself more than his own.
—Marcus Aurelius Antoninus

We are so vain that we even care for the opinion of those we don't care for.
—Marie von Ebner-Eschenbach

We are very much what others think of us. The reception our observations meet with gives us courage to proceed, or damps our efforts.
—William Hazlitt

We are slow to believe that which if believed would hurt our feelings.
—Ovid

How awful to reflect that what people say of us is true.
—Logan Pearsall Smith

Let a man once see himself as others see him, and all the enthusiasm vanishes from his heart.
—Elbert Hubbard

We have not enough self-esteem to disdain the scorn of others.
—Luc de Clapiers de Vauvenargues

However we may be reproached for our vanity we sometimes need to be assured of our merits and to have our most obvious advantages pointed out to us.
—Luc de Clapiers de Vauvenargues

Our credulity is greatest concerning the things we know least about. And since we know least about ourselves, we are ready to believe all that is said about us. Hence the mysterious power of both flattery and calumny.
—Eric Hoffer

It's not only the most difficult thing to know one's self, but the most inconvenient.
—Josh Billings

"Know thyself?" If I knew myself, I'd run away.
—Johann Wolfgang von Goethe

Every man contains within himself a ghost continent—a place circled as warily as Antarctica was circled two hundred years ago by Captain James Cook.
—Loren Eiseley

Who hath sailed about the world of his own heart, sounded each creek, surveyed each corner, but that there still remains therein much terra incognita to himself?
—Thomas Fuller (I)

If you wish to be miserable, think about yourself; you will be as wretched as you choose.
—Charles Kingsley

Self-inspection—the best cure for self-esteem.
—Author Unknown

Retire into thyself, and then thou wilt blush to find how little there is.
—Persius

Whatever you may be sure of, be sure of this: that you are dreadfully like other people.
—James Russell Lowell

Every man supposes himself not to be fully understood or appreciated.
—Ralph Waldo Emerson

It so often happens that others are measuring us by our past self while we are looking back on that self with a mixture of disgust and sorrow.
—George Eliot

When people do not respect us we are sharply offended; yet deep down in his private heart no man much respects himself.
—Mark Twain

It is a malady confined to man, and not seen in any other creatures, to hate and despise ourselves.
—Michel de Montaigne

I have always disliked myself at any given moment; the total of such moments is my life.
—Cyril Connolly

We are all serving a life sentence in the dungeon of self.
—Cyril Connolly

What other dungeon is so dark as one's own heart! What jailer so inexorable as one's self!
—Nathaniel Hawthorne

I am always with myself, and it is I who am my tormentor.
—Count Leo Tolstoy

We are all so afraid, we are all so alone, we all need so much from the outside the assurance of our worthiness to exist.
—Ford Madox Ford

We love in others what we lack ourselves, and would be everything but what we are.
—Richard Henry Stoddard

However vain we seem, we still need sometimes to be assured of our worth.
—Luc de Clapiers de Vauvenargues

We are less hurt by the contempt of fools than by the lukewarm approval of men of intelligence.
—Luc de Clapiers de Vauvenargues

We should seek the respect of others less eagerly if we were more certain of deserving it.
—Luc de Clapiers de Vauvenargues

The most accomplished persons have usually some defect, some weakness in their characters, which diminishes the lustre of their brighter qualifications.
—Junius

It is difficult to esteem a man as highly as he would wish.
—Luc de Clapiers de Vauvenargues

Life, I fancy, would very often be insupportable, but for the luxury of self-compassion.
—George Gissing

To be human is to have one's little modicum of romance secreted away in one's composition. One never ceases to make a hero of one's self—in private.
—Mark Twain

Everything without tells the individual that he is nothing; everything within persuades him that he is everything.
—Ximénès Doudan

The most vulnerable and yet most unconquerable of things is human vanity; nay, through being wounded its strength increases and can grow to giant proportions.
—Friedrich Wilhelm Nietzsche

The vanity of human life is like a rivulet, constantly passing away, and yet constantly coming on.
—Alexander Pope

The strongest passions allow us some rest, but vanity keeps us in perpetual motion.
—Jonathan Swift

There are no grades of vanity, there are only grades of ability in concealing it.
—Mark Twain

Self-love is the greatest of all flatterers.
—François de La Rochefoucauld

A man's own vanity is a swindler that never lacks a dupe.
—Honoré de Balzac

Men are found to be vainer on account of those qualities which they fondly believe they have than of those which they really have.
—Vincent Voiture

Vanity plays lurid tricks with our memory.
—Joseph Conrad

Men are very vain, and they hate nothing more than being thought so.
—Jean de La Bruyère

Such is the infatuation of self-love, that, though in the general doctrine of the vanity of the world all men agree, yet almost every one flatters himself that his own case is to be an exception from the common rule.
—Hugh Blair

Vanity finds in self-love so powerful an ally that it storms, as it were by a *coup de main*, the citadel of our heads.
—Charles Caleb Colton

Self-love is a cup without any bottom.
—Oliver Wendell Holmes, Sr.

Whatever discoveries have been made in the region of self-love, many areas remain unexplored.
—François de La Rochefoucauld

Our first love, and last love, is self-love.
—Christian Nestell Bovee

Whatever good we are told about ourselves, we learn nothing new.
—François de La Rochefoucauld

We would rather run ourselves down than not speak of ourselves at all.
—François de La Rochefoucauld

Self-love is a busy prompter.
—Samuel Johnson

Self-love is the most delicate and the most tenacious of our sentiments: a mere nothing will wound it, but nothing can kill it.
—Author Unknown

This self-love is the instrument of our preservation; it resembles the provision for the perpetuity of mankind:—it is necessary, it is dear to us, it gives us pleasure, and we must conceal it.
—François Marie de Voltaire

The most difficult secret for a man to keep is his own opinion of himself.
—Marcel Pagnol

There is false modesty, but there is no false pride.
—Jules Renard

Pride is an over-estimation of oneself by reason of self-love.
—Benedict Baruch Spinoza

It would seem that nature, which has so wisely ordered the organs of our bodies for our happiness, has also given us pride to spare us the mortification of knowing our imperfections.
—François de La Rochefoucauld

Wounded vanity knows when it is mortally hurt; and limps off the field, piteous, all disguises thrown away. But pride carries its banner to the last; and fast as it is driven from one field unfurls it in another.
—Helen Hunt Jackson

We can believe almost anything if it be necessary to protect our pride.
—Douglas A. Thom

There is this paradox in pride—it makes some men ridiculous, but prevents others from becoming so.
—Charles Caleb Colton

Pride, when wit fails, steps in to our defense,
And fills up all the mighty void of sense.
—Alexander Pope

One thing pride has which no other vice that I know of has; it is an enemy to itself; and a proud man cannot endure to see pride in another.
—Owen Feltham

Likeness begets love, yet proud men hate one another.
—Thomas Fuller (II)

Pride will spit in pride's face.
—Thomas Fuller (II)

The very pride that makes us condemn failings from which we think we are exempt leads us to despise good qualities we do not possess.
—François de La Rochefoucauld

Whenever Nature leaves a hole in a person's mind, she generally plasters it over with a thick coat of self-conceit.
—Henry Wadsworth Longfellow

Conceit is just as natural a thing to human minds as a center is to a circle.
—Oliver Wendell Holmes, Sr.

Conceit is the most contemptible and one of the most odious qualities in the world. It is vanity driven from all other shifts, and forced to appeal to itself for admiration.
—William Hazlitt

Conceit is God's gift to little men.
—Bruce Barton

I've never any pity for conceited people, because I think they carry their comfort about with them.
—George Eliot

Conceit: Self-respect in one whom we dislike.
—Ambrose Bierce

To say that a man is vain means merely that he is pleased with the effect he produces on other people. A conceited man is satisfied with the effect he produces on himself.
—Max Beerbohm

Talk about conceit as much as you like. It is to human character what salt is to the ocean; it keeps it sweet and renders it endurable. Say rather that it is the natural unguent of the sea-fowls plumage, which enables him to shed the rain that falls on him and the wave in which he dips. When one has had all his conceit taken out of him, when he has lost all his illusions, his feathers will soon soak through, and he will fly no more.
—Oliver Wendell Holmes, Sr.

The anxiety we have for the figure we cut, for our personage, is constantly cropping out. We are showing off and are often more concerned with making a display than with living. Whoever feels observed observes himself.
—André Gide

Nothing is so common-place as to wish to seem remarkable.
—Oliver Wendell Holmes, Sr.

Pride makes us esteem ourselves; vanity to desire the esteem of others.
—Hugh Blair

Vanity is as ill at ease under indifference as tenderness is under a love which it cannot return.
—George Eliot

Vanity is only being sensitive to what other people probably think of us.
—Paul Valéry

None of us are as much praised or censured as we think.
—Charles Caleb Colton

One blushes oftener from the wounds of self-love than from modesty.
—Madame de Guibert

Offended vanity is the great separator in social life.
—Sir Arthur Helps

Offended self-love never forgives.
—Jean de Vizé

Offended self-love never forgets.
—Louis Jean Baptiste Vigée

It is our own vanity that makes the vanity of others intolerable to us.
—François de La Rochefoucauld

Nothing so soothes our vanity as a display of greater vanity in others; it makes us vain, in fact, of our modesty.
—Louis Kronenberger

Vanity is the quicksand of reason.
—George Sand

Self-love is often rather arrogant than blind; it does not hide our faults from ourselves, but persuades us that they escape the notice of others.
—Samuel Johnson

Humility is not my forte, and whenever I dwell for any length of time on my own shortcomings, they gradually begin to seem mild, harmless, rather engaging little things, not at all like the startling defects in other people's characters.
—Margaret Halsey

We will never find out why we irritate people, what bothers people about us, what they find ridiculous; for us our own image is our greatest mystery.
—Milan Kundera

The same faults which in others are heavy and insupportable are in ourselves imperceptible.
—Jean de La Bruyère

When we hide our failings from others, we seek to hide them from ourselves, and it is in the latter attempt that we are most successful.
—Pierre Nicole

Everyone is eagle-eyed to see another's faults or deformities.
—John Dryden

Each one of us finds in others the very faults others find in us.
—François de La Rochefoucauld

If we had no faults we should not take so much pleasure in noting those of others.
—François de La Rochefoucauld

We don't ask others to be faultless, we only ask that their faults should not incommode our own.
—Comtesse de Martel de Janville

We acknowledge our faults in order to repair by our sincerity the damage they have done us in the eyes of others.
—François de La Rochefoucauld

All censure of a man's self is oblique praise. It is in order to show how much he can spare.
—Samuel Johnson

We confess small faults, only to persuade people that we have no great ones.
—François de La Rochefoucauld

Everyone has his faults which he continually repeats; neither fear nor shame can cure him.
—Jean de La Fontaine

We are dismayed when we find that even disaster cannot cure us of our faults.
—Luc de Clapiers de Vauvenargues

Nothing will make us so charitable and tender to the faults of others as by self-examination thoroughly to know our own.
—François de Fénelon

Our good qualities are rarely loved or admired except when they are toned down by our faults. It often happens that we are more liked for our defects than for our merits.
—Joseph Joubert

We begin by trying to alter the faults of those about us, we go on to make the best of them, and perhaps end by loving them.
—Francis H. Bradley

It is in our faults and failings, not in our virtues, that we touch one another and find sympathy.
—Jerome K. Jerome

What we love and what we hate in others is ourselves, always ourselves.
—Comtesse Diane

Perhaps the rare and simple pleasure of being seen for what one is compensates for the misery of being it.
—Margaret Drabble

If we find not repose in ourselves, it is in vain to seek it
elsewhere.
—French Proverb

Our entire life, with our fine moral code and our precious
freedom, consists ultimately in accepting ourselves as we are.
—Jean Anouilh

We are what we are; we cannot be truly other than ourselves.
—Author Unknown

All human beings have gray little souls—and they all want to
rouge them up.
—Maxim Gorky

Let the world know you as you are, not as you think you should
be, because sooner or later, if you are posing, you will forget the
pose, and then where are you?
—Fanny Brice

The worst of all deceptions is self-deception.
—Plato

The greatest thing in the world is to know how to belong to
oneself.
—Michel de Montaigne

I care not so much what I am in the opinion of others as what I
am in my own; I would be rich of myself and not by borrowing.
—Michel de Montaigne

Everyone stamps his own value on himself.
—Johann Friedrich von Schiller

Every man is valued in this world as he shows by his conduct he
wishes to be valued.
—Jean de La Bruyère

Nobody holds a good opinion of a man who has a low opinion of
himself.
—Anthony Trollope

We are respected in proportion as we respect ourselves.
—Luc de Clapiers de Vauvenargues

Character—the willingness to accept responsibility for one's own life—is the source from which self-respect springs.
—Joan Didion

A good character is, in all cases, the fruit of personal exertion. It is not inherited from parents, it is not created by external advantages, it is no necessary appendage of birth, wealth, talents or station; but it is the result of one's own endeavors.
—Joel Hawes

You cannot dream yourself into a character; you must hammer and forge yourself one.
—James A. Froude

Let us not say, Every man is the architect of his own fortune; but let us say, Every man is the architect of his own character.
—George Dana Boardman

In each human heart there are a tiger, a pig, an ass, and a nightingale. Diversity of character is due to their unequal activity.
—Ambrose Bierce

A man's character is like his shadow which sometimes follows, and sometimes precedes him, and which is occasionally longer, occasionally shorter than he is.
—Author Unknown

Judge not a ship as she lies on the stocks: wait till she has accomplished a voyage. Test everything by experience. Human beings cannot be added up like a column of figures: you can only know men by living with them. The Chinese say: "Every character must be chewed to get its juice."
—Charles Haddon Spurgeon

Every man has three characters—that which he exhibits, that which he has, and that which he thinks he has.
—Alphonse Karr

To know a man, observe how he wins his object, rather than how he loses it; for when we fail our pride supports us, when we succeed, it betrays us.
—Charles Caleb Colton

Men show their character in nothing more clearly than by what they think laughable.
—Johann Wolfgang von Goethe

Nothing is more characteristic of a man than the manner in which he behaves towards fools.
—Henri Frédéric Amiel

The real character of a man is found out by his amusements.
—Sir Joshua Reynolds

The best index to a person's character is (a) how he treats people who can't do him any good, and (b) how he treats people who can't fight back.
—Abigail Van Buren

When a man is attempting to describe another person's character, he may be right or he may be wrong; but in one thing he will always succeed, that is, in describing himself.
—Samuel Taylor Coleridge

People do not seem to realize that their opinion of the world is also a confession of character.
—Ralph Waldo Emerson

As I am, so I see; use whatever language you will, you can never say anything but what you are.
—Ralph Waldo Emerson

Be your character what it will, it will be known; and nobody will take it upon your word.
—Lord Chesterfield

As daylight can be seen through very small holes, so little things will illustrate a person's character.
—Samuel Smiles

Trifles discover character more than actions of seeming importance; what one is in a little thing he is also in great.
—William Shenstone

In anything it is a mistake to think one can perform an action or behave in a certain way once and no more. What one does, one will do again, indeed has probably already done in the distant past.
—Cesare Pavese

What we do upon some great occasion will probably depend on what we already are: and what we are will be the result of previous years of self-discipline.
—Henry P. Liddon

Character is not made in a crisis—it is only exhibited.
—Robert Freeman

No change of circumstances can repair a defect of character.
—Ralph Waldo Emerson

There is something in every person's character that cannot be broken—the bony structure of his character. Wanting to change it is the same as teaching a sheep to retrieve.
—George C. Lichtenberg

Should any man tell you that a mountain had changed its place, you are at liberty to doubt it if you think fit; but if any one tells you that a man has changed his character, do not believe it.
—François Marie de Voltaire

I think character never changes; the Acorn becomes an Oak, which is very little like an Acorn to be sure, but it never becomes an Ash.
—Hester Lynch Piozzi

Character is not cut in marble; it is not something solid and unalterable. It is something living and changing, and may become diseased as our bodies do.
—George Eliot

When our character deteriorates our taste also deteriorates.
—François de La Rochefoucauld

The hell to be endured hereafter, of which theology tells, is no worse than the hell we make for ourselves in this world by habitually fashioning our characters in the wrong way.
—William James

Man's character is his fate.
—Heraclitus

To the eyes of a miser a guinea is far more beautiful than the sun, and a bag worn with the use of money has more beautiful proportions than a vine filled with grapes. The tree which moves some to tears of joy is in the eyes of others only a green thing which stands in the way. As a man is, so he sees.
—William Blake

Thoughts, even more than overt acts, reveal character.
—William Swan Plumer

The measure of a man's real character is what he would do if he knew he would never be found out.
—Thomas B. Macaulay

Character is what you are in the dark.
—Dwight Moody

We learn to curb our will and keep our overt actions within the bounds of humanity, long before we can subdue our sentiments and imaginations to the same mild tones.
—William Hazlitt

The highest possible stage in moral culture is when we recognize that we ought to control our thoughts.
—Charles Darwin

A moral being is one who is capable of reflecting on his past actions and their motives—of approving of some and disapproving of others.
—Charles Darwin

Every man has reminiscences which he would not tell to everyone, but only to his friends. He has other matters in his mind which he would not reveal even to his friends, but only to himself, and that in secret. But there are other things which a man is afraid to tell even to himself, and every decent man has a number of such things stored away in his mind. The more decent he is, the greater the number of such things in his mind.
—Fyodor Mikhailovich Dostoevsky

Whenever you are to do a thing, though it can never be known but to yourself, ask yourself how you would act were all the world looking at you, and act accordingly.
—Thomas Jefferson

Always act as if your acts were seen.
—Baltasar Grácian

Morality is observance of the laws of wholesome living. . . . In matters of morals we can hold certain assumptions: that there are some things better or worse in human affairs; that we ought to discover the better ways; that human beings are of great worth; that good should be done and evil avoided.
—Angela M. Raimo

Absolute morality is the regulation of conduct in such a way that pain shall not be inflicted.
—Herbert Spencer

To enjoy and give enjoyment, without injury to yourself or others: this is true morality.
—Sébastien R. Nicolas Chamfort

There is a raging tiger inside every man whom God put upon this earth. Every man worthy of the respect of his children spends his life building inside himself a cage to pen that tiger in.
—Murray Kempton

Do you want to know the man against whom you have the most reason to guard yourself? Your looking-glass will give you a very fair likeness of his face.
—Richard Whately

Beware of no Man more than thyself.
—Thomas Fuller (II)

Everyone has something in his nature which, if he were to express it openly, would of necessity give offence.
—Johann Wolfgang von Goethe

Everyone is a moon, and has a dark side which he never shows to anybody.
—Mark Twain

We are no more responsible for the evil thoughts which pass through our minds, than a scarecrow for the birds which fly over the seedplot he has to guard; the sole responsibility in each case is to prevent them from settling.
—John Churton Collins

In all men is evil sleeping; the good man is he who will not awaken it, in himself or in other men.
—Mary Renault

Men become bad and guilty because they speak and act without foreseeing the results of their words and deeds.
—Franz Kafka

Remember there's always a voice saying the right thing to you somewhere if you'll only listen for it.
—Thomas Hughes

Every one of us, whatever his speculative opinions, knows better than he practices, and recognizes a better law than he obeys.
—James A. Froude

Rules of society are nothing, one's conscience is the umpire.
—Madame Dudevant

The voice of conscience is so delicate that it is easy to stifle it; but it is also so clear that it is impossible to mistake it.
—Madame Germaine de Staël

Conscience is a cur that will let you get passed it but that you cannot keep from barking.
—Sébastien R. Nicolas Chamfort

Conscience is, in most men, an anticipation of the opinion of others.
—Sir Henry Taylor

It is often easier to justify one's self to others than to respond to the secret doubts that arise in one's own bosom.
—Margaret Oliphant

I have read somewhere that conscience not only sits as witness and judge within our bosoms, but also forms the prison of punishment.
—Hosea Ballou

Conscience warns us as a friend before it punishes us as a judge.
—Stanislaus I

Conscience is the mirror of our souls, which represents the errors of our lives in their full shape.
—George Bancroft

There is no witness so dreadful, no accuser so terrible as the conscience that dwells in the heart of every man.
—Polybius

The Unknown is an ocean. What is conscience? The compass of the Unknown.
—Joseph Cook

The paradoxical—and tragic—situation of a man is that his conscience is weakest when he needs it most.
—Erich Fromm

Conscience is the most changeable of guides.
—Luc de Clapiers de Vauvenargues

Conscience is thoroughly well bred and soon leaves off talking to those who do not wish to hear it.
—Samuel Butler (II)

No evil propensity of the human heart is so powerful that it may not be subdued by discipline.
—Seneca

Our whole life is startlingly moral. There is never an instant's truce between virtue and vice.
—Henry David Thoreau

If we had to tolerate in others all that we permit in ourselves, life would become completely unbearable.
—Georges Courteline

Virtue fills our heads, but vice our hearts.
—Charles Caleb Colton

Men imagine that they communicate their virtue or vice only by overt actions, and do not see that virtue or vice emit a breath every moment.
—Ralph Waldo Emerson

Virtues and vices are of a strange nature; for the more we have, the fewer we think we have.
—Author Unknown

No vice exists which does not pretend to be more or less like some virtue and does not take advantage of this assumed resemblance.
—Jean de La Bruyère

Vice knows she's ugly, so puts on her mask.
—Benjamin Franklin

It is a particular mark of vice that we feel more ashamed of our faults before our enemies than before our friends.
—Plutarch

The most fearful characteristic of vice is its irresistible fascination—the ease with which it sweeps away resolution, and wins a man to forget his momentary outlook, and his throb of penitence, in the embrace of indulgence.
—Edwin Hubbell Chapin

If a man commit an offence and repeat it, it becomes in his eyes something permitted.
—Babylonian Talmud

Many a man's vices have at first been nothing worse than good qualities run wild.
—Augustus and Julius Hare

The willing contemplation of vice is vice.
—Arabian Proverb

We tolerate without rebuke the vices with which we have grown familiar.
—Publilius Syrus

Every vice has its excuse ready.
—Publilius Syrus

Men wish to be saved from the mischiefs of their vices, but not from their vices.
—Ralph Waldo Emerson

The wolf loses his teeth, but not his inclinations.
—Spanish Proverb

We may say that vices await us on the journey of life, as hosts with whom we must successively lodge; and I doubt whether experience would enable us to avoid them were we allowed to travel the same road again.
—François de La Rochefoucauld

A few vices are sufficient to darken many virtues.
—Plutarch

We make ourselves a ladder out of our vices if we trample the vices themselves underfoot.
—Saint Augustine

Reform must come from within, not from without. You cannot legislate for virtue.
—James Cardinal Gibbons

Virtue is a state of war, and to live in it we have always to combat with ourselves.
—Jean Jacques Rousseau

Virtue is the denial of self and response to what is right and proper.
—Confucius

The strength of a man's virtue should not be measured by his special exertions, but by his habitual acts.
—Blaise Pascal

The measure of any man's virtue is what he would do, if he had neither the laws nor public opinion, nor even his own prejudices to control him.
—William Hazlitt

Perfect virtue is to do unwitnessed that which we should be capable of doing before all the world.
—François de La Rochefoucauld

Virtue has always been conceived of as a victorious resistance to one's vital desire.
—James Branch Cabell

Virtue consists, not in abstaining from vice, but in not desiring it.
—George Bernard Shaw

If better were within, better would come out.
—Thomas Fuller (II)

To many people virtue consists chiefly in repenting faults, not in avoiding them.
—George C. Lichtenberg

Many wish not so much to be virtuous, as to seem to be.
—Cicero

Virtue must be valuable, if men and women of all degrees pretend to have it.
—Edgar Watson Howe

A man has virtues enough if he deserves pardon for his faults on account of them.
—George C. Lichtenberg

Confidence in another man's virtue is no slight evidence of one's own.
—Michel de Montaigne

He hath no mean portion of virtue that loveth it in another.
—Thomas Fuller (II)

That virtue we appreciate is as much ours as another's. We see so much only as we possess.
—Henry David Thoreau

He that is good, will infallibly become better, and he that is bad, will as certainly become worse; for vice, virtue and time are three things that never stand still.
—Charles Caleb Colton

When the fight begins within himself, a man's worth something.
—Robert Browning

It is not neurotic to have conflicts. . . . Conflicts within ourselves are an integral part of human life.
—Karen Horney

We are, I know not how, double in ourselves, so that when we believe we disbelieve, and cannot rid ourselves of what we condemn.
—Michel de Montaigne

You cannot make yourself feel, but you can make yourself do right in spite of your feelings.
—Pearl S. Buck

There is only one duty, only one safe course, and that is to try to be right.
—Winston Churchill

To see what is right, and not do it, is want of courage, or of principle.
—Confucius

Be advised that every time you avoid doing right, you increase your disposition to do wrong.
—Author Unknown

There is a moral element in us that makes us like to know that we are doing wrong when we are doing it.
—Robert Lynd

It is possible to go wrong in many ways, but right in only one. The former is thus easy and the latter difficult.
—Aristotle

It is the necessities of life which generate ideas of right and wrong.
—W. Somerset Maugham

Our conduct is influenced not by our experience but by our expectation of life.
—George Bernard Shaw

Our humanity rests upon a series of learned behaviors, woven together into patterns that are infinitely fragile and never directly inherited.
—Margaret Mead

For behavior, men learn it, as they take diseases, one of another.
—Francis Bacon

Behavior is a mirror in which every one displays his image.
—Johann Wolfgang von Goethe

In great matters men try to show themselves to their best advantage; in small matters they show themselves as they are.
—Sébastien R. Nicolas Chamfort

We often do not know ourselves the grounds
On which we act, though plain to others.
—Bertolt Brecht

From his cradle to his grave a man never does a single thing
which has any first and foremost object save one—to secure peace
of mind, spiritual comfort, for himself.
—Mark Twain

We pass our life in forging fetters for ourselves, and in
complaining of having to wear them.
—Gustav Vapereau

An unrestricted satisfaction of every need presents itself as the
most enticing method of conducting one's life, but it means
putting enjoyment before caution, and soon brings its own
punishment.
—Sigmund Freud

Discretion is the perfection of reason, and a guide to us in all the
duties of life. It is only found in men of sound sense and good
understanding.
—Jean de La Bruyère

Our remedies oft in ourselves do lie.
—William Shakespeare

Our body . . . should be to us like a sick person entrusted to our
care. We must refuse it many of the worthless things it wants; . . .
we must forcefully compel it to take the helpful remedies
repugnant to it.
—Antony of Padua

It is not only what we do, but also what we do not do, for which
we are accountable.
—Molière

No human being can come into this world without increasing or
diminishing the sum total of human happiness.
—Elihu Burrit

A man's real life is that accorded to him in the thoughts of other men by reason of respect or natural love.
—Joseph Conrad

The world is a looking-glass, and gives back to every man the reflection of his own face. Frown at it and it will in turn look sourly upon you; laugh at it and with it, and it is a jolly kind companion.
—William Makepeace Thackeray

The happiness or unhappiness of men depend no less on temper than fortune.
—François de La Rochefoucauld

Our temperament decides the value of everything fortune bestows on us.
—François de La Rochefoucauld

Mutability of temper and inconsistency with ourselves is the greatest weakness of human nature.
—Joseph Addison

Nothing can bring you peace but yourself.
—Ralph Waldo Emerson

People often say that this or that person has not yet found himself. But the self is not something one finds, it is something one creates.
—Thomas Szasz

The unexamined life is not worth living.
—Socrates

No man is the worse for knowing the worst of himself.
—H. G. Bohn

What a man thinks about himself, that it is which determines, or rather indicates, his fate.
—Henry David Thoreau

What you are must always displease you, if you attain to that which you are not.
—Saint Augustine

Every man has at times in his mind the ideal of what he should be, but is not. This ideal may be high and complete, or it may be quite low and insufficient; yet in all men that really seek to improve, it is better than the actual character. Man never falls so low that he can see nothing higher than himself.
—Theodore Parker

Be always displeased with what though art, if thou desire to attain to what though art not; for where thou hast pleased thyself, there thou abidest.
—Francis Quarles

The most precious of all possessions, is power over ourselves; power to withstand trial, to bear suffering, to front danger; power over pleasure and pain; power to follow our convictions, however resisted by menace and scorn; the power of calm reliance in scenes of darkness and storms. He that has not a mastery over his own inclinations; he that knows not how to resist the importunity of present pleasure or pain, for the sake of what reason tells him is fit to be done, wants the true principle of virtue and industry, and is in danger of never being good for anything.
—John Locke

The man who makes everything that leads to happiness depend upon himself, and not upon other men, has adopted the very best plan for living happily. This is the man of moderation, the man of manly character and wisdom.
—Plato

There's only one corner of the universe you can be certain of improving, and that's your own self. So you begin there, not

outside, not on other people. That comes afterwards, when you've worked on your own corner.
—Aldous Huxley

Somewhere along the line of development we discover what we really are, and then we make our real decision for which we are responsible. Make that decision primarily for yourself because you can never really live anyone else's life, not even your own child's. The influence you exert is through your own life and what you become yourself.
—Anna Eleanor Roosevelt

Remember that you are but an actor, acting whatever part the Master has ordained. It may be short or it may be long. If he wishes you to represent a poor man, do so heartily; if a cripple, or a magistrate, or a private man, in each case act your part with honor.
—Epictetus

Who we are and how we are are less important than what we are.
—Author Unknown

Whatever games are played with us, we must play no games with ourselves, but deal in our privacy with the last honesty and truth.
—Ralph Waldo Emerson

The test of a civilized person is first self-awareness, and then depth after depth of sincerity in self-confrontations.
—Clarence Day

What we must decide is perhaps how we are valuable rather than how valuable we are.
—Edgar Z. Friedenberg

You are unique, and if that is not fulfilled, then something has been lost.
—Martha Graham

If you have anything really valuable to contribute to the world it will come through the expression of your own personality, that

single spark of divinity that sets you off and makes you different from every other living creature.
—Bruce Barton

If a man does not keep pace with his companions, perhaps it is because he hears a different drummer. Let him step to the music which he hears, however measured or far away.
—Henry David Thoreau

Resolve to be thyself: and know, that he
Who finds himself, loses his misery.
—Matthew Arnold

How many cares one loses when one decides not to be something but to be someone.
—Coco Chanel

What you think of yourself is much more important than what others think of you.
—Seneca

Our own heart, and not other men's opinions of us, forms our true honor.
—Johann Friedrich von Schiller

Make the most of yourself for that is all there is of you.
—Author Unknown

Do not make yourself so big, you are not so small.
—Yiddish Proverb

Everybody must learn this lesson somewhere—that it costs something to be what you are.
—Shirley Abbott

Be careful how you live. You may be the only Bible some person ever reads.
—William J. Toms

Each heart is a world. You find all within yourself that you find without. To know yourself you have only to set down a true statement of those that ever loved or hated you.
—Johann Kaspar Lavater

Such Is Life

PART 13

MIDDLE AGE

Everyone else my age is an adult,
whereas I am merely in disguise.
—Margaret Atwood

Such Is Life

Man arrives as a novice at each age of his life.
—Sébastien R. Nicholas Chamfort

Whoever, in middle age, attempts to realize the wishes and hopes of his early youth, invariably deceives himself. Each ten years of a man's life has it own fortunes, its own hopes, its own desires.
—Johann Wolfgang von Goethe

At 30 a man should know himself like the palm of his hand, know the exact number of his defects and qualities, know how far he can go, foretell his failures—be what he is. And, above all, accept these things.
—Albert Camus

As we advance in life we learn the limits of our abilities.
—Author Unknown

After thirty, a man wakes up sad every morning, excepting perhaps five or six, until the day of his death.
—Ralph Waldo Emerson

Which of us that is thirty years old has not had his Pompeii? Deep under ashes lies Life, Youth, the careless sports, the pleasures and passions, the darling joy.
—William Makepeace Thackeray

We are living at an important and fruitful moment now, for it is clear to men that the images of adult manhood given by the popular culture are worn out; a man can no longer depend on them. By the time a man is thirty-five he knows that the images of the right man, the tough man, the true man which he received in high school do not work in life.
—Robert Bly

As we reach mid-life in the middle thirties or early forties, we are not prepared for the idea that time can run out on us, or for the startling truth that if we don't hurry to pursue our own definition

of a meaningful existence, life can become a repetition of trivial maintenance duties.
—Gail Sheehy

It's helpful to look at your life and ask: "If I had one more year to live, what would I do?" We all have things we want to achieve. Don't just put them off—do them now.
—John Goddard

To hold the same views at forty as we held at twenty is to have been stupefied for a score of years, and take rank, not as a prophet, but as an unteachable brat, well birched and none the wiser.
—Robert Louis Stevenson

At 20 years of age the will reigns; at 30 the wit; at 40 the judgment.
—Benjamin Franklin

We don't understand life any better at forty than at twenty, but we know it and admit it.
—Ernest Renan

A fool at forty is a fool indeed.
—Edward Young

If a man reach forty and yet be disliked by his fellows, he will be so to the end.
—Confucius

The first forty years of life give us the text: the next thirty supply the commentary.
—Arthur Schopenhauer

After a certain number of years our faces become our biographies.
—Cynthia Ozick

Today is my forty-third birthday. I have thus long passed the peak of life where the waters divide.
—Esaias Tegnér

It seems . . . as though the second half of a man's life is made up of nothing but the habits he has accumulated during the first half.
—Fyodor Mikhailovich Dostoevsky

Habituation is a falling asleep or fatiguing of the sense of time; which explains why young years pass slowly, while later life flings itself faster and faster upon its course.
—Thomas Mann

Middle-age is Janus-faced. As we look back on our accomplishments and our failures to achieve the things we wanted, we look ahead to the time we have left to us. . . . Our children are gaining life, and our parents are losing it.
—Dr. Stanley H. Cath

What you have become is the price you paid to get what you used to want.
—Mignon McLaughlin

We did not change as we grew older; we just became more clearly ourselves.
—Lynn Hall

The heart never grows better by age; I fear rather worse; always harder. A young liar will be an old one; and a young knave will only be a greater knave as he grows older.
—Lord Chesterfield

As we advance in life the circles of our pains enlarges, while that of our pleasures contracts.
—Madame Anne Sophie Swetchine

When our parents are living we feel that they stand between us and death; when they are gone, we ourselves are in the forefront of the battle.
—Author Unknown

You will find as you grow older that the weight of rages will press harder and harder upon the employer.
—William Archibald Spooner

Whenever a man's friends begin to compliment him about looking young, he may be sure that they think he is growing old.
—Washington Irving

If you pull out a gray hair seven will come to its funeral.
—Pennsylvania German Proverb

You never really feel older than other people but only different, to our advantage or disadvantage, in some particular; whereas we always do feel definitely younger than other people.
—J. B. Priestly

After a certain age, men never become really intimate, let their relations with each other be ever so close.
—Anthony Trollope

Middle age is when you've met so many people that every new person you meet reminds you of someone else.
—Ogden Nash

Middle age: when you're sitting at home on Saturday night and the telephone rings and you hope it isn't for you.
—Ogden Nash

Middle age is when you have a choice of two temptations and choose the one that will get you home earlier.
—Author Unknown

(Middle age is) the time when a man is always thinking that in a week or two he'll feel just as good as ever.
—Don Marquis

Maturity is the time of life when, if you had the time, you'd have the time of your life.
—Author Unknown

The first half of life consists of the capacity to enjoy without the chance; the last half consists of the chance without the capacity.
—Mark Twain

Of middle age the best that can be said is that a middle-aged person has likely learned to have a little fun in spite of his troubles.
—Don Marquis

The youth gets together the materials to build a bridge to the moon, or, perchance, a palace or temple on the earth, and, at length, the middle-aged man concludes to build a woodshed with them.
—Henry David Thoreau

Age is the most terrible misfortune that can happen to any man; other evils will mend, this is every day getting worse.
—George James

Forty is the old age of youth; fifty the youth of old age.
—Victor Hugo

He that is not handsome at twenty, nor strong at thirty, nor rich at forty, nor wise at fifty, will never be handsome, strong, rich, or wise.
—Author Unknown

At thirty man suspects himself a fool,
Knows it at forty, and reforms his plan;
At fifty chides his infamous delay, . . .
Resolves; and re-resolves; then dies the same.
—Edward Young

The process of maturing is an art to be learned, an effort to be sustained. By the age of fifty you have made yourself what you are, and if it is good, it is better than your youth.
—Marya Mannes

A man of fifty is responsible for his face.
—Edwin M. Stanton

A man of fifty looks as old as Santa Claus to a girl of twenty.
—William Feather

Men, like peaches and pears, grow sweet a little before they begin
to decay.
—Oliver Wendell Holmes, Sr.

The years between fifty and seventy are the hardest. You are
always being asked to do things, and you are not decrepit enough
to turn them down.
—T. S. Eliot

Hope is the last gift given to man, and the only gift not given to
youth. Youth is pre-eminently the period in which a man can be
lyric, fanatical, poetic; but youth is a period in which a man can
be hopeless. The end of every episode is the end of the world. But
the power of hoping through everything, the knowledge that the
soul survives its adventures, that great inspiration comes to the
middle aged.
—G. K. Chesterton

The problem for some can involve how you maintain your
humanity in the face of bitterness . . . about yourself and your
perceived failures, or your wish that the world were a better place
for yourself and your children to live in. One compensation is to
integrate and to broaden one's perspective. A new vital
connection can be made with the grandchildren, for example, or
in passing on one's knowledge to the next generation. There are
very few things you can do to defy the aging process. Keeping
your hopes alive is definitely one of them.
—Dr. Stanley H. Cath

The daily wearing away of life, with its ever shrinking remainder,
is not the only thing we have to consider. For even if a man's
years be prolonged, we must still take into account that it is
doubtful whether his mind will continue to retain its capacity for
the understanding of business, or for the contemplative effort
needed to apprehend things divine and human. The onset of
senility may involve no loss of respiratory or alimentary powers,
or of sensations, impulses and so forth; nevertheless, the ability

to make full use of his faculties . . . or to make any other of the decisions that require the exercise of a practical intellect, is already on the wane. We must press on, then, in haste; not simply because every hour brings us nearer to death, but because even before then our powers of perception and comprehension begin to deteriorate.

—Marcus Aurelius Antoninus

Such Is Life

PART 14

HUMANITY

I consider the soul of man as the ruin
of a glorious pile of buildings;
where, amidst great heaps of rubbish,
you meet with noble fragments of sculpture,
broken pillars and obelisks,
and a magnificence in confusion.
—Sir Richard Steele

Such Is Life

A man is a god in ruins.
—Ralph Waldo Emerson

Every man is odd.
—William Shakespeare

Every man is an original and solitary character. None can either understand or feel the book of his own life like himself.
—Richard Cecil

A wonderful fact to reflect upon, that every human creature is constituted to be that profound secret and mystery to every other.
—Charles Dickens

Do we really know anybody? Who does not wear one face to hide another?
—Frances Marion

You must look into people as well as at them.
—Lord Chesterfield

Many individuals have, like uncut diamonds, shining qualities beneath a rough exterior.
—Juvenal

A man is like a bit of Labrador spar, which has no lustre as you turn it in your hand, until you come to a particular angle; then it shows deep and beautiful colors.
—Ralph Waldo Emerson

We do not learn to know men through their coming to us. To find out what sort of persons they are, we must go to them.
—Johann Wolfgang von Goethe

Man is subject to innumerable pains and sorrows by the very nature of humanity, and yet, as if nature had not sown evils enough in life, we are continually adding grief to grief and aggravating the common calamity by our cruel treatment of one another.
—Joseph Addison

Human history is the sad result of each one looking out for himself.
—Julio Cortázar

The glare, the heat, and noise, this congeries of individuals without sympathy, and dishes without flavor; this is society.
—Benjamin Disraeli

There is not a more mean, stupid, dastardly, pitiful, selfish, spiteful, envious, ungrateful animal than the Public. It is the greatest of cowards for it is afraid of itself.
—William Hazlitt

Society is a madhouse whose wardens are the officials and police.
—August Strindberg

What is meant by a "knowledge of the world" is simply an acquaintance with the infirmities of men.
—Charles Dickens

It is a sorry business to inquire into what men think, when we are every day uncomfortably confronted with what they do.
—Michael Arlen

All that I care to know is that a man is a human being—that is enough for me; he can't be any worse.
—Mark Twain

Man: An animal so lost in rapturous contemplation of what he thinks he is as to overlook what he indubitably ought to be.
—Ambrose Bierce

Of all created creatures man is the most detestable. . . . He is the only creature that has a nasty mind.
—Mark Twain

What is man? A miserable little pile of secrets.
—André Malraux

There is no man so good, who, were he to submit all thoughts and actions to the laws, would not deserve hanging ten times in his life.
—Michel de Montaigne

Many might go to heaven with half the labour they go to hell.
—Ben Jonson

I never wonder to see men wicked, but I often wonder to see them not ashamed.
—Jonathan Swift

One of the worst things about life is not how nasty the nasty people are. You know that already. It is how nasty the nice people can be.
—Anthony Powell

I have long since come to believe that people never mean half of what they say, and that it is best to disregard their talk and judge only their actions.
—Dorothy Day

We judge others by their words and deeds, ourselves by our thoughts and our intentions.
—Comtesse Diane

A man must be both stupid and uncharitable who believes there is no virtue or truth but on his own side.
—Joseph Addison

Men are not against you; they are merely for themselves.
—Gene Fowler

We must not indulge in unfavourable views of mankind, since by doing it we make bad men believe that they are no worse than others, and we teach the good that they are good in vain.
—Walter Savage Landor

It is a great mistake to think that anybody is either an angel or a devil.
—Anthony Trollope

Good and bad men are each less so than they seem.
—Samuel Taylor Coleridge

As it is said of the greatest liar that he tells more truth than falsehood, so it may be said of the worst man that he does more good than evil.
—Samuel Johnson

I wonder how anyone can have the face to condemn others when he reflects upon his own thoughts.
—W. Somerset Maugham

There is as much difference between us and ourselves as between us and others.
—Michel de Montaigne

When we come to judge others it is not by ourselves as we really are that we judge them, but by an image that we have formed of ourselves from which we have left out everything that offends our vanity or would discredit us in the eyes of the world.
—W. Somerset Maugham

That which we call sin in others is experiment for us.
—Ralph Waldo Emerson

Charity: An amiable quality of the heart which moves us to console in others the sins and vices to which ourselves are addicted.
—Ambrose Bierce

Just as those who practice the same profession recognize each other instinctively, so do those who practice the same vice.
—Marcel Proust

Experience tells us that each man most keenly and unerringly detects in others the vice which he is most familiar himself.
—Frederick William Robertson

Everybody likes to see somebody else get caught for the vices practiced by themselves.
—Marya Mannes

Never put much confidence in such as put no confidence in others. A man prone to suspect evil is mostly looking in his neighbor for what he sees in himself. As to the pure all things are pure, even so to the impure all things are impure.
—Augustus and Julius Hare

The better a man is, the less ready is he to suspect wickedness in others.
—Cicero

Speak well of every one if you speak of them at all—none of us are so very good.
—Elbert Hubbard

A man had rather have a hundred lies told of him, than one truth which he does not wish should be told.
—Samuel Johnson

A truth that's told with bad intent
Beats all the lies you can invent.
—William Blake

Nothing makes a man or body of men as mad as the truth. If there is no truth in it they laugh it off.
—Will Rogers

An injurious truth has no merit over an injurious lie. Neither should ever be uttered.
—Mark Twain

Never throw mud. You may miss your mark, but you must have dirty hands.
—Joseph Parker

Leave other people's mistakes where they lie.
—Marcus Aurelius Antoninus

Let us think often of our own sin, and we shall be lenient to the sins of others.
—François de Fénelon

Teach me to feel another's woe,
    To hide the fault I see:
That mercy I to others show,
    That mercy show to me
—Alexander Pope

There is no readier way for a man to bring his own worth into question, than by endeavoring to detract from the worth of other men.
—John Tillotson

I never yet heard man or woman much abused that I was not inclined to think the better of them, and to transfer the suspicion or dislike to the one who found pleasure in pointing out the defects of another.
—Jane Porter

A man never discloses his own character so clearly as when he describes another's.
—Jean Paul Richter

When certain persons abuse us, let us ask ourselves what description of characters it is that they admire; we shall often find this a very consolatory question.
—Charles Caleb Colton

Even the lion has to defend himself against flies.
—Author Unknown

Let us believe neither half of the good people tell us of ourselves, nor half the evil they say of others.
—Jean-Antoine Petit-Senn

There is so much good in the worst of us, and so much bad in the best of us, that it behooves all of us not to talk about the rest of us.
—Edward Wallis Hoch

There are few occasions in which we should make a bad bargain by giving up the good that is said about us on condition that nothing bad may be said.
—François de La Rochefoucauld

I never hitherunto knewe man so good and vertuous which hath not been subject to the malice and slaunders of some one.
—Stefano Guazzo

There are two modes of establishing our reputation; to be praised by honest men, and to be abused by rogues.
—Charles Caleb Colton

What people say behind your back is your standing in the community.
—Edgar Watson Howe

Many a man's reputation would not know his character if they met on the street.
—Elbert Hubbard

The best-loved man or maid in the town would perish with anguish could they hear all that their friends say in the course of a day.
—John Hay

I hold it to be a fact, that if all persons knew what each said of the other, there would not be four friends in the world.
—Blaise Pascal

A man usually has no idea what is being said about him. The entire town may be slandering him, but if he has no friends he will never hear about it.
—Honoré de Balzac

It takes your enemy and your friend, working together, to hurt you to the heart; one to slander you and the other to get the news to you.
—Mark Twain

He who slanders an absent friend, he who does not defend him when he is attacked, he who seeks eagerly to raise the senseless laugh and acquire the fame of wit, he who cannot keep a friend's secret; that man is a scoundrel. Mark him and avoid him.
—Horace

There are two things for which animals are to be envied: they know nothing of future evils, or of what people say of them.
—François Marie de Voltaire

I know nothing swifter in life than the voice of rumor.
—Plautus

Nothing is so swift as calumny; nothing is more easily uttered; nothing more readily received; nothing more widely dispersed.
—Cicero

When rumors are spread abroad, they are always believed. There is an excitement and a pleasure in believing them. If the accused one be near enough to ourselves to make the accusation a matter of personal pain, of course we disbelieve. But, if the distance be beyond this, we are almost ready to think that anything may be true of anybody.
—Anthony Trollope

How large a portion of chastity is sent out of the world by distant hints, nodded away and cruelly winked into suspicion, by the envy of those that are past all temptations of it themselves. How often does the reputation of a helpless creature bleed by a report that the party propagating it beholds with pity, and is sorry for it, and hopes that it may not be true, but in the meantime gives it her pass, that at least it may have fair play in the world, to be believed or not, according to the charity of those into whose hands it shall happen to fall.
—Laurence Sterne

The average man does not get pleasure out of an idea because he thinks it is true; he thinks it is true because he gets pleasure out of it.
—H. L. Mencken

Gossip is when you hear something you like about someone you don't.
—Earl Wilson

No matter what you do, someone always knew you would.
—Author Unknown

Scandal is but amusing ourselves with the faults, foibles, follies and reputations of our friends.
—Royall Tyler

The only time people dislike gossip is when you gossip about them.
—Will Rogers

Great numbers of moderately good people think it fine to talk scandal; they regard it as a sort of evidence of their own goodness.
—Frederick William Faber

If you can't say anything good about someone, sit right here by me.
—Alice Roosevelt Longworth

Gossip is vice enjoyed vicariously.
—Elbert Hubbard

All men seek esteem; the best by lifting themselves, which is hard to do, the rest by shoving others down, which is much easier.
—Mary Renault

Absent: Exposed to the attacks of friends and acquaintances; defamed; slandered.
—Ambrose Bierce

Take no part with scandalizers; thou knowest not thy turn among them.
—Thomas Fuller (II)

Who speaks ill of others to you will speak ill of you to others.
—German Proverb

Listen not to a tale-bearer or slanderer, for he tells thee nothing out of good will, but as he discovereth of the secrets of others, so he will of thine in turn.
—Socrates

Slanderers are like flies that pass all over a man's good parts to light only on his sores.
—Rule of Life

Lies are as communicative as fleas; and truth is as difficult to lay hold upon as air.
—Walter Savage Landor

Even when it brings some truth with it, rumor is not free from the flaw of falsehood, for it ever takes away from, adds to, and alters the truth.
—Tertullian

Gossiping and lying go together.
—Thomas Fuller (II)

Every man is bound to leave a story better than he found it.
—Mrs. Ward

Do we ever hear the most recent fact related exactly in the same way by the several people who were at the same time eyewitnesses of it? No. One mistakes, another misrepresents, and others warp it a little to their own turn of mind, or private views.
—Lord Chesterfield

When the world has once got hold of a lie, it is astonishing how hard it is to get it out of the world. You beat it about the head, till it seems to have given up the ghost, and lo! the next day it is as healthy as ever.
—Edward G. Bulwer-Lytton

Calumny is like the wasp that worries you, which it is not best to try to get rid of unless you are sure of slaying it, for otherwise it returns to the charge more furious than ever.
—Sébastien R. Nicholas Chamfort

Never chase a lie. Let it alone, and it will run itself to death. I can work out a good character much faster than anyone can lie me out of it.
—Lyman Beecher

Have patience awhile; slanders are not long-lived. Truth is the child of time; ere long she shall appear to vindicate thee.
—Immanuel Kant

The man who fears no truths has nothing to fear from lies.
—Thomas Jefferson

No one can disgrace us but ourselves.
—Josiah Gilbert Holland

The greatest friend of truth is Time.
—Charles Caleb Colton

Everyone suffers wrongs for which there is no remedy.
—Edgar Watson Howe

To be wronged is nothing unless you continue to remember it.
—Confucius

The remedy for wrongs is to forget them.
—Publilius Syrus

He that cannot forgive others breaks the bridge over which he must pass himself; for every man needs to be forgiven.
—Lord Herbert of Cherbury

There's no real making amends in this world, any more you can mend a wrong subtraction by doing your addition right.
—George Eliot

Never does the human soul appear so strong as when it foregoes revenge and dares to forgive an injury.
—Edwin Hubbell Chapin

The weak can never forgive. Forgiveness is the attribute of the strong.
—Mohandas K. Gandhi

The brave only know how to forgive; it is the most refined and generous pitch of virtue human nature can arrive at. Cowards have done good and kind actions—cowards have even fought, nay, sometimes even conquered; but a coward never forgave. It is not in his nature; the power of doing it flows only from a strength and greatness of soul, conscious of its own force and security, and above the little temptations of resenting every fruitless attempt to interrupt its happiness.
—Laurence Sterne

A wise man will make haste to forgive, because he knows the true value of time, and will not suffer it to pass away in unnecessary pain.
—Samuel Johnson

It is easier for the generous to forgive than for the offender to ask forgiveness.
—James Thomson

I can forgive, but I cannot forget, is only another way of saying, I will not forgive. Forgiveness ought to be like a canceled note— torn in two, and burned up, so that it never can be shown against one.
—Henry Ward Beecher

Compassion will cure more sins than condemnation.
—Henry Ward Beecher

It is human nature to think wisely and act foolishly.
—Anatole France

Make no judgments where you have no compassion.
—Anne McCaffery

Life teaches us to be less harsh with ourselves and with others.
—Johann Wolfgang von Goethe

In this world, you must be a bit too kind in order to be kind enough.
—Pierre Carlet de Marivaux

Kindness is loving people more than they deserve.
—Joseph Joubert

Kindness is the golden chain by which society is bound together.
—Johann Wolfgang von Goethe

An inexhaustible good nature is one of the most precious gifts of heaven, spreading itself like oil over the troubled sea of thought, and keeping the mind smooth and equable in the roughest weather.
—Washington Irving

Kindness in words creates confidence. Kindness in thinking creates profoundness. Kindness in giving creates love.
—Lao-Tzu

We should do good whenever we can and do kindness at all times, for at all times we can.
—Joseph Joubert

There never was any heart truly great and generous that was not also tender and compassionate.
—Robert South

The best portion of a good man's life is his little, nameless, unremembered acts of kindness and of love.
—William Wordsworth

In the intercourse of social life, it is by little acts of watchful kindness recurring daily and hourly, by words, tones, gestures, looks, that affection is won and preserved.
—George Augustus Sala

A word of kindness is seldom spoken in vain, while witty sayings are as easily lost as the pearls slipping from a broken string.
—George D. Prentice

Kindness is a language the dumb can speak and the deaf can hear and understand.
—Christian Nestell Bovee

Wherever there is a human being there is an opportunity for kindness.
—Seneca

No act of kindness, no matter how small, is ever wasted.
—Æsop

Kindness can become its own motive. We are made kind by being kind.
—Eric Hoffer

Everyone is a prisoner of his own experiences. No one can eliminate prejudices—just recognize them.
—Edward R. Murrow

The responsibility of tolerance lies with those who have the wider vision.
—George Eliot

Tolerance is the oil which takes the friction out of life.
—Wilbert E. Scheer

A great many people think they are thinking when they are merely rearranging their prejudices.
—William James

Beware prejudices. They are like rats, and men's minds are like traps; prejudices get in easily, but it is doubtful if they ever get out.
—Lord Francis Jeffrey

Prejudice is a raft onto which the shipwrecked mind clambers and paddles to safety.
—Ben Hecht

Prejudice squints when it looks, and lies when it talks.
—Duchess d'Abrantes

Prejudice is the child of ignorance.
—William Hazlitt

Even when we fancy we have grown wiser, it is only, it may be, that new prejudices have displaced old ones.
—Christian Nestell Bovee

It is never too late to give up our prejudices.
—Henry David Thoreau

Acquaintance softens prejudice.
—Æsop

People only see what they are prepared to see.
—Ralph Waldo Emerson

A man has generally the good or ill qualities which he attributes to mankind.
—William Shenstone

Just as much as we see in others we have in ourselves.
—William Hazlitt

Wise men appreciate all men, for they see the good in each and know how hard it is to make anything good.
—Baltasar Grácian

If you expect perfection from people your whole life is a series of disappointments, grumblings and complaints. If, on the contrary, you pitch your expectations low, taking folks as the inefficient

creatures which they are, you are frequently surprised by having them perform better than you had hoped.
—Bruce Barton

Every man, however good he may be, has a yet better man dwelling in him, which is properly himself, but to whom nevertheless he is often unfaithful. It is to this interior and less mutable being that we should attach ourselves, not to the changeable, everyday man.
—Wilhelm von Humboldt

Since the generality of persons act from impulse much more than from principle, men are neither so good nor so bad as we are apt to think them.
—Augustus and Julius Hare

What an absurd thing it is to pass over all the valuable parts of a man, and fix our attention on his infirmities.
—Joseph Addison

It is only imperfection that complains of what is imperfect. The more perfect we are, the more gentle and quiet we become towards the defects of others.
—François de Fénelon

As I know more of mankind I expect less of them, and am ready now to call a man a good man upon easier terms than I was formerly.
—Samuel Johnson

Tolerance comes with age. I see no fault committed that I myself could not have committed at some time or other.
—Johann Wolfgang von Goethe

I know by my own pot how other's boil.
—French Proverb

If you will please people, you must please them in their own way; and as you cannot make them what they should be, you must take them as they are.
—Lord Chesterfield

There is no dearth of charity in the world in giving, but there is comparatively little exercised in thinking and speaking.
—Sir Phillip Sidney

One learns people through the heart, not the eyes or the intellect.
—Mark Twain

It is a common error, of which a wise man will beware, to measure the worth of our neighbor by his conduct toward ourselves. How many rich souls might we not rejoice in the knowledge of, were it not for our pride!
—Jean Paul Richter

True kindness presupposes the faculty of imagining as one's own the suffering and joys of others.
—André Gide

There is no man in this world without some manner of tribulation or anguish, though he be king or pope.
—Thomas á Kempis

There is in every human countenance either a history or a prophecy, which must sadden, or at least soften, every reflecting observer.
—Samuel Taylor Coleridge

If the internal griefs of every man could be read, written on his forehead, how many who now excite envy, would appear to be objects of pity?
—Metastasio

None know the weight of another's burden.
—George Herbert

Every man is entitled to be valued by his best moment.
—Ralph Waldo Emerson

We can scarcely hate anyone that we know.
—William Hazlitt

PART 15

THE HUMAN CONDITION

Ships that pass in the night, and speak each other in passing;
Only a signal shown and a distant voice in the darkness;
So on the ocean of life we pass and speak one another,
Only a look and a voice; then darkness again and silence.
—Henry Wadsworth Longfellow

Unless we remember we cannot understand.
—Edward M. Forster

How we remember, what we remember and why we remember form the most personal map of our individuality.
—Christina Baldwin

We do not remember days, we remember moments.
—Cesare Pavese

Sit in reverie, and watch the changing color of the waves that break upon the ideal seashore of the mind.
—Henry Wadsworth Longfellow

Memories are hunting-horns, whose noise dies away in the wind.
—Guillaume Apollinaire

The leaves of memory seemed to make a mournful rustling in the dark.
—Henry Wadsworth Longfellow

Footfalls echo in the memory
Down the passage which we did not take
Towards the door we never opened
Into the rosegarden.
—T. S. Eliot

Man is the only animal that laughs and weeps; for he is the only animal that is struck by the difference between what things are and what they might have been.
—William Hazlitt

Everything intercepts us from ourselves.
—Ralph Waldo Emerson

Always driven towards new shores, or carried hence without hope of return, shall we never, on the ocean of age, cast anchor for even a day?
—Alphonse de Lamartine

Our dreams are never realized and as soon as we see them betrayed we realize that the intensest joys of our life have nothing to do with reality. No sooner do we see them betrayed than we are consumed with regret for the time when they glowed within us. And in this succession of hopes and regrets our life slips by.
—Natalia Ginzburg

We live between two dense clouds—the forgetting of what was and the uncertainty of what will be.
—Anatole France

Nothing but infinite pity is sufficient for the infinite pathos of human life.
—Author Unknown

We are all of us calling and calling across the incalculable gulfs which separate us even from our nearest friends.
—David Grayson

The world, in its best state, is nothing more than a larger assembly of beings, combining to counterfeit happiness which they do not feel, employing every art and contrivance to embellish life, and to hide their real condition from the eyes of one another.
—Samuel Johnson

We all live in a house on fire, no fire department to call; no way out, just the upstairs window to look out of while the fire burns the house down with us trapped, locked in it.
—Tennessee Williams

Each one of us must suffer long to himself before he can learn that he is but one in a great community of wretchedness which has been pitilessly repeating itself from the foundation of the world.
—William Dean Howells

Gnaw the bone which is fallen to thy lot.
—Ben Syra

There is nothing that men love better, or manage worse, than their lives.
—Jean de La Bruyère

The world is nothing but a great desire to live and a great dissatisfaction with living.
—Heraclitus

Life is not lost by dying; life is lost minute by minute, day by dragging day, in all the thousand small uncaring ways.
—Stephen Vincent Benét

Opportunities flit by while we sit regretting the chances we have lost, and the happiness that comes to us we heed not, because of the happiness that is gone.
—Jerome K. Jerome

Ah, how many regrets does the length of life incur.
—Publilius Syrus

Sighs for follies said and done
Twist our narrow days.
—W. H. Auden

Regret is an odd emotion because it comes only upon reflection. Regret lacks immediacy, and so its power seldom influences events when it could do some good.
—William O'Rourke

Not to understand a treasure's worth till time has stolen away the slighted good, is cause of half the poverty we feel, and makes the world the wilderness it is.
—William Cowper

One doesn't recognize in one's life the really important moments—not until it's too late.
—Agatha Christie

The most decisive actions of our life—I mean those that are most likely to decide the whole course of our future—are more often than not, unconsidered.
—André Gide

Regrets are as personal as fingerprints.
—Margaret Culkin Banning

There's nothing half so real in life as the things you've done . . . inexorably, unalterably done.
—Sara Teasdale

This is a hard and precarious world, where every mistake and infirmity must be paid for in full.
—Clarence Day

One of the greatest weaknesses of those who suffer misfortune through their own fault is that they almost always try to find excuses before looking for the remedies; as a result they often find remedies too late.
—Cardinal de Retz

Man is born with a tendency to detect a maximum of contributory negligence in other people's misfortunes, and nothing but blind chance in his own.
—Arthur Schnitzler

It is seldom that God sends such calamities upon man as men bring upon themselves and suffer willingly.
—Jeremy Taylor

Misfortunes always come in by a door that has been left open for them.
—Czech Proverb

One misfortune always carries another on its back.
—Dutch Proverb

There is a chill air surrounding those who are down in the world, and people are glad to get away from them, as from a cold room.
—George Eliot

The usual fortune of complaint is to excite contempt more than pity.
—Samuel Johnson

The world is quickly bored by the recital of misfortune, and willingly avoids the sight of distress.
—W. Somerset Maugham

We exaggerate misfortune and happiness alike. We are never either so wretched or so happy as we say we are.
—Honoré de Balzac

Depend upon it that if a man talks of his misfortunes there is something in them that is not disagreeable to him; for where there is nothing but pure misery there never is any recourse to the mention of it.
—Samuel Johnson

Remember that in all miseries lamenting becomes fools, and action, wise folk.
—Sir Phillip Sidney

A stumble may prevent a fall.
—Thomas Fuller (II)

There exist some evils so terrible and some misfortunes so horrible that we dare not think of them, whilst their very aspect makes us shudder; but if they happen to fall on us, we find ourselves stronger than we imagined; we grapple with our luck, and behave better than we expected we should.
—Jean de La Bruyère

As there is no worldly gain without some loss, so there is no worldly loss without some gain. If thou hast lost thy wealth, thou hast lost some trouble with it; if thou are degraded from thy honor, thou art likewise freed from the stroke of envy, if sickness hath blurred thy beauty, it hath delivered thee from pride. Set the allowance against the loss and thou shalt find no great loss; he loses little or nothing that reserves himself.
—Francis Quarles

Life is thick sown with thorns, and I know no other remedy than to pass quickly through them. The longer we dwell on our misfortunes, the greater is their power to harm us.
—François Marie de Voltaire

If all our misfortunes were laid in one common heap whence everyone must take an equal portion, most people would be contented to take their own and depart.
—Socrates

No scene of life but teems with mortal woe.
—Sir Walter Scott

Dwelling on the negative simply contributes to its power.
—Shirley MacLaine

Some of the best lessons we ever learn we learn from our mistakes and failures. The error of the past is the wisdom and success of the future.
—Tryon Edwards

We should face reality and our past mistakes in an honest, adult way. Boasting of glory does not make glory, and singing in the dark does not dispel fear.
—King Hussein (Jordan)

Our bravest and best lessons are not learned through success, but through misadventure.
—Amos Bronson Alcott

Mistake, error, is the discipline through which we advance.
—William Ellery Channing

We often discover what *will* do, by finding out what will not do; and probably he who never made a mistake never made a discovery.
—Samuel Smiles

Be not ashamed to confess that you have been in the wrong. It is but owning what you need not be ashamed of—that you now have more sense than you had before, to see your error; more humility to acknowledge it, more grace to correct it.
—Jeremiah Seed

It is only an error in judgment to make a mistake, but it shows infirmity of character to adhere to it when discovered.
—Christian Nestell Bovee

Man is made for error; it enters his mind naturally, and he discovers a few truths only with the greatest effort.
—Frederick the Great

All men are liable to error; and most men are, in many points, by passion or interest, under temptation to it.
—John Locke

Error is not a fault of our knowledge, but a mistake of our judgment, giving assent to that which is not true.
—John Locke

It is almost as difficult to make a man unlearn his errors as his knowledge. Mal-information is more hopeless than non-information; for error is always more busy than ignorance.
—Charles Caleb Colton

Mistakes live in the neighborhood and therefore delude us.
—Sir Rabindranath Tagore

Man's lives consist mostly of their making the same mistake over and over again.
—Siegfried Trebitsch

The keenest sorrow is to recognize ourselves as the sole cause of all our adversities.
—Sophocles

Ah, trouble, trouble, there are two different kinds . . . there's the one you give and the other you take.
—Kay Boyle

It's not the tragedies that kill us, it's the messes.
—Dorothy Parker

There's no limit to how complicated things can get, on account of one thing always leading to another.
—E. B. White

Sometimes in life situations develop that only the half-demented can get out of.
—François de La Rochefoucauld

One cannot manage too many affairs: like pumpkins in the water, one pops up while you try to hold down the other.
—Alfred North Whitehead

Chaos is the score upon which reality is written.
—Henry Miller

Woes cluster; rare are solitary woes;
They love a train, they tread each others heel.
—Edward Young

When one is past, another care we have,
Thus woe succeeds a woe, as wave a wave.
—Robert Herrick

The new trouble always has precedence over those which are of earlier date.
—Anthony Trollope

Too much happens. . . . Man performs, engenders so much more than he can or should have to bear. That's how he finds he can bear anything.
—William Faulkner

We do not do what we want and yet we are responsible for what we are—that is the fact.
—Jean Paul Sartre

We do what we must, and call it by the best names.
—Ralph Waldo Emerson

When the world has once begun to use us ill, it afterwards continues the same treatment with less scruple or ceremony, as men do a whore.
—Jonathan Swift

When an elephant is in trouble, even a frog will kick him.
—Hindu Proverb

The drowning man is not troubled by rain.
—Persian Proverb

The descent from the terrible to the ridiculous is little by little.
—Longinus

The thought that we are enduring the unendurable is one of the things that keep us going.
—Molly Haskell

A man must learn to endure that patiently which he cannot avoid conveniently.
—Michel de Montaigne

Endurance is patience concentrated.
—Thomas Carlyle

Whatever necessity lays upon thee, endure: whatever she commands, do.
—Johann Wolfgang von Goethe

The manner in which one endures what must be endured is more important than the thing that must be endured.
—Dean Acheson

When a storm blows, sent by the gods, we needs must endure it, toiling without complaint.
—Æschylus

There are some things you learn best in calm, and some in storm.
—Willa Cather

In the great storms of life we act like the captain of a ship who, under the stress of a hurricane, lightens the ship of its heaviest cargo.
—Honoré de Balzac

A great pilot can sail even when his canvas is rent.
—Seneca

If the wind will not serve, take to the oars.
—Latin Proverb

I am not afraid of storms for I am learning how to sail my ship.
—Louisa May Alcott

Stars may be seen from the bottom of a deep well when they cannot be discerned from the top of a mountain. So are many things learned in adversity which the prosperous man dreams not of.
—Charles Haddon Spurgeon

There is a strength of quiet endurance as significant of courage as the most daring feats of prowess.
—Henry Theodore Tuckerman

We must make the best of those ills which cannot be avoided.
—Alexander Hamilton

The best way out of a difficulty is through it.
—Author Unknown

Everything has two handles: one by which it may be borne, another by which it cannot.
—Epictetus

The weather-cock on the church spire, though made of iron, would soon be broken by the storm-wind if it . . . did not understand the noble art of turning to every wind.
—Heinrich Heine

Our strength often increases in proportion to the obstacles imposed upon it.
—Paul De Rapin

Difficulties strengthen the mind, as labor does the body.
—Seneca

Adversity has the effect of eliciting talents, which, in prosperous circumstances, would have lain dormant.
—Horace

Crises refine life. In them you discover what you are.
—Allan K. Chalmers

Adversity introduces a man to himself.
—Author Unknown

It is by the presence of mind in untried emergencies that the native metal of man is tested.
—James Russell Lowell

The gem cannot be polished without friction, nor man perfected without trials.
—Chinese Proverb

He knows not his own strength that hath not met adversity.
—Ben Jonson

We come to know best what men are, in their worst jeopardies.
—Daniel

It is more useful to watch a man in times of peril, and in adversity to discern what kind of man he is; for then at last the words of truth are drawn from the depths of his heart, and the mask is torn off; reality remains.
—Lucretius

Affliction appears to be the guide to reflection; the teacher of humility; the parent of repentance; the nurse of faith; the strengthener of patience, and the promoter of charity.
—Author Unknown

Adversity is the trial of principle. Without it a man hardly knows whether he is honest or not.
—Henry Fielding

Calamity is the perfect glass wherein we truly see and know ourselves.
—Sir William Davenant

Every calamity is a spur and a valuable hint.
—Ralph Waldo Emerson

Problems are messages.
—Shakti Gawain

Affliction comes to us, not to make us sad but sober; not to make us sorry but wise.
—Henry Ward Beecher

Affliction, like the iron-smith, shapes as it smites.
—Christian Nestell Bovee

We acquire the strength we have overcome.
—Ralph Waldo Emerson

What does not destroy me makes me stronger.
—Friedrich Wilhelm Nietzsche

Strength is born in the deep silence of long-suffering hearts; not amid joy.
—Felicia Hemans

It is not the so-called blessings of life, its sunshine and calm and pleasant experiences that make men, but its rugged experiences, its storms and tempests and trials. Early adversity is often a blessing in disguise.
—William Mathews

The school of adversity is a very good school, provided you don't matriculate too early and continue too long.
—Louis K. Anspacher

Though all afflictions are evils in themselves, yet they are good for us, because they discover to us our disease and tend to our cure.
—John Tillotson

Here is the secret of inspiration. Tell yourself that thousands and tens of thousands of people, not very intelligent and certainly no more intelligent than the rest of us, have mastered problems as difficult as those that now baffle you.
—William Feather

To support the burden, you must strive with head erect.
—Ovid

Keep up appearances whatever you do.
—Charles Dickens

When any calamity has been suffered, the first thing to be remembered, is, how much has been escaped.
—Samuel Johnson

The worst thing you can possibly do is worrying and thinking about what you could have done.
—George C. Lichtenberg

If you have had bad luck, don't lie down and let it kick you.
—David Harum

There is nothing good or bad but thinking makes it so.
—William Shakespeare

Comparison, more than reality, makes men happy or wretched.
—Thomas Fuller (II)

The circumstances of others seem good to us, while ours seem good to others.
—Publilius Syrus

People are always blaming their circumstances for what they are. I don't believe in circumstances. The people who get on in this world are the people who get up and look for the circumstances they want, and, if they can't find them, make them.
—George Bernard Shaw

Circumstances are the rulers of the weak; they are but the instruments of the wise.
—Samuel Lover

Man is not the creature of circumstances. Circumstances are the creatures of men.
—Benjamin Disraeli

Circumstances are like clouds continually gathering and bursting—while we are laughing the seed of some trouble is put into the wide arable land of events—while we are laughing it sprouts, it grows, and suddenly bears a passion fruit which we must pluck.
—John Keats

It is our relation to circumstances that determines their influence over us. The same wind that carries one vessel into port may blow another off shore.
—Christian Nestell Bovee

The wind and the waves are always on the side of the ablest navigators.
—Edward Gibbon

There is nothing in life so irrational, that good sense and chance may not set it to rights; nothing so rational, that folly and chance may not utterly confound it.
—Johann Wolfgang von Goethe

Think naught a trifle, though it small appear;
Small sands the mountain, moments make the year,
And trifles life.
—Edward Young

A grain of sand leads to the fall of a mountain when the moment has come for the mountain to fall.
—Ernest Renan

The displacement of a little sand can change occasionally the course of deep rivers.
—Manuel González Prada

Little strokes fell great oaks.
—Benjamin Franklin

It is the little bits of things that fret and worry us; we can dodge an elephant, but we can't dodge a fly.
—Josh Billings

A mere trifle consoles us, for a mere trifle distresses us.
—Blaise Pascal

Trifles make up the happiness or the misery of mortal life. The majority of men slip into their graves without having encountered on their way thither any signal catastrophe or exaltation of fortune or feeling.
—Alexander Smith

In the end, what effect your life most deeply are things too simple to talk about.
—Nell Blaine

It will generally be found that men who are constantly lamenting their ill luck are only reaping the consequences of their own

neglect, mismanagement, and improvidence, or want of application.
—Samuel Smiles

As long as we are lucky we attribute it to our smartness; our bad luck we give the gods credit for.
—Josh Billings

Prudence is a good thing; forethought is wisdom.
—Croesus

Hindsight is far more accurate than foresight.
—Kathleen Knight

Experience is the name everyone gives to their mistakes.
—Oscar Wilde

Experience is the name men give to their follies or their sorrows.
—Alfred de Musset

Experience: The wisdom that enables us to recognize as an undesirable old acquaintance the folly that we have already embraced.
—Ambrose Bierce

Experience, the only logic sure to convince a diseased imagination and restore it to rugged health.
—Mark Twain

Experience is a school where a man learns what a big fool he has been.
—Josh Billings

Every man's experience of today is that he was a fool yesterday and the day before yesterday. To-morrow he will most likely be of exactly the same opinion.
—Charles Mackay

Experience is a jewel, and it had need be so, for it is often purchased at an infinite rate.
—William Shakespeare

Experience is a hard teacher because she gives the test first, the lesson afterwards.
—Vernon Saunders Law

Each succeeding day is the scholar of that which went before it.
—Publilius Syrus

Experience is never limited, and it is never complete; it is an immense sensibility, a kind of huge spider-web of the finest silken threads suspended in the chamber of consciousness, and catching every air-borne particle in its tissue.
—Henry James

To most men, experience is like the stern lights of a ship, which illumines only the track it has passed.
—Samuel Taylor Coleridge

Experience is not what happens to a man. It is what a man does with what happens to him.
—Aldous Huxley

Men are wise in proportion, not to their experience, but to their capacity for experience.
—George Bernard Shaw

We should be careful to get out of an experience only the wisdom that is in it—and stop there; lest we be like the cat that sits down on a hot stove-lid. She will never sit down on a hot stove-lid again—and that is well; but also she will never sit down on a cold one anymore.
—Mark Twain

Our experience is composed rather of illusions lost than of wisdom gained.
—Joseph Roux

What is experience? A poor little hut constructed from the ruins of the palace of gold and marble called our illusions.
—Joseph Roux

Men heap together the mistakes of their lives, and create a monster they call Destiny.
—John Oliver Hobbes

We make our own fortunes and we call them fate.
—Benjamin Disraeli

I often feel, and ever more deeply I realize, that fate and character are the same conception.
—Novalis

What a man thinks of himself, that it is which determines, or rather indicates, his fate.
—Henry David Thoreau

Some people's lives are affected by what happens to their person or their property; but for others fate is what happens to their feelings and their thoughts—that and nothing more.
—Willa Cather

It is to be remarked that a good many people are born curiously unfitted for the fate awaiting them on this earth.
—Joseph Conrad

Many men would take the death-sentence without a whimper to escape the life-sentence which fate carries in her other hand.
—T. E. Lawrence

We are little better than straws upon the water: we may flatter ourselves that we swim, when the current carries us along.
—Lady Mary Wortley Montagu

Fate leads the willing, and drags along those who hang back.
—Seneca

When Fate wills that something should come to pass, she sends forth a million of little circumstances to clear and prepare the way.
—William Makepeace Thackeray

Whatsoe'er we perpetrate,
We do but row, we are steered by fate.
—Samuel Butler (I)

For what are men who grasp at praise sublime,
But bubbles on the rapid stream of time,
That rise, and fall, that swell, and are no more,
Born, and forgot, ten thousand an hour?
—Edward Young

Why shouldn't things be largely absurd, futile, and transitory. They are so, and we are so, and they and we go very well together.
—George Santayana

Nothing is pure and entire of a piece. All advantages are attended with disadvantages. A universal compensation prevails in all conditions of being and existence.
—David Hume

Every man in the world is better than some one else. And not as good as some one else.
—William Saroyan

We're all of us guinea pigs in the laboratory of God. Humanity is just a work in progress.
—Tennessee Williams

The whole world is a desperate joke, and to be human is an outrage. The soul man is endowed with is most cruelly abused; he is deceived, led on with untold promises. He carries within him the momentousness of his existence, a longing for eternity. And what is his fate? Fear and flight; mortal danger from first to last. That tiny, borrowed flame is forever threatened with extinction.
—Milán Füst

Of all the creatures that creep and breathe on earth there is none more wretched than man.
—Homer

Man believes himself always greater than he is, and is esteemed less than he is worth.
—Johann Wolfgang von Goethe

Description of man. Dependence, desire for independence, needs.
—Blaise Pascal

The state of man: inconstancy, boredom, anxiety.
—Blaise Pascal

We all never tell things. And we all never tell the same things. They aren't secrets. They're conditions. As much as we may all hate to admit it, I'm afraid we all live the same worlds inside.
—Scott Bradfield

We are monads, incapable of reciprocal messages, or capable only of truncated messages, false at their departure, misunderstood on their arrival.
—Primo Levi

No human creature is understood by any other human creature. At the most, from habit, patience, interest, friendship, they accept or tolerate each other.
—Hippolyte A. Taine

Everybody is a burden to other people. It is the way of life.
—Anthony Trollope

We are born into a world where alienation awaits us.
—Ronald David Laing

We enter the world alone, we leave it alone.
—James A. Froude

You come into the world alone and you go out of the world alone yet it seems to me you are more alone while living than even going and coming.
—Emily Carr

One can suffer a convulsion of one's entire nature, and, unless it makes some noise, no one notices. It's not just that we are incurious; we completely lack any sense of each other's existences,
—Elizabeth Bowen

Solitude is the profoundest fact of the human condition. Man is the only being who knows he is alone.
—Octavio Paz

Loneliness is and always has been the central and inevitable experience of every man.
—Thomas Wolfe

To be adult is to be alone.
—Jean Rostand

The whole conviction of my life now rests upon the belief that loneliness, far from being a rare and curious phenomenon, peculiar to myself and to a few other solitary men, is the central and inevitable fact of human existence.
—Thomas Wolfe

We're all of us sentenced to solitary confinement inside our own skins, for life.
—Tennessee Williams

We all come to dinner, but each has a room to himself.
—Walter Bagehot

God made everything out of the void, but the void shows through.
—Paul Valéry

Every man bears the whole stamp of the human condition.
—Michel de Montaigne

Men are born to trouble at first, and are exercised in it all their days. There is a cry at the beginning of life and a groan at the end of it.
—William D. Arnot

This world is but a thoroughfare full of woe,
And we pilgrims passing to and fro.
—Geoffrey Chaucer

The world is a great ocean, upon which we encounter more tempestuous storms than calms.
—Edgar Allan Poe

Believe everything you hear said of the world; nothing is too impossibly bad.
—Honoré de Balzac

It is a wild and miserable world!
    Thorny, and full of care,
Which every fiend can make his prey at will.
—Percy Bysshe Shelley

We must expect everything and fear everything from time and men.
—Luc de Clapiers de Vauvenargues

I hate mankind, for I think myself one of the best of them, and I know how bad I am.
—Samuel Johnson

There are times when one would like to hang the whole human race, and finish the farce.
—Mark Twain

I begin where most people end, with a full conviction of the emptiness of all sorts of ambition, and the unsatisfactory nature of all human pleasures.
—Alexander Pope

So full is the world of calamity, that every source of pleasure is polluted.
—Samuel Johnson

We must laugh before we are happy for fear of dying without laughing at all.
—Jean de La Bruyère

The world is a gambling table so arranged that all who enter the casino must play and all must lose more or less heavily in the long run, though they win occasionally by the way.
—Samuel Butler (II)

Trust not the world, for it never payeth what it promiseth.
—Saint Augustine

Ah, what a dusty answer gets the soul
When hot for certainties in this our life!
—George Meredith

We read the world wrong and say that it deceives us.
—Sir Rabindranath Tagore

One sees the past better than it was; one finds the present worse than it is; and hopes for a future happier than it will be.
—Madame d'Epinay

Every age has its troubles: everyone dislikes his own time of life.
—Ausonius

No lot is altogether happy.
—Horace

There are only two or three human stories and they go on repeating themselves as fiercely as if they never happened before.
—Willa Cather

Man is a mere character in a comedy.
—Jean de La Bruyère

The earth's a stage which God and nature do with actors fill.
—Thomas Heywood

Life furnishes the stage, and we set the scene.
—Meditations In Wall Street

The world's a stage: We act but can't rehearse.
—David McCord

Life is a stranger's sojourn, a night at an inn.
—Marcus Aurelius Antoninus

For the world, I count it not an inn, but an hospital; and a place not to live, but to die in.
—Sir Thomas Browne

Humanity is composed but of two categories, the invalids and the nurses.
—Walter Sickert

We die every day; every moment deprives us of a portion of life and advances us a step toward the grave; our whole life is only a long and painful sickness.
—Jean Baptiste Massillon

The living are the dead on a holiday.
—Maurice Maeterlinck

Old and young, we are all on our last cruise.
—Robert Louis Stevenson

The world itself is but a large prison out of which some daily are led to execution.
—Sir Walter Raleigh

The state of man is not unlike that of a fish hooked by an angler. Death allows us a little line. We flounce, and sport, and vary our situation. But when we would extend our schemes, we discover our confinement, checked and limited by a superior hand, who drags us from our element whenever he pleases.
—William Shenstone

Imagine a number of men in chains, all under sentence of death, some of whom are each day butchered in the sight of the others; those remaining see their own condition in that of their fellows, and looking at each other with grief and despair await their turn. This is an image of the human condition.
—Blaise Pascal

Life is like a beautiful and winding lane, on either side bright flowers, beautiful butterflies, and tempting fruits, which we scarcely pause to admire and taste, so eager are we to hasten to an opening which we imagine will be more beautiful still. But by degrees, as we advance, the trees grow bleak, the flowers and butterflies fail, the fruits disappear, and we find we have arrived—to reach a desert waste.
—George Augustus Sala

Every human being on this earth is born with a tragedy, and it isn't original sin. He's born with the tragedy that he has to grow up. That he has to leave the nest, the security, and go out to do battle. He has to lose everything that is lovely and fight for a new loveliness of his own making, and it's a tragedy. A lot of people don't have the courage to do it.
—Helen Hayes

Everyone must row with the oars he has.
—English Proverb

Destiny is not a matter of chance, it is a matter of choice; it is not a thing to be waited for, it is a thing to be achieved.
—William Jennings Bryan

We who lived in concentration camps can remember the men who walked through the huts comforting others, giving away their last piece of bread. They may have been few in number, but they offer sufficient proof that everything can be taken from a man but one thing: the last of human freedoms—to choose one's attitude in any given set of circumstances, to choose one's own way.
—Victor Frankl

He who chooses the beginning of a road chooses the place it leads to. It is the means that determine the end.
—Harry Emerson Fosdick

One day Alice came to a fork in the road and saw a Cheshire cat in a tree.
　"Which road do I take?" she asked.
　His response was a question: "Where do you want to go?"
　"I don't know," Alice answered.
　"Then," said the cat, "it doesn't matter."
—Lewis Carroll

When you have to make a choice and don't make it, that in itself is a choice.
—William James

Wherever we are, it is but a stage on the way to do something else, and whatever we do, however well we do it, it is only the preparation to do something else that may be different.
—Robert Louis Stevenson

Do not feel certain of anything.
—Bertrand Russell

All things human change.
—Alfred, Lord Tennyson

It is not unconscious changes made in their lives by men and women—a new job, a new town, a divorce—which really shape them, like the chapter headings in a biography, but a long, slow mutation of emotion, hidden, all-penetrative; something by which they may be so taken up that the practical outward changes of their lives in the world, noted with surprise, scandal or envy by others, pass almost unnoticed by themselves. This

gives a shifting quality to the whole surface of life; decisions made with reason and the tongue may never be made valid by the heart.
—Nadine Gordimer

People change and forget to tell each other.
—Lillian Hellman

How hard it is to escape from places. However carefully one goes they hold you—you leave little bits of yourself fluttering on the fences—little rags and shreds of your very life.
—Katherine Mansfield

Our yesterdays follow us; they constitute our life, and they give character and force and meaning to our present deeds.
—Joseph Parker

Could we know what men are most apt to remember, we might know what they are most apt to do.
—Lord Halifax

The best way to suppose what may come, is to remember what is past.
—Lord Halifax

Memory is the diary we all carry about with us.
—Oscar Wilde

Recollection is the only paradise from which we cannot be turned out.
—Jean Paul Richter

The music in my heart I bore
Long after it was heard no more.
—William Wordsworth

Pleasure is the flower that fades; remembrance is the lasting perfume.
—Marquis de Boufflers

How cruelly sweet are the echoes that start
When memory plays an old tune on the heart.
—Eliza Cook

Everybody needs his memories. They keep the wolf of insignificance from the door.
—Saul Bellow

I suspect that it is not without significance that the word remembering can be formed as *re-membering*. By its very nature the act of remembering is to offer a thing of patches, to try to put together again a once seamless garment of events totally and immediately experienced but now tattered by time.
—Herbert O'Driscoll

The memory represents to us not what we choose but what it pleases.
—Michel de Montaigne

The charm, one might say the genius, of memory is that it is choosy, chancy and temperamental; it rejects the edifying cathedral and indelibly photographs the small boy outside chewing a hunk of melon in the dust.
—Elizabeth Bowen

Memory is a net; one finds it full of fish when he takes it from the brook; but a dozen miles of water have run through it without sticking.
—Oliver Wendell Holmes, Sr.

Our memories are card indexes consulted, and then put back in disorder by authorities whom we do not control.
—Cyril Connolly

We find a little of everything in our memory; it is a kind of pharmacy or chemical laboratory in which chance guides our hand now to a calming drug and now to a dangerous poison.
—Marcel Proust

Memory seldom fails when its first office is to show us the tombs of our buried hopes.
—Countess of Blessington

Joy's recollection is no longer joy, while sorrow's memory is sorrow still.
—Lord Byron

Obligations, hatreds, injuries—What did I expect memories to be? And I was forgetting remorse. I have a complete past now.
—Jean Anouilh

What beastly incidents our memories insist on cherishing! . . . the ugly and disgusting . . . the beautiful things we have to keep in diaries to remember!
—Eugene O'Neill

Memory is a capricious and arbitrary creature. You never can tell what pebble she will pick up from the shore of life to keep among her treasures, or what inconspicuous flower of the field she will preserve as the symbol of "thoughts that do often lie too deep for tears." . . . And yet I do not doubt that the most important things are always the best remembered.
—Henry Van Dyke

The things we remember best are those better forgotten.
—Baltasar Grácian

Nothing fixes a thing so intensely in the memory as the wish to forget it.
—Michel de Montaigne

To want to forget something is to think of it.
—French Proverb

A retentive memory may be a good thing, but the ability to forget is the true token of greatness.
—Elbert Hubbard

Sometimes what we call "memory" and what we call "imagination" are not so easily distinguished.
—Leslie Marmon Silko

Nostalgia is a seductive liar.
—George Ball

It isn't so astonishing, the number of things I can remember, as the number of things I can remember that aren't so.
—Mark Twain

Memories are like stones, time and distance erode them like acid.
—Ugo Betti

That memory is the book of judgment, from some opium experiences of mine, I can believe. I have, indeed, seen the same thing asserted in modern books, and accompanied by a remark which I am convinced is true, mainly: that the dread book of account, which the Scriptures speak of is, in fact, the mind itself of each individual. Of this, at least, I feel assured—that there is no such thing as forgetting possible to the mind; a thousand incidents may and will interpose a veil between our present consciousness and the secret inscriptions on the mind; accidents of the same sort will rend away this veil; but whether veiled or unveiled, the inscription remains forever; just as the stars seem to withdraw before the common light of day; whereas, in fact, we all know that it is the light which is drawn over them as a veil, and that they are waiting to be revealed, when the obscuring daylight shall have withdrawn.
—Thomas De Quincey

Of one power even God is deprived, and that is the power of making what is past never to have been.
—Agathon

Each has his past shut in him like the leaves of a book known to him by heart and his friends can only read the title.
—Virginia Woolf

Keep off your thoughts of things that are past and done
For thinking of the past wakes regret and pain.
—Arthur Waley

If everybody remembered the past, nobody would ever forgive anybody.
—Robert Lynd

Time cures sorrows and squabbles because we all change, and are no longer the same persons. Neither the offender nor the offended is the same.
—Blaise Pascal

The years teach much which the days never knew.
—Ralph Waldo Emerson

If we could have a little patience, we should escape much mortification; time takes away as much as it gives.
—Madam Marie de Sévigné

God has commanded time to console the unhappy.
—Joseph Joubert

The powers of Time as a comforter can hardly be overstated; but the agency by which he works is exhaustion.
—Letitia Landon

There is nothing that time does not either soothe or conquer.
—Publilius Syrus

Wherever anything lives, there is, open somewhere, a register in which time is being inscribed.
—Henri Bergson

In theory, one is aware that the earth revolves, but in practice one does not perceive it; the ground upon which one treads seems not to move, and one can live undisturbed. So it is with time in one's life.
—Marcel Proust

Time is a river, the resistless flow of all created things. One thing no sooner comes in sight than it is hurried past and another is borne along, only to be swept away in its turn.
—Marcus Aurelius Antoninus

You cannot step twice into the same stream. For as you are stepping in, other and yet other waters flow on.
—Heraclitus

Time bears away all things, even the mind.
—Virgil

There are few things which time does not distort; many which it removes.
—Varro

Many are always praising the by-gone time, for it is natural that the old should extol the days of their youth; the weak, the time of their strength; the sick, the season of their vigor; and the disappointed, the spring-tide of their hopes.
—Caleb Bingham

Th' past always looks betther thin it was. It's only pleasant because it isn't here.
—Finley Peter Dunne

What was hard to endure is sweet to recall.
—Continental Proverb

It is sadder to find the past again and to find it inadequate to the present than it is to have it elude you and remain forever a harmonious conception of memory.
—F. Scott Fitzgerald

The past is the region of sobs. The future is the realm of song.
—Oscar Wilde

Present: The part of eternity dividing the domain of disappointment from the realm of hope.
—Ambrose Bierce

Future: that period of time in which our affairs prosper, our friends are true and our happiness is assured.
—Ambrose Bierce

We are never present with, but always beyond ourselves. Fear, desire, and hope are still pushing us on towards the future.
—Michel de Montaigne

Let each of us examine his thoughts; he will find them wholly concerned with the past or the future. We almost never think of the present, and if we do think of it, it is only to see what light it throws on our plans for the future. The present is never our end. The past and present are our means, the future alone our end. Thus we never actually live, but hope to live, and since we are always planning how to be happy, it is inevitable that we should never be so.
—Blaise Pascal

We all think we can choose when a choice comes, but our choice is really made not at the moment, but by our life hitherto. You choose according to that which you have chosen a hundred times before: Your destiny is not that which you will do, but that which you have done. Your future lies behind you, in your past.
—Edward Frederick Benson

I believe
the future is only the past again,
entered through another gate.
—Arthur Wing Pinero

Man to the last is but a froward child;
So eager for the future, come what may,
And to the present so insensible.
—Samuel Rogers

The habit of looking to the future and thinking that the whole meaning of the present lies in what it will bring forth is a precious one. There can be no value in the whole unless there is value in the parts.
—Bertrand Russell

The future is purchased by the present.
—Samuel Johnson

Much may be done in those little shreds and patches of time, which every day produces, and which most men throw away, but which nevertheless will make at the end of it no small deduction from the life of man.
—Charles Caleb Colton

Time is at once the most valuable and the most perishable of all our possessions.
—John Randolph

Dost thou love life? Then do not squander time, for that is the stuff life is made of.
—Benjamin Franklin

You will never "find" time for anything. If you want time you must make it.
—Charles Buxton

Nought treads so silent as the foot of time.
—Edward Young

Ah! the clock is always slow;
It is later than you think.
—Robert W. Service

There are two golden days in the week upon which and about which I never worry. . . . One of these days is yesterday. Yesterday with all its cares and frets, with all . . . its mistakes and blunders has passed forever beyond the reach of my recall . . . . And the other day I do not worry about is tomorrow. Tomorrow with all its possible adversities, . . . its failures and mistakes, is as far beyond the reach of my mastery as is its dead sister yesterday.
—Robert J. Burdette

We can easily manage, if we will only take, each day, the burden appointed for it. But the load will be too heavy for us if we carry yesterday's burden over again to-day, and then add the burden of the morrow to the weight before we are required to carry it.
—John Newton

God will not suffer man to have a knowledge of things to come; for if he had prescience of his prosperity, he would be careless; and if understanding of his adversity, he would be despairing and senseless.
—Saint Augustine

   The best
Thing we can do is to make wherever we're lost in
look as much like home as we can.
—Christopher Fry

Cease to ask what the morrow will bring forth, and set down as gain each day that Fortune grants.
—Horace

Enjoy the blessings of the day if God sends them: and the evils bear patiently and sweetly; for this day only is ours: we are dead to yesterday, and not born to tomorrow.
—Jeremy Taylor

Never let the future disturb you. You will meet it, if you have to, with the same weapons of reason which today arm you against the present.
—Marcus Aurelius Antoninus

Don't let what happened yesterday inhibit what is happening today or will happen tomorrow. It's ancient history, and nothing you can do will change it. Stick to the present and the future; look to the past only when you can do it rationally and objectively as a way to improve on the other two. . . . The bottom line: Keep your eyes on the road, and use your rearview mirror only to avoid trouble.
—Daniel Meacham

Do not look where you fell, but where you slipped.
—African Proverb

No matter how far you have gone on a wrong road, turn back.
—Turkish Proverb

We know what we are, but not what we may be.
—William Shakespeare

PART 16

LIFE

All the world's a stage,
And all the men and women merely players.
They have their exits and their entrances,
And one man in his time plays many parts. . . .
—William Shakespeare

Such Is Life

O God, thy sea is so great, and my boat is so small.
—Author Unknown

We sail within a vast sphere, ever drifting in uncertainty, driven from end to end.
—Blaise Pascal

To every man his own life is a mystery.
—Latin Proverb

Very few live by choice. Every man is placed in his present condition by causes which acted without his foresight, and with which he did not always willingly cooperate; and therefore you will rarely meet one who does not think the lot of his neighbor better than his own.
—Samuel Johnson

The retrospect of life swarms with lost opportunities.
—Sir Henry Taylor

Real life is, to most men, a long second-best, a perpetual compromise between the ideal and the possible.
—Bertrand Russell

   There comes
For ever something between us and what
We deem our happiness.
—Lord Byron

Man is never happy, but spends his whole life in striving after something which he thinks will make him so; he seldom attains his goal, and when he does, it is only to be disappointed; he is mostly shipwrecked in the end, and comes into harbor with masts and rigging gone.
—Arthur Schopenhauer

None of us can help the things life has done to us. They're done before you realize it, and once they're done they make you do other things until at last everything comes between you and what you'd like to be, and you have lost your true self forever.
—Eugene O'Neill

Life is a very sad piece of buffoonery, because we have . . . the need to fool ourselves continuously by the spontaneous creation of a reality (one for each and never the same for everyone) which, from time to time, reveals itself to be vain and illusory.
—Luigi Pirandello

We live, not as we wish to, but as we can.
—Menander of Athens

Life carries us places, like rivers and winds carry things, often against our own will.
—Scott Bradfield

Life is a continued struggle to be what we are not, and to do what we cannot.
—William Hazlitt

The life of every man is a diary in which he means to write one story, and writes another; and his humblest hour is when he compares the volume as it is with what he hoped to make it.
—Sir James Matthew Barrie

Everything that happens to us leaves some trace behind; everything contributes imperceptibly to make us what we are.
—Johann Wolfgang von Goethe

Life is a long lesson in humility.
—Sir James Matthew Barrie

We spend our years as a tale that is told.
—Psalms

Youth is a blunder; manhood a struggle; old age a regret.
—Benjamin Disraeli

Man spends his life in reasoning on the past, in complaining of the present, in fearing for the future.
—Antoine Rivarol

We are born crying, live complaining, and die disappointed.
—Thomas Fuller (II)

Life is the garment we continually alter, but which never seems to fit.
—David McCord

Life is the continuous adjustment of internal relations to external relations.
—Herbert Spencer

The art of life lies in a constant readjustment to our surroundings.
—Okakura Kakuzo

Life is for most of us a continuous process of getting used to things we hadn't expected.
—Author Unknown

Life is just one damn thing after another.
—Elbert Hubbard

It is not true that life is one damned thing after another—it is one damn thing over and over.
—Edna St. Vincent Millay

Life is a constant oscillation between the sharp horns of a dilemma.
—H. L. Mencken

Life is not a spectacle or a feast; it is a predicament.
—George Santayana

Life is the art of drawing sufficient conclusions from insufficient premises.
—Samuel Butler (II)

Life is like playing a violin in public and learning the instrument as one goes along.
—Samuel Butler (II)

The hardest thing to learn in life is which bridge to cross and which to burn.
—Bertrand Russell

Life is a crowded superhighway with bewildering cloverleaf exits on which a man is liable to find himself speeding back in the direction he came from.
—Peter De Vries

Life must be lived forwards, but can only be understood backwards.
—Sören Kierkegaard

Every man is his own ancestor, and every man is his own heir. He devises his own future, and he inherits his own past.
—Frederick Henry Hedge

Life is a battle and a sojourning in a strange land.
—Marcus Aurelius Antoninus

The art of living is more like that of wrestling than of dancing; the main thing is to stand firm and be ready for an unforeseen attack.
—Marcus Aurelius Antoninus

A man's life is like a house on fire—it flares up, it blazes fearsomely, and then it comes crashing down.
—Milán Füst

Most people's lives—what are they but trails of debris, long trails of debris with nothing to clean it all up but, finally, death?
—Tennessee Williams

What are the facts? Not those in Homer, Shakespeare, or even the Bible. The facts for most of us are a dark street, crowds, hurry, commonplaceness, loneliness, and, worse than all, a terrible doubt which can hardly be named as to the meaning and purpose of the world.
—Samuel Rutherford

This business of petty inconvenience and indignity, of being kept waiting about, of having to do everything at other people's convenience, is inherent in working-class life. A thousand influences constantly press a working man into a *passive* role. He does not act, he is acted upon.
—George Orwell

Human life is nothing but a perpetual illusion; there is nothing but mutual deception and flattery. No one talks about us in our presence as he would in our absence. Human relations are only based on this mutual deception; and few friendships would survive if everyone knew what his friend said about him behind his back.
—Blaise Pascal

That's what it was to be alive. To move about in a cloud of ignorance; to go up and down trampling on the feelings of those about you. To spend and waste time as though you had a million years. To be always at the mercy of one self-centered passion, or another.
—Thornton Wilder

No man lives without jostling and being jostled; in all ways he has to elbow himself through the world, giving and receiving offence.
—Thomas Carlyle

Life is an adventure in forgiveness.
—Norman Cousins

The art of life is to know how to enjoy a little and to endure much.
—William Hazlitt

Life is a journey, not a home; a road, not a city of habitation; and the enjoyments and blessings we have are but little inns on the roadside of life, where we may be refreshed for a moment, that we may with new strength press on to the end.
—Author Unknown

Life, alas, is one long test of endurance.
—Milán Füst

Life is a series of relapses and recoveries.
—George Ade

Life is a disease; and the difference between one man and another is the stage of the disease at which he lives.
—George Bernard Shaw

Life is a hospital in which every patient is possessed by the desire of changing his bed. One would prefer to suffer near the fire, and another is certain he would get well if he were by the window.
—Charles Baudelaire

We do not know either unalloyed happiness or unmitigated misfortune. Everything in this world is a tangled yarn; we taste nothing in its purity; we do not remain two moments in the same state. Our affections as well as bodies, are in perpetual flux.
—Jean Jacques Rousseau

A little vanity and a little pleasure make up the lives of most men and women.
—Joseph Joubert

There is pleasure enough in this life to make us wish to live, and pain enough to reconcile us to death when we can live no longer.
—Author Unknown

My notions about life are much the same as they are about traveling; there is a good deal of amusement on the road, but, after all, one wants to be at rest.
—Robert Southey

Life often seems like a long shipwreck, of which the debris are friendship, glory, and love; the shores of existence are strewn with them.
—Madame Germaine de Staël

A moral character is attached to autumnal scenes. The flowers fading like our hopes, the leaves falling like our years, the clouds fleeting like our illusions, the light diminishing like our intelligence, the sun growing colder like our affections, the rivers becoming frozen like our lives—all bear secret relations to our destinies.
—François de Chateaubriand

Nature! We are surrounded by her and locked in her clasp: powerless to leave her, and powerless to come closer to her. Without asking us or warning us she takes us into the whirl of her dance, and hurries on with us until we are weary and fall from her arms.
—Johann Wolfgang von Goethe

Life is one long process of getting tired.
—Samuel Butler (II)

Life for most of us is full of steep stairs to go puffing up and, later, of shaky stairs to totter down; and very early in the history of stairs must have come the invention of banisters.
—Louis Kronenberger

You fall out of your mother's womb, you crawl across open country under fire, and drop into your grave.
—Quentin Crisp

Life is one long struggle in the dark.
—Lucretius

Life is half spent, before we know what it is.
—George Herbert

Life is a foreign language: all men mispronounce it.
—Christopher Morley

Such Is Life

The uttered part of a man's life bears to the unuttered, unconscious part a small unknown proportion. He himself never knows it, much less do others.
—Thomas Carlyle

Life is constantly weighing us in very sensitive scales, and telling every one of us precisely what his real weight is to the last grain of dust.
—James Russell Lowell

Life does not consist mainly—or even largely—of facts and happenings. It consists mainly of the storm of thoughts that is forever blowing through one's head.
—Mark Twain

Life consists in what a man is thinking of all day.
—Ralph Waldo Emerson

Our life is what our thoughts make of it.
—Marcus Aurelius Antoninus

I have always disliked myself at any given moment; the total of such moments is my life.
—Cyril Connolly

Life is for each man a solitary cell whose walls are mirrors.
—Eugene O'Neill

Life is full of internal dramas, instantaneous and sensational, played to an audience of one.
—Anthony Powell

Life is a tragedy wherein we sit as spectators for a while and then act our part in it.
—Jonathan Swift

What a fine comedy this would be if one did not play a part in it!
—Denis Diderot

Life is a tragedy for those who feel, and a comedy for those who think.
—Jean de La Bruyère

378

Life is a tragedy when seen in close-up, but a comedy in long-shot.
—Sir Charles Chaplin

There was never yet an uninteresting life. Such a thing is an impossibility. Inside of the dullest exterior there is a drama, a comedy, a tragedy.
—Mark Twain

There has rarely passed a life of which a judicious and faithful narrative would not be useful.
—Samuel Johnson

Pythagoras used to say life resembles the Olympic Games; a few men strive their muscles to carry off a prize; others bring trinkets to sell to the crowd for a profit; and some there are who seek no further advantage than to look at the show and see how and why everything is done. They are spectators of other men's lives in order better to judge and manage their own.
—Michel de Montaigne

Our lives are waves that come up out of the ocean of eternity, break upon the beach of earth, and lapse back to the ocean of eternity. Some are sunlit, some run in storm and rain; one is a quiet ripple, another is a thunderous breaker; and once in many centuries comes a great tidal wave that sweeps over continents; but all go back to the sea and lie equally level there.
—Austin O'Malley

The sum of things is ever being renewed, and mortals live dependent one upon another. Some nations increase, others diminish, and in a short space the generations of living creatures are changed and like runners pass on the torch of life.
—Lucretius

Human life may be likened to the flowers on yonder tree. The wind blows down the flowers, of which some are caught by the screens and scattered on the beautifully decorated mats and cushions, while others are blown over the fence and dropped on the dump heap.
—Fan Chen

Life is an onion and one peels it crying.
—French Proverb

What is your life more than a short day in which the sun hardly rises before it is lost in the utter darkness of the cold night?
—Andres Fernandes de Andrada

One life; a little gleam of time between two eternities; no second chance for us forever more.
—Thomas Carlyle

Brief and powerless is man's life; on him and all his race the slow, sure doom falls pitiless and dark.
—Bertrand Russell

Life is terribly deficient in form. Its catastrophes happen in a wrong way and to the wrong people. There is a grotesque horror about its comedies, and its tragedies seem to culminate in farce.
—Oscar Wilde

What is life but a series of uninspired follies?
—George Bernard Shaw

Nothing can exceed the vanity of our existence, but the folly of our pursuits. We wept when we came into the world, and every day tells us why.
—Oliver Goldsmith

We live, as we dream—alone.
—Joseph Conrad

Life is perhaps most wisely regarded as a bad dream between two awakenings, and every day is a life in miniature.
—Eugene O'Neill

Life is a dream, but somewhat less changeable.
—Blaise Pascal

We sleep, but the loom of life never stops; and the pattern which was weaving when the sun went down is weaving when it comes up to-morrow.
—Henry Ward Beecher

Each day is a little life; every waking and rising a little birth, every fresh morning a little youth, every going to rest and sleep a little death.
—Arthur Schopenhauer

There is no cure for birth and death save to enjoy the interval.
—George Santayana

Life in itself is neither good nor evil, it is the scene of good or evil, as you make it.
—Michel de Montaigne

He who asks of life nothing but the improvement of his own nature is less liable than anyone else to miss and waste life.
—Henry Frédéric Amiel

Life consists not in holding good cards but in playing those you do hold well.
—Josh Billings

Life is like a game of Whist. I don't enjoy the game much: but I like to play my cards well, and see what will be the end of it.
—George Eliot

There are many people who reach their conclusions about life like schoolboys; they cheat their master by copying the answer out of a book without having worked out the sum for themselves.
—Sören Kierkegaard

Each man must look to himself to teach him the meaning of life. It is not something discovered: it is something molded.
—Antoine de Saint-Exupéry

Life is a process of becoming, a combination of states we have to go through. Where people fail is that they wish to elect a state and remain in it. This is a kind of death.
—Anaïs Nin

The ultimate value of life depends upon awareness, and the power of contemplation rather than upon mere survival.
—Aristotle

Life is not long, and too much of it must not pass in idle deliberation how it shall be spent.
—Samuel Johnson

We must live as we think, otherwise we shall end up by thinking as we have lived.
—Paul Bourget

Life is the soul's nursery—its training place for the destinies of eternity.
—William Makepeace Thackeray

Life is the childhood of our immortality.
—Johann Wolfgang von Goethe

We are involved in a life that passes understanding and our highest business is our daily life.
—John Cage

We do all stand in the front ranks of the battle every moment of our lives; where there is a brave man there is the thickest of the fight, there the post of honor.
—Henry David Thoreau

Life shrinks or expands in proportion to one's courage.
—Anaïs Nin

However mean your life is, meet it and live it; do not shun it and call it hard names. It is not so bad as you are.
—Henry David Thoreau

All of the animals, excepting man, know that the principle business of life is to enjoy it.
—Samuel Butler (II)

Life is a play! 'Tis not its length, but its performance that counts.
—Seneca

The web of your life is of a mingled yarn, good and ill together.
—William Shakespeare

Do not take life too seriously; you will never get out of it alive.
—Elbert Hubbard

Nothing happens to you that hasn't happened to somebody else.
—William Feather

Remember this,—that very little is needed to make a happy life.
—Marcus Aurelius Antoninus

The best use of life is to spend it for something that outlasts life.
—William James

If we really want to live, we'd better
    start at once to try;
If we don't it doesn't matter, we'd better
    start to die.
—W. H. Auden

Life cannot wait until the sciences have explained the universe scientifically. We cannot put off living until we are ready. The most salient characteristic of life is its coerciveness: it is always urgent, "here and now" without any possible postponement. Life is fired at us point blank.
—Jose Ortega Y Gasset

Defer not joys thou mayest not win from fate:
    Judge only what is past to be thine own.
Cares with a linked chain of sorrow wait.
    Mirth tarries not; but soon on wing is flown.
With both hands hold it—clasped in full embrace,

Still from thy breast it oft will glide away!
To say "I mean to live" is follies place:
    Tomorrow's life comes late: live, then, today.
—Martial

Begin at once to live, and count each separate day as a separate life.
—Seneca

Life itself is a party; you join after it's started and you leave before it's finished.
—Elsa Maxwell

Drink and sing, an inch before us is black night.
—Japanese Proverb

PART 17

OLD AGE

To know how to grow old is
the master-work of wisdom,
and one of the most difficult chapters
in the great art of living.
—Henry Frédéric Amiel

Such Is Life

The wine of life keeps oozing drop by drop,
The leaves of life keep falling one by one.
—Omar Khayyám

Soon you will have forgotten the world, and the world will have forgotten you.
—Marcus Aurelius Antoninus

It is time to be old,
To take in sail.
—Ralph Waldo Emerson

A single breaker may recede; but the tide is evidently coming in.
—Thomas B. Macaulay

Age, with stealing steps, hath clawed me.
—William S. W. Vaux

Sixty is not a bad age—unless in perspective, when no doubt it is contemplated by the majority of us with mixed feelings. It is a calm age; the game is practically over by then; and standing aside one begins to remember with a certain vividness what a fine fellow one used to be. I have observed that, by an amiable attention of providence, most people at sixty begin to take a romantic view of themselves. Their very failures exhale a charm of peculiar potency. And indeed the hopes of the future are a fine company to live with, exquisite forms, fascinating if you like, but—so to speak—naked, stripped for a run. The robes of glamour

are luckily the property of the immovable past which, without them, would sit, a shivery sort of thing, under the gathering shadows.
—Joseph Conrad

There never has been an intelligent person of the age of sixty who would consent to live his life over again. His or anyone else's.
—Mark Twain

I walk in the garden, I look at the flowers and shrubs and trees and discover in them an exquisiteness of contour, a vitality of edge or a vigor of spring as well as an infinite variety of color that no artifact I have seen in the last sixty years can rival. . . . Each day, as I look, I wonder where my eyes were yesterday.
—Bernard Berenson

You must keep busy. Continue working if you can, or develop an interest that you can pursue as though it were a livelihood. Too many people look on retirement as a permanent vacation. They find that the vacation ends after a few weeks or months, leaving an empty future. Activity is the only antidote.
—B. F. Skinner

It is better to wear out than to rust out.
—Bishop Richard Cumberland

Age seldom arrives smoothly or quickly. It's more often a succession of jolts.
—Jean Rhys

Growing old is not a gradual decline, but a series of drops, full of sorrow, from one ledge to another below it.
—Logan Pearsall Smith

For years I wanted to be older, and now I am.
—Margaret Atwood

Age and wedlock we all desire and repent of.
—Thomas Fuller (II)

We hope to grow old, and yet we dread old age.
—Jean de La Bruyère

Old age is the most unexpected of all the things that can happen to a man.
—Leon Trotsky

A person is always startled when he hears himself seriously called an old man for the first time.
—Oliver Wendell Holmes, Jr.

Man resembles the fruit of the tree, which, though it escape injury during its growth, yet must decay at maturity.
—Salomon Ibn Gabirol

I wasted time, and now time doth waste me.
—William Shakespeare

Age is not all decay; it is the ripening, the swelling, of the fresh life within, that withers and bursts the husk.
—George MacDonald

Old age has a great sense of calm and freedom. When the passions have relaxed their holds, you have escaped not from one master but from many.
—Plato

All the passions are extinguished with old age.
—François Marie de Voltaire

Old age is a tyrant who forbids at the penalty of death all the pleasures of youth.
—François de La Rochefoucauld

After a man passes sixty, his mischief is mainly in his head.
—Edgar Watson Howe

Is it not strange that desire should so many years outlive performance?
—William Shakespeare

The old man, especially if he is in society, in the privacy of his thoughts, though he may protest the opposite, never stops believing that, through some irregular exception of the universal rule, he can in some unknown and inexplicable way still make an impression on women.
—Giacomo Leopardi

The passions of the young are the vices in the old.
—Joseph Joubert

Age—that period of life in which we compound for the vices that we still cherish by reviling those that we no longer have the enterprise to commit.
—Ambrose Bierce

The more the pleasures of the body fade away, the greater to me is the pleasure and charm of conversation.
—Plato

Old men delight in giving good advice as a consolation for the fact that they can no longer set bad examples.
—François de La Rochefoucauld

There is a wicked inclination in most people to suppose an old man decayed in his intellect. If a young or middle-aged man, when leaving a company, does not recollect where he laid his hat, it is nothing; but if the same inattention is discovered in an old man, people will shrug up their shoulders and say, "His memory is going."
—Samuel Johnson

When the ox stumbles, all whet their knives.
—Yiddish Proverb

The young man is deliberately odd and prides himself on it; the old man is unintentionally so, and it mortifies him.
—Jean Paul Richter

Youth, which is forgiven everything, forgives itself nothing: age, which forgives itself everything, is forgiven nothing.
—George Bernard Shaw

All sorts of allowances are made for the illusions of youth; and none, or almost none, for the disenchantments of age.
—Robert Louis Stevenson

If youth knew what to do, and age could do what it knows, no man would ever be poore.
—Randle Cotgrave

A young boy is a theory, an old man is a fact.
—Edgar Watson Howe

We must not take the faults of our youth into our old age, for old age brings with it its own defects.
—Johann Wolfgang von Goethe

The blemishes of the mind, like those of the face, increase by age.
—François de La Rochefoucauld

My experience is that as soon as people are old enough to know better, they don't know anything at all.
—Oscar Wilde

Age imprints more wrinkles in the mind than it does on the face.
—Michel de Montaigne

As one grows older, one becomes wiser and more foolish.
—François de La Rochefoucauld

The older I grow the more I distrust the familiar doctrine that age brings wisdom.
—H. L. Mencken

People always fancy that we must become old to become wise; but, in truth, as years advance, it is hard to keep ourselves as wise as we were.
—Johann Wolfgang von Goethe

It is a man's own fault, it is from want of use, if his mind grows torpid in old age.
—Samuel Johnson

The evening of life brings with it its lamp.
—Joseph Joubert

When I was younger I could remember anything, whether it happened or not, but I am getting old and soon I shall remember only the latter.
—Mark Twain

We are never done with thinking about our parents, I suppose, and come to know them better long after they are dead than we ever did when they were alive.
—May Sarton

No matter how old a mother is, she watches her middle-aged children for signs of improvement.
—Florida Scott-Maxwell

She never outgrows the burden of love, and to the end she carries the weight of hope for those she bore. Oddly, very oddly, she is forever surprised and even faintly wronged that her sons and daughters are just people, for many mothers hope and even expect that their newborn child will make the world better, will somehow be a redeemer. Perhaps they are right, and they can believe that the rare quality they glimpsed in the child is active in the adult.
—Florida Scott-Maxwell

An old man loved is winter with flowers.
—German Proverb

A woman is as old as she looks to a man that likes to look at her.
—Finley Peter Dunne

Man is old when he begins to hide his age; woman, when she begins to tell hers.
—Author Unknown

The woman who tells her age is either too young to have anything to lose or too old to have anything to gain.
—Chinese Proverb

Beauty and ugliness disappear equally under the wrinkles of age; one is lost in them, the other hidden.
—Jean-Antoine Petit-Senn

To keep the heart unwrinkled, to be hopeful, cheerful, reverent— that is to triumph over old age.
—Thomas Bailey Aldrich

Age does not depend upon years, but upon temperament and health. Some men are born old, and some never grow so.
—Tryon Edwards

Age . . . is a matter of feeling, not of years.
—George William Curtis

When we are out of sympathy with the young, then I think our work in this world is over.
—George MacDonald

The quarrels of friends in the latter part of life are never truly reconciled.
—William Shenstone

Very soon you will be dead; but even yet you are not single-minded, nor above disquiet; not yet unapprehensive of harm from without; not yet charitable to all men, nor persuaded that to do justly is the only wisdom.
—Marcus Aurelius Antoninus

Our wishes lengthen as our sun declines.
—Edward Young

As we grow old we slowly come to believe that everything will turn out badly for us, and that failure is in the nature of things; but then we do not much mind what happens to us one way or the other.
—Isak Dinesen

I used to dread getting older because I thought I would not be able to do all the things I wanted to do, but now that I am older I find that I don't want to do them.
—Nancy Astor

No snow falls lighter than the snow of age; but none lies heavier, for it never melts.
—Author Unknown

All the best sands of my life are somehow getting into the wrong end of the hourglass. If I could only reverse it! Were it in my power to do so, would I?
—Thomas Bailey Aldrich

Old age is like flying a plane through a storm. Once you're aboard, there's nothing you can do.
—Golda Meir

It is not the end of joy that makes old age sad, but the end of hope.
—Jean Paul Richter

Age and sorrow have the gift of reading the future by the sad past.
—Frederick William Farrar

We look back on our life as a thing of broken pieces, because our mistakes and failures are always the first to strike us, and outweigh in our imagination what we have accomplished and attained.
—Johann Wolfgang von Goethe

I remember my youth and the feeling that will never come back anymore—the feeling that I could last forever, outlast the sea, the earth, and all men; the deceitful feeling that lures us on to perils, to love, to vain effort—to death; the triumphant conviction of strength, the heat of life in the handful of dust, that glow in the heart that with every year grows dim, grows cold, grows small, and expires—and expires, too soon, too soon—before life itself.
—Joseph Conrad

We must tooth and nail retain the use of this life's pleasures, which our years snatch from us one after another.
—Michel de Montaigne

The passing years steal from us one thing after another. They have stripped me of mirth, love, feasting, play.
—Horace

We do not die wholly at our deaths: we have moldered away gradually long before. Faculty after faculty, interest after interest, attachment after attachment disappear: we are torn from ourselves while living.
—William Hazlitt

The damps of autumn sink into the leaves and prepare them for the necessity of their fall; and thus insensibly are we, as years close around us, detached from our tenacity of life by the gentle pressure of recorded sorrow.
—Walter Savage Landor

The troubles of age were intended . . . to wean us gradually from our fondness for life the nearer we approach to the end.
—Jonathan Swift

Old age brings along with its uglinesses the comfort that you will soon be out of it,—which ought to be substantial relief to such discontented pendulums as we are. To be out of the war, out of debt, out of the drouth, out of the blues, out of the dentist's hands, out of the second thoughts, mortifications, and remorses that inflict such twinges and shooting pains,—out of the next

winter, and the high prices, and company below your ambitions,—surely these are soothing hints.
—Ralph Waldo Emerson

An old man will either make the best of the fact that he is what he is, a lamentable wreck of his former self, or he won't. But what should he do if he doesn't make the best of it? There remains nothing but to pretend not to be what he is. There remains nothing but to create, by means of a difficult pretense, everything that he no longer is, that has been lost: to invent, create, and demonstrate his gaiety, vitality, and friendliness; to evoke his youthful self and to try to merge with it and have it replace what he has become.
—Milan Kundera

When you are forty, half of you belongs to the past. . . . And when you are seventy, nearly all of you.
—Jean Anouilh

Threescore years and ten is enough; if a man can't suffer all the misery he wants in that time, he must be numb.
—Josh Billings

To be seventy years old is like climbing the Alps. You reach a snow-crowned summit, and you see behind you the deep valley stretching miles and miles away, and before you other summits higher and whiter, which you may have the strength to climb, or may not. Then you sit down and meditate and wonder which it will be.
—Henry Wadsworth Longfellow

Being over seventy is like being engaged in a war. All our friends are going or gone and we survive amongst the dead and dying as on a battlefield.
—Muriel Spark

All of us, as the years slip by, face increasingly the problem of living with the abiding subtractions of death. These create gaps which cannot be filled and leave us suddenly lonely in the midst of crowds.
—John Mason Brown

The surest sign of age is loneliness.
—Amos Bronson Alcott

What is the worst of woes that wait on age?
What stamps the wrinkle deeper on the brow?
To view each loved one blotted from Life's page,
And be alone on earth, as I am now.
—Lord Byron

When death consents to let us live a long time, it takes successively as hostages all those we loved.
—Ninon de Lenclos

Old age is an island surrounded by death.
—Juan Montalvo

Two or three have died in the last two twelve months, and so many parts of me have been numbed. One sees a picture, reads an anecdote, starts a casual fancy, and thinks to tell of it to this person in preference to every other—the person is gone whom it would have peculiarly suited. It won't do for another. Every departure destroys a class of sympathies.
—Charles Lamb

The deep pain that is felt at the death of every friendly soul arises from the feeling that there is in every individual something which is inexpressible, peculiar to him alone, and is, therefore, absolutely and *irretrievably* lost.
—Arthur Schopenhauer

The loss of a beloved deserving friend is the hardest trial of philosophy.
—Lady Mary Wortley Montagu

We never know the true value of friends. While they live we are too sensitive to their faults: when we have lost them we only see their virtues.
—Augustus and Julius Hare

When a friend is carried to his grave, we at once find excuses for every weakness, and palliations of every fault; we recollect a thousand endearments which before glided off our minds without impression, a thousand favours unrepaid, a thousand duties unperformed, and wish, vainly wish, for his return, not so much that we may receive as that we may bestow happiness, and recompense that kindness which before we never understood.

There is not, perhaps, to a mind well instructed, a more painful occurrence than the death of one whom we have injured without reparation. Our crime seems now irretrievable; it is indelibly recorded, and the stamp of fate is fixed upon it. We consider, with the most afflictive anguish, the pain which we have given and now cannot alleviate, and the losses which we have caused and now cannot repair.
—Samuel Johnson

Old memories are so empty when they cannot be shared.
—Jewelle Gomez

Nothing so reconciles us to the thought of our own death, as the prospect of one friend after another dropping around us.
—Seneca

One dies as often as one loses loved ones.
—Publilius Syrus

Since Penelope Noakes of Duppas Hill is gone, there is no one who will ever call me Nellie again.
—An Old Lady

The most I ever did for you was to outlive you.
But that is much.
—Edna St. Vincent Millay

Our trials grow with our years.
—Johann Wolfgang von Goethe

One evil in old age is that, as your time is come, you think every little illness is the beginning of the end. When a man expects to be arrested, every knock at the door is an alarm.
—Sydney Smith

It would be well if old age diminished our perceptibilities to pain in the proportion that it does our sensibilities to pleasure; and if life has been termed a feast, those favoured few are the most fortunate guests who are not compelled to sit at the table when they can no longer partake of the banquet. But the misfortune is, that body and mind, like man and wife, do not always agree to die together. It is bad when the mind survives the body; and worse still when the body survives the mind; but when both these survive our spirits, our hopes, and our health, this is worst of all.
—Charles Caleb Colton

Age does not make us childish, as they say. It only finds us true children still.
—Johann Wolfgang von Goethe

The old—like children—talk to themselves, for they have reached that hopeless wisdom of experience which knows that though one were to cry it in the streets to multitudes, or whisper it in the kiss to one's beloved, the only ears that can ever hear one's secret are one's own.
—Eugene O'Neill

When you become senile, you won't know it.
—Bill Cosby

In a dream you are never eighty.
—Anne Sexton

Looking back at the age of eighty-eight I see clearly that I achieved practically nothing. The world today and the history of the human anthill during the last fifty-seven years would be exactly the same if I had played ping-pong instead of sitting on

committees and writing books and memoranda. . . . I must have in a long life ground through between a hundred and fifty thousand and two hundred thousand hours of perfectly useless work.
—Leonard Woolf

A man over ninety is a great comfort to all his elderly neighbors: he is a picket-guard at the extreme outpost: and young folks of sixty or seventy feel that the enemy must get by him before he can come near their camp.
—Oliver Wendell Holmes, Jr.

No one is so old that he does not think he could live another year.
—Cicero

There are times when one grows impatient for death. There is a sweetness in being gathered to one's fathers. The very phrase is restful. Dying sounds more active; it recalls doing, and one is so tired of doing.
—Israel Zangwill

I am sick of this way of life. The weariness and sadness of old age make it intolerable. I have walked with death in hand, and death's own hand is warmer than my own. I don't wish to live any longer.
—W. Somerset Maugham

What has puzzled us before seems less mysterious, and the crooked paths look straighter as we approach the end.
—Jean Paul Richter

The last time you're doing something—knowing you're doing it for the last—makes it even more alive than the first.
—Gloria Naylor

One must grow old. Do not weep, do not join supplicating hands, do not revolt; one must grow old. Repeat this word, not as a cry of despair, but as a signal for a necessary departure. Look at yourself, look at your eyelids, your lips, raise from your temples the curls of your hair: already you are beginning to drift away from your life, don't forget it, one must grow old! . . . Go away slowly, slowly, without tears; forget nothing! Take with you your health, your cheerfulness, your coquetry, the small amount of kindness that rendered life less bitter for you. . . . Go away adorned.
—Colette

What a wonderful life I've had! I only wish that I'd realized it sooner.
—Colette

If Winter comes, can Spring be far behind?
—Percy Bysshe Shelley

Such Is Life

PART 18

DEATH

A man has not time to subdue his passions,
establish his soul in virtue, and come
up to the perfection of his nature,
before he is hurried off the stage.
—Joseph Addison

Such Is Life

"Farewell," says the dying man to his reflection in the mirror that is held up to him. "We shall not meet again."
—Paul Valéry

The day is done, and the darkness
   Falls from the wings of night,
As a feather is wafted downward
   From an eagle in his flight.
—Henry Wadsworth Longfellow

The naked map of life is spread out before me, and in the emptiness and desolation I see death coming to meet me.
—William Hazlitt

Every moment of life is a step towards death.
—Pierre Corneille

Death never takes the wise man by surprise; he is always ready to go.
—Jean de La Fontaine

One should be ever booted and spurred and ready to depart.
—Michel de Montaigne

To neglect at any time preparation for death is to sleep on our post at a siege; to omit it in old age is to sleep at an attack.
—Samuel Johnson

It is a myth to think death is just for the old. Death is there from the beginning.
—Herman Feifel

He whom the Gods love dies young.
—Menander of Athens

Death is as near to the young as to the old; here is all the difference: death stands behind the young man's back, before the old man's face.
—Reverend T. Adams

It is possible to provide security against other ills, but as far as death is concerned, we men all live in a city without walls.
—Epicurus

Death is the black camel that kneels once at every man's door.
—Turkish Proverb

Death is the sound of distant thunder at a picnic.
—W. H. Auden

Death only comes once, and we are aware of it every moment of our lives; dreading it is more painful than enduring it.
—Jean de La Bruyère

Nature has lent us life, as we do a sum of money; only no certain day is fixed for payment. What reason then to complain if she demands it at pleasure, since it was on this condition that we received it?
—Cicero

While I thought I was learning how to live, I have been learning how to die.
—Leonardo Da Vinci

Man is a watch, wound up at first but never
Wound up again: once down, he's down forever.
—Robert Herrick

Death takes us piecemeal, not at a gulp.
—Seneca

First our pleasures die—and then
Our hopes, and then our fears—and when
These are dead, the debt is due,
Dust claims dust—and we die too.
—Percy Bysshe Shelley

Death surprises us in the midst of our Hopes.
—Thomas Fuller (II)

Death is not the greatest loss in life. The greatest loss is what dies inside us while we live.
—Norman Cousins

Most persons have died before they expire—died to all earthly longings, so that the last breath is only, as it were, the locking of the door of the already deserted mansion.
—Oliver Wendell Holmes, Sr.

Our repugnance to death increases in proportion to our consciousness of having lived in vain.
—William Hazlitt

We all live in suspense, from day to day, from hour to hour; in other words, we are the hero of our own story. We cannot believe that it is finished, that we are "finished," even though we may be so; we expect another chapter, another installment, tomorrow or next week.
—Mary McCarthy

No one has ever died who was ready to die.
—Antiphanes

It is not death, it is dying that alarms me.
—Michel de Montaigne

Dying is ceasing to be afraid.
—William Wycherley

Men fear Death, as children fear to go in the dark; and as that natural fear in children is increased with tales, so is the other.
—Francis Bacon

If death be terrible, the fault is not in death, but thee.
—Author Unknown

I'm not afraid of death. It's the stake one puts up in order to play the game of life.
—Jean Giraudoux

Fear not death, for it is your destiny.
—Ben Sira

Reason thus with life:
If I do lose thee, I do lose a thing
That none but fools would keep.
—William Shakespeare

Death is not a foe, but an inevitable adventure.
—Sir Oliver Lodge

Dying is a wild night and a new road.
—Emily Dickinson

Death is a law and not a punishment. Three things ought to console us for giving up life—the friends we lost, the few persons worthy of being loved whom we leave behind us, finally the memory of our stupidities and the assurance that they are now going to stop.
—John Dubos

The conscience of a dying man calumniates his life.
—Luc de Clapiers de Vauvenargues

Conscience, though ever so small a worm while we live, grows suddenly into a serpent on our deathbed.
—Douglas Jerrold

In the depth of the anxiety of having to die is the anxiety of being eternally forgotten.
—Paul Tillich

He was comforted by one of the simpler emotions which some human beings are lucky enough to experience. He knew when he died he would be watched by someone he loved.
—Noel Annan

Men are never convinced of your reasons, of your sincerity, of the seriousness of your sufferings, except by your death.
—Albert Camus

It is very singular, how the fact of a man's death often seems to give people a truer idea of his character, whether for good or evil, than they have ever possessed while he was living and acting among them. Death is so genuine a fact that it excludes falsehood or betrays its emptiness; it is a touch-stone that proves the gold, and dishonors the baser metal.
—Nathaniel Hawthorne

Death is a thing of grandeur. It brings instantly into being a whole new network of relations between you and the ideas, the desires, the habits of the man now dead. It is a rearrangement of the world.
—Antoine de Saint-Exupéry

"After she was dead I loved her." That is the story of every life— and death.
—Gore Vidal

We understand death for the first time when he puts his hand upon one whom we love.
—Madame Germaine de Staël

We mortals realize the value of our blessings only when we have lost them.
—Plautus

The most painful death in all the world is the death of a child. When a child dies, when one child dies—not the 11 per 1000 we talk about statistically, but the one that a mother held briefly in her arms—he leaves an empty place in a parent's heart that will never heal.
—Thomas H. Kean

When death strikes down the innocent and young, for every fragile form from which he lets the panting spirit free, a hundred virtues rise, in shapes of mercy, charity, and love, to walk the world and bless it. Of every tear that sorrowing mortals shed on such green graves, some good is born, some gentler nature comes.
—Charles Dickens

To a father, when his child dies, the future dies; to a child, when his parents die, the past dies.
—Berthold Auerbach

When our parents are living we feel that they stand between us and death; when they go, we move to the edge of the unknown.
—R. I. Fitzhenry

After my mother's death I began to see her as she had really been. . . . It was less like losing someone than discovering someone.
—Nancy Hale

It is of no avail to weep for the loss of a loved one, which is why we weep.
—Solon

The bitterest tears shed over graves are for words left unsaid and deeds left undone.
—Harriet Beecher Stowe

When the veil of death has been drawn between us and the objects of our regard, how quick-sighted do we become to their merits, and how bitterly do we remember words, or even looks, of unkindness which may have escaped in our intercourse with them! How careful should such thoughts render us in the fulfill-

ment of those offices of affection with may yet be in our power to perform! For who can tell how soon the moment may arrive when repentance cannot be followed by reparation?
—Bishop Reginald Heber

When death, the great reconciler, has come, it is never our tenderness we repent of, but our severity.
—George Eliot

When we lose one we love, our bitterest tears are called forth by the memory of hours when we loved not enough.
—Maurice Maeterlinck

A man's dying is more the survivor's affair than his own.
—Thomas Mann

Ah! surely Nothing dies but Something mourns!
—Lord Byron

Mourning is not forgetting. . . . It is an undoing. Every minute tie has to be untied and something permanent and valuable recovered and assimilated from the dust.
—Margery Allingham

I hate funerals, and would not attend my own if it could be avoided, but it is well for every man to stop once in a while to think of what sort of a collection of mourners he is training for his final event.
—Robert T. Morris

Those who die a lingering death are never so bitterly lamented; they have been mourned in advance.
—Comtesse Diane

You will not die because you're ill, but because you're alive.
—Seneca

When a man dies, and his kin are glad of it, they say, "He is better off."
—Edgar Watson Howe

There is none so fortunate that there will not be one or two standing at his deathbed who will welcome the evil befalling him.
—Marcus Aurelius Antoninus

Everyone is born a king, and most people die in exile.
—Oscar Wilde

Death is in my sight today
As when a man desires to see home
When he has spent many years in captivity.
—The Man Who Was Tired of Life

I have lived in doubt, I die in anxiety, I know not whither I go.
—Author Unknown

Our hope of immortality does not come from any religions, but nearly all religions come from that hope.
—Robert Green Ingersoll

When illusions are over, when the distractions of sense, the vagaries of fancy, the tumults of passion have dissolved even before the body is cold, which once they so thronged and agitated, the soul merges into intellect, intellect into conscience, conscience into the unbroken, awful solitude of its own personal accountability; and though the inhabitants of the universe were within the spirit's ken, this personal accountability is as strictly alone and unshared as if no being were throughout immensity but the spirit and its God.
—Henry Giles

To work hard, to live hard, to die hard, and then go to hell after all would be too damned hard.
—Carl Sandburg

If God knows all I do not fear Him.
—Comtesse Diane

If I ever reach heaven I expect to find three wonders there: first, to meet some I had not thought to see there; second, to miss

some I had expected to see there; and third, the greatest surprise of all, to find myself there.
—John Newton

Heaven will be no heaven to me if I do not meet my wife there.
—Andrew Jackson

After your death you will be what you were before your birth.
—Arthur Schopenhauer

That day, which you fear as being the end of all things, is the birthday of your eternity.
—Seneca

You must die, but not as often as you have wished.
—Publilius Syrus

Sometimes death is a punishment; often a gift; it has been a favor to many.
—Seneca

Death is not the greatest of ills; it is worse to want to die, and not be able to.
—Sophocles

Death always comes too early or too late.
—English Proverb

We bring our years to an end, as it were a tale that is told.
—Book of Common Prayer

After the game the king and the pawn go in the same box.
—Italian Proverb

How very little the world misses anybody! How soon the chasm left by the best and wisest men closes!
—Thomas B. Macaulay

How frighteningly few are the persons whose death would spoil our appetite and make the world seem empty.
—Eric Hoffer

No man is an island entire of itself; every man is part of the main. . . . Any man's death diminishes me because I am involved in mankind, and therefore never send to know for whom the bell tolls; it tolls for thee.
—John Donne

In a harbor, two ships sailed: one setting forth on a voyage, the other coming home to port. Everyone cheered the ship going out, but the ship sailing in was scarcely noticed. To this, a wise man said: "Do not rejoice over a ship setting out to sea, for you cannot know what terrible storms it may encounter and what fearful dangers it may have to endure. Rejoice rather over the ship that has safely reached port and brings its passengers home in peace."

And this is the way of the world: When a child is born, all rejoice; when someone dies, all weep. We should do the opposite. For no one can tell what trials and travails await a newborn child; but when a mortal dies in peace, we should rejoice, for he has completed a long journey, and there is no greater boon than to leave this world with the imperishable crown of a good name.
—Babylonian Talmud

Judge none blessed before his death.
—Ecclesiasticus

Good-by world . . . good-by to clocks ticking . . . and Mama's sunflowers. And food and coffee. And new-ironed dresses and hot baths . . . and sleeping and waking up. Oh, earth, you're too wonderful for anybody to realize you.
—Thornton Wilder

The play is done; the curtain drops,
　　Slow falling to the prompter's bell:
A moment yet the actor stops,
　　And looks around, to say farewell.
It is an irksome word and task:
　　And, when he's laughed and said his say,
He shows, as he removes the mask,
　　A face that's anything but gay.
—William Makepeace Thackeray

The hour of departure has arrived, and we go our ways—I to die, and you to live. Which is the better, God only knows.
—Socrates

In death itself there can be nothing terrible, for the act of death annihilates sensation; but there are many roads to death, and some of them justly formidable, even to the bravest: but so various are the modes of going out of the world, that to be born may have been a more painful thing than to die, and to live may prove a more troublesome thing than either.
—Charles Caleb Colton

Why is it harder to think of his going to nothing than to think of his coming from nothing? One direction is just as dark as the other.
—Anne Morrow Lindbergh

The thought of life that ne'er shall cease
Has something in it like despair.
—Henry Wadsworth Longfellow

Life would be as insupportable without the prospect of death, as it would be without sleep.
—Countess of Blessington

Whoever has lived long enough to find out what life is knows how deep a debt of gratitude we owe to Adam, the first great benefactor of our race. He brought death into the world.
—Mark Twain

Death, the only immortal who treats us all alike, whose peace and refuge are for all. The soiled and the pure, the rich and the poor, the loved and the unloved.
—Mark Twain

The gods conceal from men the happiness of death, that they may endure life.
—Lucan

All say, "How hard it is that we have to die"—a strange complaint to come from the mouths of people who have had to live.
—Mark Twain

The stroke of death is as a lover's pinch,
Which hurts and is desired.
— William Shakespeare

Death, the refuge, the solace, the best and kindliest and most prized friend and benefactor of the erring, the forsaken, the old and weary and broken of heart. . . .
—Mark Twain

Death is the liberator of him whom freedom cannot release; the physician of him whom medicine cannot cure; the comforter of him whom time cannot console.
—Charles Caleb Colton

All was ended now, the hope and the fear and the sorrow, all the aching of heart, the restless, unsatisfied longing, all the dull, deep pain, and constant anguish of patience.
—Henry Wadsworth Longfellow

Is there another life? Shall I awake and find this all a dream? There must be, we cannot be created for this sort of suffering.
—John Keats

From too much love of living,
    From hope and fear set free,
We thank with brief thanksgiving
    Whatever Gods may be,
That no life lives forever,
That dead men rise up never;
That even the weariest river
    Winds somewhere safe to sea.
—Algernon Charles Swinburne

Death is for many of us the gate of hell; but we are inside on the way out, not outside on the way in.
—George Bernard Shaw

When you take the wires of the cage apart, you do not hurt the bird but help it. You let it out of its prison. How do you know that death does not help me when it takes the wires of my cage down?—that it does not release me, and put me into some better place, and better condition of life?
—Bishop Randolph S. Foster

No one knows but that death is the greatest of all human blessings.
—Plato

Life is a great surprise. I do not see why death should not be an even greater one.
—Vladimir Nabokov

Each night is but the past day's funeral, and the morning his resurrection: Why then should our funeral sleep be otherwise than our sleep at night?
—Arthur Warwick

It is not without reason that we are taught to study even our sleep for the resemblance it has with death. How easily we pass from waking to sleeping. With how little sense of loss we lose consciousness of the light and of ourselves! Perhaps the faculty of sleep, which deprives us of all action and all feeling, might seem useless and contrary to nature, were it not that thereby Nature teaches us that she has made us for dying and living alike, and from the start of life presents to us the eternal state that she reserves for us after we die, to accustom us to it and take away our fear of it.
—Michel de Montaigne

We sometimes congratulate ourselves at the moment of waking from a troubled dream; it may be so at the moment after death.
—Nathaniel Hawthorne

I am fully convinced that the soul is indestructible, and that its activity will continue through eternity. It is like the sun, which, to our eyes, seems to set in the night; but it has in reality gone to diffuse its light elsewhere.
—Johann Wolfgang von Goethe

Such Is Life

As the evening twilight fades away, the sky is filled with stars, invisible by day.
—Henry Wadsworth Longfellow

    How well he fell asleep!
Like some proud river, widening toward the sea;
Calmly and grandly, silently and deep,
    Life joined eternity.
—Samuel Taylor Coleridge

You will wake, and remember, and understand.
—Robert Browning

The rest is silence.
—William Shakespeare

The dog barks, but the caravan moves on.
—Arabian Proverb

PART 19

LAST WORDS

Soon the light of the skies
Will be gone from my eyes.
Soon the black night will creep,
Bringing smooth dreamless sleep.
Gone—the struggle and strife
Of the sad dream of life.
—Madame Louise Serment

Such Is Life

It is today, my dear, that I take a perilous leap.
—François Marie de Voltaire

I am about to take my last voyage, a great leap in the dark.
—Thomas Hobbes

All my possessions for a moment of time.
—Queen Elizabeth I

All this will soon pass away as a dream.
—Charles Burney

I must go in, the fog is rising.
—Emily Dickinson

I have lived too long. I want to go home.
—Joseph Clare

I believe . . . I'm going to die. I love the rain. I want the feeling of it on my face.
—Katherine Mansfield

I am leaving at last a world where the heart must either break or turn to bronze.
—Sébastien R. Nicholas Chamfort (before his suicide)

I was born without knowing why, I have lived without knowing why, and I am dying without knowing why or how.
—Pierre Gassendi

Oh God! What then is man?
—Johann Barneveldt

I am so very tired of all this. I am tired of all of you.
—Monsieur Störr

I am going to seek a great perhaps. Draw the curtain: the farce is played out.
—François Rabelais

This is the last of earth! I am content.
—John Quincy Adams

I have enjoyed a world which, though wicked enough in all conscience, is perhaps as good as worlds unknown.
—John J. Audubon

This is the best of all possible worlds.
—Arthur Brisbane

I don't know what I may seem to the world. But as to myself, I seem to have been only a boy playing on the seashore and diverting myself in now and then finding a smoother pebble or prettier shell than the ordinary, whilst the ocean of truth lay all undiscovered before me.
—Sir Isaac Newton

My life has been faulty, but God will judge me by my intentions.
—Henry Charles Peerson

I have tried so hard to do the right. . . .
—Grover Cleveland

Everything has gone *wrong*, my girl!
—Arnold Bennett

Soul of my soul, now I am going alone. I grieve for your helplessness. But what is the use. Every torture that I have inflicted, every sin that I have committed, every wrong that I have done I carry the consequences with me. Strange that I came with nothing into the world and now go away with this stupendous caravan of sin.
—Aurungzebe

God will help me . . . I am so tired!
—Julia Ward Howe

A little while and I will be gone from you. Whither I cannot tell. From now here we come, into now here we go. What is life? It is the flash of a firefly in the night. It is the breath of a buffalo in the wintertime. It is as the little shadow that runs across the grass and loses itself in the sunset.
—Isapwo Muksika Crowfoot

Lord, what things I lie here and remember.
—George Browne MacDonald

Is this dying, is this all? Is this what I feared when I prayed against a hard death? Oh, I can bear this, I can bear it!
—Cotton Mather

I'm not afraid anymore.
—George S. Kaufman

When you come to the hedge that we must all go over, it isn't so bad. You feel sleepy, you don't care. Just a little dreamy anxiety, which world you're really in, that's all.
—Stephen Crane

I am seeing things that you know nothing of.
—William Allingham

I am crossing a beautiful wide river and the opposite shore is coming nearer and nearer.
—General George Meade

What, can this be death? Is it come already? I see it, I see it! The gates are wide open. Beautiful, beautiful.
—Solomon Foot

Do you hear the music?
—Jacob Boehm

Oh, I hear such beautiful voices, and the children are the loudest.
—Mary-Anne Schimmelpenninck

I see Mother.
—Sir Charles Eliot

Clasp my hand, dear friend, I am dying.
—Conte Vittorio Alfieri

Hold me in your arms.
—Sir Charles Bell

Such Is Life

It is very hard, my children, I no longer see you. Remember me,
love me always.
—Charles Nodier

I will remember you in my dreams.
—Jonah Ustinov

We shall meet again.
—Madame Recamier

PART 20

MORAL

"Tut, tut, child!" said the Duchess,
"Everything's got a moral, if only you can find it."
—Lewis Carroll

Such Is Life

Many grains of incense fall on the same altar: one sooner, another later—it makes no difference.
—Marcus Aurelius Antoninus

Everything is only for a day, both that which remembers and that which is remembered.
—Marcus Aurelius Antoninus

The days come and go like muffled and veiled figures sent from a distant friendly party, but they say nothing, and if we do not use the gifts they bring, they carry them as silently away.
—Ralph Waldo Emerson

We are all fellow passengers on a dot of earth. And each of us, in the span of time, has really only a moment among our companions.
—Lyndon Baines Johnson

We are not permitted to choose the frame of our destiny. But what we put into it is ours.
—Dag Hammarskjöld

We must not, in trying to think about how we can make a big difference, ignore the small daily differences we can make which, over time, add up to big differences that we often cannot foresee.
—Marian Wright Edelman

Oh, if at every moment of our lives we could know the consequences of some of the utterings, thoughts and deeds that seem so trivial and unimportant at the time! And should we not conclude from such examples that there is no such thing in life as unimportant moments devoid of meaning for the future?
—Isabelle Eberhardt

Nothing is ours outright, as a gift; we have to perform for ourselves even those of our actions which seem most passive. The humble Sancho Panza kept suggesting this on all occasions, by repeating his proverb: "If they give you the cow, you have to carry the rope." All we are given is possibilities—to make ourselves one thing or another.
— Jose Ortega Y Gasset

The value of life lies, not in the length of days, but in the use we make of them; a man may live long, yet very little. Satisfaction in life depends not on the number of your years, but on your will.
—Michel de Montaigne

They that deserve nothing should be content with anything. Bless God for what you have, and trust God for what you want. If we cannot bring our condition to our mind, we must bring our mind to our condition: if a man is not content in the state he is in, he will not be content in the state he would be in.
—Erskine Mason

What fools we are! "He has spent his life in idleness," we say; "I have done nothing today." What, have you not lived? That is not only the fundamental but the most honorable of your occupations. "If I had been given an opportunity to manage great affairs, I might have shown what I can do." Have you been able to meditate and manage your own life? Then you have performed the greatest work of all. . . .

It is our duty to compose our character, not to compose books and to win, not battles and provinces, but order and tranquility for our conduct of life.

Our great and glorious masterpiece is to live to the purpose.
—Michel de Montaigne

Believe that life is worth living, and your belief will help create the fact.
—William James

You do not have to ignore problems in order to be happy, but you need to remind yourself constantly that the insurmountable difficulties of today are the solved problems of tomorrow.
—Cardinal Heenan

Reflect upon your present blessings of which every man has many; not on your past misfortunes, of which all men have some.
—Charles Dickens

Look well into thyself; there is a source which will always spring up if thou wilt search there.
—Marcus Aurelius Antoninus

Nothing happens to any man that he is not formed by nature to bear.
—Marcus Aurelius Antoninus

Be thou like the bird perched upon some frail thing, although he feels the branch bending beneath him, yet loudly sings, knowing full well that he has wings.
—Madame de Gasparin

Be content with what you are, and wish not change; nor dread your last day, nor long for it.
—Martial

Do not despair—many are happy much of the time; more eat than starve, more are healthy than sick, more curable than dying; not so many dying as dead; and one of the thieves was saved. Hell's bells and all's well—half the world is at peace with itself, and so is the other half; vast areas are unpolluted; millions of children grow up without suffering deprivation, and millions, while deprived and cruelly treated, none the less grow up. No laughter is sad and many tears are joyful.
—Tom Stoppard

To be honest, to be kind—to earn a little and to spend a little less, to make upon the whole a family happier for his presence, to renounce when that shall be necessary and not be embittered, to keep a few friends, but these without capitulation—above all, on the same grim condition, to keep friends with himself—here is a task for all that a man has of fortitude and delicacy.
—Robert Louis Stevenson

Here lies one who meant well, tried a little, failed much:—surely that may be his epitaph of which he need not be ashamed.
—Robert Louis Stevenson

Have patience with all things, but chiefly have patience with yourself. Do not lose courage in considering your own imperfections, but instantly set about remedying them—every day begin the task anew.
—Saint Francis de Sales

Make yourself necessary to somebody.
—Ralph Waldo Emerson

I've never met a person, I don't care what his condition, in whom I could not see possibilities. I don't care how much a man may consider himself a failure, I believe in him, for he can change the thing that is wrong in his life any time he is ready and prepared to do it. Whenever he develops the desire, he can take away from his life the thing that is defeating it. The capacity for reformation and change lies within.
—Preston Bradley

The world has no room for cowards. We must all be ready somehow to toil, to suffer, to die. And yours is not the less noble because no drum beats before you when you go out into your daily battlefields, and no crowds shout about your coming when you return from your daily victory or defeat.
—Robert Louis Stevenson

Not in the clamour of the crowded street,
Not in the shouts and plaudits of the throng,
But in ourselves, are triumph and defeat.
—Henry Wadsworth Longfellow

Finish every day and be done with it. You have done what you could. Some blunders and absurdities no doubt crept in; forget them as soon as you can.
—Ralph Waldo Emerson

Go placidly amid the noise and the haste, and remember what peace there may be in silence. As far as possible without surrender, be on good terms with all persons. Speak your truth quietly and clearly, and listen to others, even the dull and the ignorant; they too have their story. Be yourself. Especially do not feign affection. Neither be cynical about love; for in the face of all aridity and disenchantment it is as perennial as the grass. Take kindly the counsel of the years, gracefully surrendering the things of youth. Nurture strength of spirit to shield you in sudden misfortune. But do not distress yourself with imaginings. Many fears are born of fatigue and loneliness. Beyond a wholesome discipline, be gentle with yourself. You are a child of the universe

no less than the trees and the stars; you have a right to be here. And whether or not it is clear to you, no doubt the universe is unfolding as it should. Therefore be at peace with God, whatever you conceive Him to be, and whatever your labours and aspirations, in the noisy confusion of life keep peace with your soul. With all its sham, drudgery and broken dreams, it is still a beautiful world.
—Max Ehrmann

Whilst ye are upon the earth, enjoy the good things that are here (to that end were they given) and be not melancholy, and wish yourself in heaven.
—John Selden

Look not mournfully into the Past. It comes not back again. Wisely improve the Present. It is thine. Go forth to meet the shadowy Future, without fear, and with a manly heart.
—Henry Wadsworth Longfellow

Love all, trust a few. Do wrong to none.
—William Shakespeare

Treat people as if they were what they ought to be and you help them to become what they are capable of being.
—Johann Wolfgang von Goethe

The little I have seen of the world teaches me to look upon the errors of others in sorrow, not in anger. When I take the history of one poor heart that has sinned and suffered, and think of the struggles and temptations it has passed through, the brief pulsations of joy, the feverish inquietude of hope and fear, the pressure of want, the desertion of friends, I would fain leave the erring soul of my fellow-man with Him from whose hands it came.
—Henry Wadsworth Longfellow

To understand is to forgive, even oneself.
—Alexander Chase

How can we venture to judge others when we know so well how ill-equipped they are for judging us.
—Comtesse Diane

Every one of these hundreds of millions of human beings is in some form seeking happiness. . . . Not one is altogether trustworthy nor altogether consistent; and not one is altogether vile. . . . Not a single one but has at some time wept.
—Herbert George Wells

The love of our neighbor in all its fullness simply means being able to say to him, "What are you going through?"
—Simone Weil

If we could read the secret history of our enemies, we should find in each man's life sorrow and suffering enough to disarm all hostility.
—Henry Wadsworth Longfellow

Life that ever needs forgiveness has for its first duty to forgive.
—Edward G. Bulwer-Lytton

Forgiveness is the act of admitting we are like other people.
—Christina Baldwin

When you see a man in distress, recognize him as a fellow man.
—Seneca

A tender-hearted, compassionate disposition, which inclines men to pity and to feel the misfortunes of others, and which is incapable of involving any man in ruin and misery, is, of all tempers of mind, the most amiable; and though it seldom receives much honour, is worthy of the highest.
—Henry Fielding

The worst sin towards our fellow creatures is not to hate them, but to be indifferent to them; that's the essence of inhumanity.
—George Bernard Shaw

More hearts pine away in secret anguish for unkindness from those who should be their comforters, than for any other calamity in life.
—Edward Young

The blossom cannot tell what becomes of its odor, and no man can tell what becomes of his influence and example, that roll away from him, and go beyond his ken on their perilous mission.
—Henry Ward Beecher

Kind looks, kind words, kind acts, and warm handshakes—these are secondary means of grace when men are in trouble and are fighting their unseen battles.
—John Hall

Do not believe that he who seeks to comfort you lives untroubled among the simple and quiet words that sometimes do you good. His life has much difficulty and sadness. . . . Were it otherwise he would never have been able to find those words.
—Rainer Maria Rilke

One must be very fond of people and trust them if one is not to make a mess of life.
—Edward M. Forster

Never give up on anybody.
—Hubert H. Humphrey

Every one of us is the child of somebody.
—Pierre de Beaumarchais

Be kind, for everyone you meet is fighting a hard battle.
—Philo

A loving person lives in a loving world. A hostile person lives in a hostile world: everyone you meet is your mirror.
—Ken Keyes, Jr.

It's a hard, sad life for most people. Don't scorn the simple things that give them pleasure.
—D. Sutten

Beware how you take away hope from any human being.
—Oliver Wendell Holmes, Sr.

No human being can really understand another, and no one can arrange another's happiness.
—Graham Greene

Every possession and every happiness is but lent by chance for an uncertain time, and may therefore be demanded back the next hour.
—Arthur Schopenhauer

Never part without loving words to think of during your absence. It may be that you will not meet again in life.
—Jean Paul Richter

Treasure each other in the recognition that we do not know how long we shall have each other.
—Joshua Loth Liebman

Adapt yourself to the things among which your lot has been cast and love sincerely the fellow creatures with whom destiny has ordained that you shall live.
—Marcus Aurelius Antoninus

Whatever you do . . . love those who love you.
—François Marie de Voltaire

Spend these fleeting moments on earth as Nature would have you spend them, and then go to your rest with a good grace, as an olive falls in its season, with a blessing for the earth that bore it and a thanksgiving to the tree that gave it life.
—Marcus Aurelius Antoninus

No star is ever lost we once have seen,
We may always be what we might have been.
—Adelaide A. Proctor

He conquers who endures.

—Persius

Such Is Life

So it is, and such is life.

—Charles Dickens

Such Is Life

INDEX

One may recollect generally that certain thoughts or facts are to be found in a certain book; but without a good index such a recollection may be hardly more available than that of the cabin-boy who knew where the ship's tea kettle was because he saw it fall overboard. In truth a very large part of every man's reading falls overboard, and unless he has good indexes he will never find it again.
—Horace Binney

Such Is Life

D

G

M

No two people read the same book.

—Edmund Wilson

Such Is Life

ACKNOWLEDGEMENTS

This book began as a seed of an idea for a completely different type of project. I wanted to collect a few helpful maxims and aphorisms and handwrite them in a small book to present to my younger sister, Kathy Brzezina. I felt that were I to find profound words of wisdom to guide me in life's vicissitudes, I would share them with Kathy to aid her in increasing the happiness of her own journey. This small kernel continued to grow in my mind...

Kathy, this gift is complete now, and I offer it to you with love.

Several people were gracious enough to read and comment on this manuscript during its long development. I would like to thank my wife, Zusia and our daughters Leilah Scheys and Ashlei Watson for their gentle encouragement and the clarity and wisdom of their observations. I also wish to express my deep gratitude to my friends Jim and Donna Doestch, Daniel Martin, Dennis and Melanie Girard and Gail Anderson for their continued support and ceaseless proofreading.

All of you contributed in many ways to this project, but not least in that I learned so much of life's lessons and bounty in your company.

Such Is Life